LIBRARY MARKETING THAT WORKS!

Suzanne Walters

Neal-Schuman Publishers, Inc.

NEW YORK   LONDON

Published by Neal-Schuman Publishers, Inc.
100 William Street, Suite 2004
New York, NY 10038

ISBN: 1-55570-473-5

Printed and bound in the United States of America.

The paper used in this publication meets the minimum requirements of American National Standard for Information Sciences—Permanence of Paper for Printed Library Materials, ANSI Z39.48-1992.

"Power Card" and the Power Card™ design are trademarks or registered trademarks of Reliant Energy, Inc., used by permission.

A cataloging record for this title is available from the Library of Congress (record number 2002035988).

DEDICATION

To Chandranath Sen, MD, Chairman of the Department of Neurosurgery at St. Luke's-Roosevelt Hospital Center and Beth Israel Medical Center, and Codirector of the Center for Cranial Base Surgery at St. Luke's-Roosevelt Hospital Center, in New York City, for whom the impossible is ordinary. He sets the standard for excellence in his field. He is both an artist and a scientist in the science of neurosurgery, without whose skill, this book would not have been possible.

Also, to my many librarian friends in public and medical libraries who searched through literature and electronic resources. They demonstrated the persistence, knowledge, and skills so familiar in the library field. Their searching provided me with information about valuable resources and contacts in the field of neurosurgery.

Contents

Part I: Strategic Planning

Part II: Marketing Planning Processes

Part III: New Directions in Marketing

Appendixes: Marketing Tools You Can Use

List of Figures

List of Brainstorming Questions and Worksheets

List of Success Stories

Preface

Library Marketing That Works! is not just another book for library professionals. It provides both information about and tools for marketing your library using means like advocacy, programming, fundraising, partnering, public relations, community building, advertising, and much more. This book is a tool for renewing and perhaps even reshaping your library's services and changing its image in the community and among local business and government leaders. Such a task is a challenge, but the goal of this book is to make it all work, to bring it together in a way that any library director or team can manage.

To relate the tools of marketing to daily library activity, I divide *Library Marketing That Works!* into three parts. Part I covers strategic planning for libraries, Part II outlines the specifics of a marketing plan, and Part III explores new directions in marketing. The parts can be used as a whole or individually as you address the specific problems your library faces.

Part I, Strategic Planning, includes a process for formulating mission, vision, and values statements that will get your library focused and on the road to success. It forces you to take a critical look at your library, your products and services, your customers and community, and even your competition. Vision and mission statements are typical in libraries, but they rarely address marketing and positioning your library. This is the process for getting your bearings and setting a course.

You discover the nuts-and-bolts of applying marketing to your work in Part II, Market Planning Processes, the core of *Library Marketing That Works!* Through these three chapters, you will learn to identify customers in general and in specific terms through segmentation, identifying their decision-making processes, and conducting market research. You will learn to use the six Ps—Product, Place, Price, Promotion, Positioning, and Politics—to make every program and service your library provides a success with your community. Finally, you will learn to advertise, develop effective public relations, and get your name out in the media. Appendix A includes two sample plans to show you a model for executing two different types of market planning processes. This process is not about turning a library into a business, it's about getting families to your Mommy and Me classes, students to your after school program, and seniors to your day programs. It is about putting your library back into the minds of people, politicians, and businesses, and this will reap its own rewards.

Part III, New Directions in Marketing, introduces new concepts like relationship marketing, the new customer service culture, partnerships, special marketing strategies for donors and voters, and new technology marketing tools like database marketing and the Web.

The format of *Library Marketing That Works!* encourages your immediate participation. Brainstorming activities, worksheets, and questions, appear throughout the book to get you thinking about the library's possibilities and problems. You can fill out these sheets individually, or use them in large group workshops to bring your full staff's ideas to the table. Together these Brainstorms will become a working document, to which your library can refer to solve problems, readdress issues, and evaluate progress. Each Brainstorm includes examples to prompt your thinking, to help you consider angles and answers you might not otherwise have included. Success stories illustrate each point and give your library concrete ideas for future programs and activities.

The companion CD-ROM is the perfect tool for involving staff, board members, and volunteers in the process. Included on the CD is the full set of Brainstorms, questions and worksheets, that you can duplicate and distribute, and a One-Day Marketing Workshop including a PowerPoint presentation and handouts. This Workshop has been used successfully at a number of libraries and will help bring your staff's ideas together for the benefit of your library.

This is an ambitious book, but it is also a necessary book. As government funding, corporate donations, and demographics change throughout the country, a successful marketing plan can help save your library in difficult times.

Acknowledgments

Charles Harmon, the Director of Publishing at Neal-Schuman, wrote me a note asking if I would update my original marketing manual that was first published in 1990. At the time, I was recovering from brain surgery and was not employed by any library. I hesitated in responding to him, but then I thought that I could use various libraries and library programs to illustrate marketing concepts. In many marketing textbooks, various corporations are used, so why not try to use different libraries?

The stories I obtained were astounding. Libraries shined with sophistication, clarity, creativity, determination, enthusiasm, and gut-level drive. Their level of expertise in the marketing area had grown significantly in these past ten years. Their examples and stories are just plain heartwarming and inspirational. Librarians everywhere were enthusiastic and generous in sharing their stories. They provided information and materials, and reviewed copy, for which I am very grateful. Some of them even wrote their own copy. We exchanged e-mails, telephone calls, lunch, and tours. The Success Stories are the result. They not only illustrate marketing concepts, but they also serve as a great inspiration to me and librarians everywhere. I'm sure that they will do the same for you.

I would like to thank the following people for their help in research or providing stories:

Angel Fire Library
Angel Fire, New Mexico
Debby Clanton, Board President
Becky Marshall, Library Director

Aurora Public Library
Aurora, Colorado
Tom Nicholas, Director of Library & Recreation Services
Bette Yager, Reference & BRC supervisor
Mary C. Garcia, Administrative Secretary

Berkeley Public Library
Berkeley, California
Jeri Ewart, Supervising Librarian
Adam Broner, Tool Library

Bill and Melinda Gates Foundation
Seattle, Washington
Richard Akeroyd, Former Director, International Library Initiatives

Brooklyn Public Library
Brooklyn, New York
Beth Weinstein, Director, Marketing and Communications
Valerie Geiss, Manager, Media Relations and Communications

Hennepin County Library
Richfield, Minnesota
Patrick Jones, Director of Outreach Services

Denver Public Library, Blair-Caldwell African American Research Library
Denver, Colorado
Dr. Rick J. Ashton, City Librarian

Charleszine (Terry) Nelson, Senior Librarian

Celeste Jackson, Manager of Public Relations

Douglas County Libraries
Castle Rock, Colorado
Jamie LaRue, Library Director
Katie Klossner, Community Relations Manager

Friends and Foundation of the San Francisco Public Library
San Francisco, California
Martin Gomez, Executive Director
Deborah Doyle, Chair

Friends of the Saint Paul Public Library
Saint Paul, Minnesota
Peter D. Pearson, President

Houston Public Library
Houston, Texas
Andrea Lapsley, Assistant Director, Marketing and Development

Information Today, Inc.
Medford, New Jersey
Kathy Dempsey, Editor, *Computers in Libraries* magazine and
***Marketing Library Services* newsletter**

Laramie County Library System
Cheyenne, Wyoming
Lucie Osborn, Library Director
Susan Vittitow, Director, Laramie County Library Foundation
Troy Rumpf, Public Relations Specialist

Mississippi Library Commission
Jackson, Mississippi
Sharman B. Smith, Executive Director

New Mexico State Library
Santa Fe, New Mexico
Richard Akeroyd, State Librarian
Stephanie Rawlings Gerding, Library Development Office, Continuing Education Director

North Carolina State University Libraries
Raleigh, North Carolina
May Chang, Web Development Librarian

Public Library of Charlotte and Mecklenburg County
Charlotte, North Carolina
Robin Bryan, Brarydog Coordinator
Helene Blowers, Director of Web Services

Queens Borough Public Library
Jamaica, New York
Gary Strong, Library Director
Joanne King, Public Relations Department
Thomas E. Alford, Deputy Director, Customer Service

Rampart Library District, Woodland Park Public Library
Woodland Park, Colorado
Sharon Quay, Library Director

Reliant Energy
Houston, Texas
Cathy Guy, Manager, Corporate Community Relations and Vice President of Reliant Resource Foundation
Robert W. Gibbs, Jr., Director, Corporate Community Relations and President of Reliant Resources Foundation

Richmond Public Library
Richmond, British Columbia, Canada
Cate McNeely, Deputy Chief Librarian
Mark Ellis, Coordinator of Reference and Information Services
Shirley Lew, Web Coordinator
Shelly Civikin, Head of Readers Advisory

Ruby M. Sisson Memorial Library
Pagosa Springs, Colorado
Lenore Bright, Library Director

Ruidoso Public Library
Ruidoso, New Mexico
Phyllis Reed, Library Director

San Jose Public Library
San Jose, California
Dave Genesy, Innovative Library Services Manager
Lorraine Oback, Marketing Communications Director

Seattle Public Library Foundation
Seattle, Washington
Terry Collings, Executive Director
Jonna Ward, Community Campaign Director

Shelby County Public Libraries, Harrison Regional Library System
Columbia, Alabama
Mary Hedricks, Supervisor

Sweetwater County Library System
Green River, Wyoming
Paul Holland, Director

Tattered Cover Bookstore
Denver, Colorado
Joyce Mestis, Owner

University of Denver
Denver, Colorado
R. Bruce Hutton, PhD, Professor of Marketing, Marketing Department

West Virginia Library Commission
Charleston, West Virginia
James D. Waggoner, Deputy Director

Part 1
Strategic Planning

CHAPTER 1

Begin with Powerful Mission, Vision, and Values Statements

Long Range Plans, Strategic Plans, and Understanding Your Library

Libraries, like other institutions and businesses, require different types of planning to be successful. Individual planning processes vary—depending on the size and budget of your library. Most medium to large libraries have a long-range plan in place. It usually establishes significant items like the budget and policies, and will be as general or detailed as the library director and staff desires. While long range planning focuses our eyes on the horizon, strategic planning is a process that concentrates on specific goals and objectives in strategic areas for the next 3–5 years. The library director, key staff players, the board of directors, trustees, foundation members are involved in a participatory planning process, through which they identify a series of quantifiable goals.

A strategic plan sets its sights on the big picture of the long-range plan, while working on very precise and focused ways to accomplish the goals it embodies for your institution's future. If your library has a long-range plan in place, you should review it before beginning to work on your your present long-range plan. Please do not let the daunting prospect of the process of implementing a strategic plan inhibit the fun and creative brainstorming recommended in this chapter. If you do not have a long-range plan, then you can approach this strategic planning as a totally fresh experience.

The specifics of a strategic plan come from ideas that you must generate. You begin first by creating a strategic mind-set, and then sharpen the focus by following the step-by-step guide. It begins with writing or rewriting powerful mission, vision, and values statements. Next, you perform a SWOT (strengths, weaknesses, opportunities, and threats) analysis of the library. Finally, you can create long-term goals using the findings of the SWOT analysis.

Create a Strategic Mind-Set

Thinking of your library strategically might be a new experience for some librarians and library stakeholders. Remember that library services do not remain static. New information products are available every day. Think how libraries have had to change in the last ten or twenty years. Think of the impact of technology, the variety of new products and services. Libraries must change and continue to change in order to grow. Change is inevitable. In fact, the very pace of change is accelerating. You can't just sit back and think that the work is done.

What are the benefits of a strategic planning process?

- It gives you an accurate, timely, complete, and objective snapshot of the library today.

- It exposes and encourages creativity, enthusiasm, bonding, and loyalty among staff in all areas of the library.

- It creates a performance standard against which you can measure future progress.

- It evaluates differing opinions among the director, management team, staff, board, and auxiliary groups.

- It develops respect for each other's responsibility and what each needs to accomplish to achieve the goals.

- It improves communication and builds a management team.

- It provides broader context and awareness for why problems exist.

- It develops a sense of ownership by all the participants.

- It provides a glue that keeps board and staff together.

- It develops a common vision.

Write an Effective Mission Statement

How do you begin developing a strategic marketing approach to your library, its programs and services, its funding opportunities, and its role in the community? It all starts with writing an effective mission statement. Even if you already have a mission statement, you should periodically reevaluate it. Mission statements can be vibrant and succinct—defining the purpose of the library, the role of the library in the community, and the ways the library benefits its customers.

A powerful mission statement will provide a clear course for the marketing planning process, by helping you identify your library's priorities. Traditionally, libraries have tried to be all things to all people. But in this world of diminishing resources and increasing technological sophistication, it is impossible to meet everyone's every need. In defining which needs you will meet, your mission statement will address these four Ws:

- Who are you serving?

- What are you doing to serve your customers?

- When are your services available?

- Where are your parameters of service?

More specifically, a mission statement will explore the following questions about your library:

1. What service business are you in?
    - How do you provide information?
    - How do you provide recreation?
    - How do you provide education?
    - How do you provide entertainment?

2. Who uses your products and services?
    - Who are your primary customers?
    - Do you serve as the children's guide to learning?
    - Do you serve as the student's resource for information?
    - Do you serve as the small business's information guide?
    - Are you a research facility?

3. How well does your system work?
    - How well are you doing?
    - What measurement tools do you employ to measure customer satisfaction?
    - How do you try to understand customer needs?

4. How does your library compare to other institutions?
    - Who is your competition for funding?
    - Who is your competition for services and programs?

5. What might the future hold?

- What are your growth markets?

- What new products and services should you develop to meet customer needs?

- What is your niche in the market place?

- Are there special niches that your library is uniquely qualified to develop?

Getting Ready to Write

There is no one "right" way to write or rewrite a mission statement. It is part analytical and rational, part creative and intuitive. Use the following worksheets as a map to explore the many areas that define your library.

☀ BRAINSTORMING 1.1 WHAT IS YOUR INSTITUTION?

Remember, in the mission statement, we are describing the four basic Ws. Those include who we are serving, with what, when, and where. Let's begin by describing your institution as it is at this time. These questions help the participants realize the scope of the library's offerings. They answer the "What" question. Use these questions to investigate the basic question: What service business are you in?

- What is your library's role in the community?

  Examples: community center, archival repository, research facility

- How does your library offer information?

  Examples: Web site, database, card catalog

- How does your library promote education?

  Examples: books clubs, after school programs, tutor times

- How does your library encourage life-long learning?

  Examples: computer education, senior services, lectures

- What is the library's role as a cultural institution within the community?

  Examples: partners with arts council, traveling exhibits, plays/performances

- What is the library's role in building the community?

  Examples: makes meeting rooms available, hosts socials

☀ BRAINSTORMING 1.2 WHAT ARE YOUR PRODUCTS?

Use these questions to investigate the basic question: What products and services do you offer your customers?

- What products does your library hold?

  Examples: books, videos, databases, Internet access

- What services do you offer?

  Examples: circulation, interlibrary loan, telephone reference

☀ BRAINSTORMING 1.3 HOW DO YOU DELIVER?

Use these questions to investigate the basic question: How do you deliver your library's products and services?

- How does your community get your products?

  Examples: walk in clients, bookmobile, virtual

- What characteristics do your customers expect in the responses they receive when utilizing your products and services?

  Examples: friendly, instructional, patient

- What characteristics do your customers actually encounter when utilizing your products and services?

  Examples: rushed, friendly, judgmental

☀ BRAINSTORMING 1.4 WHO ARE YOUR CUSTOMERS?

Use these questions to investigate the basic question: Who do you serve?

- What are the ages of your users?

  Examples: seniors, toddlers, teens

- What are the occupations of your users?

  Examples: students, small business people, unemployed

- What are ethnic/social groups of your users?

  Examples: Hispanics, gays and lesbians, homeless

☼ BRAINSTORMING 1.5 WHAT DO YOU DO WELL?

Use these questions to realize your library's distinctive competencies. Distinctive competencies are, quite simply, those things that you do really well. Some of these questions can be answered by looking through your answers to brainstorming questions 1.1–1.4. Each of these questions requires an honest, thoughtful answer that may take some time.

- Which customers do you serve exceptionally well (think specifically)?

  Examples: freshman high school students, Hispanic senior citizens

- Which products and or services do your customers use most?

  Examples: online databases, children's nonfiction, new fiction titles

- Which services have earned your library awards or recognition?

- Which services do your customers compliment?

- Which services make your staff proud?

The following brainstorming sessions ask you to look forward or think hypothetically. The preceding questions had concrete answers that could be checked by facts. The questions listed below will help you develop the forward-looking mission and vision statements key to successful strategic planning.

☼ BRAINSTORMING 1.6 WHAT QUALITIES DO YOU ENCOURAGE IN YOUR STAFF?

- What do you look for when hiring people?

  Examples: intelligent, vibrant, social

- What do you look for when promoting people?

  Examples: leadership, creativity, integrity

- What do you like about your team?

  Examples: teamwork, commitment, energetic

☼ BRAINSTORMING 1.7 HOW CAN YOU TRY TO UNDERSTAND CUSTOMER NEEDS?

- What studies can you conduct?

  Examples: circulation statistics, telephone surveys, tally of Web site visitors

- How can you listen to your customers?

  Examples: focus groups, comment cards, complaint calls

- Where can you get customer service ideas?

  Examples: professional journals, business magazines, on-site observations

☼ BRAINSTORMING 1.8 WHAT IS YOUR COMPETITION?

Use these questions to identify your current situation, but also try to uncover ways to distinguish yourself and set your library apart from the competition.

- Who is drawing from your funding sources?

  Examples: other city agencies, charities

- Who is providing similar programs and services?

  Examples: author readings at the bookstore, online resources, after school programs

- What is taking customers away?

  Examples: community center, other public events

- What is keeping you from your customers?

  Examples: weather, location, hours of operation

☼ BRAINSTORMING 1.9 WHAT AREAS OFFER YOU POTENTIAL GROWTH OPPORTUNITIES?

- What groups do you want to serve better?
- What programs do you want to implement?
- What programs do you want to improve?

 BRAINSTORMING 1.10 WHAT STANDS OUT?

- What questions did you answer unanimously?
- What questions sparked debate?
- What answers are most emblematic of your library?
- What answers make you proud?
- What answers make you embarrassed?

BRAINSTORMING 1.11 WHAT GOES FORWARD?

- What are the two or three values that best describe your library today?
- What are the two or three values that you want to describe your library in the future?

BRAINSTORMING 1.12 WHAT IS THE MISSION OF YOUR LIBRARY?

Examples:

Denver Public Library,   **Denver, Colorado**

The mission of the Denver Public Library is to help people of our community to achieve their full potential.

Douglas County Library System,   **Douglas County, Colorado**

The Douglas County Library system provides resources for learning and leisure to build communities and improve lives in Douglas County.

Queens Borough Public Library,   **Jamaica, New York**

The mission of the Queen Borough Public Library is to provide quality services, resources and lifelong learning opportunities through books and a variety of other formats to meet the informational, educational, cultural and recreation needs and interests of its diverse and changing population.

The library is a forum for all points of view and adheres to the principle of intellectual freedom as expressed in the library Bill of Rights formulated by the American Library Association.

Richmond Public Library,   **Richmond, British Columbia, Canada**

The mission of the Richmond public library is to provide access to informational, educational, cultural and recreational library materials and services in a variety of formats and technologies; to be responsive to the public library needs of the community and to uphold the public's freedom of access to information.

Write a mission statement for your library:

_____

_____

_____

_____

_____

_____

_____

_____

Write an Effective Vision Statement

A vision statement is a vivid and compelling description of your library's future. A powerful vision statement encompasses an inspiring intention for your institution—express its purpose and promise. Where your mission statement described the very best your library offers now, your vision statement should say where you want to be in the future and how you plan to get there.

The stirring nature of an effective vision statement will become a powerful motivational tool for the staff and stakeholders. There are no rules to writing a good vision statement. It can be long or short. One note of caution while writing: although it's good to "dream big"—also try to think realistically.

🔅 BRAINSTORMING 1.13 WHAT IS THE FUTURE OF YOUR LIBRARY?

- Where do you see your library products and services in five years?

  Examples: new technology, increased outreach and programming, larger circulating collection

- Who will be the customers of your library?

  Examples: senior citizens, first generation Hispanics, children under age five

- What new sources might fund your library?

  Examples: new fee-based services, library café, lottery

- How will your library be a leader?

  Examples: new senior programs, new community activities

- What will your building/facility need or become?

  Examples: remodeled meeting rooms, more Internet connections, new compact shelves

 BRAINSTORMING 1.14 WHAT IS THE VISION OF YOUR LIBRARY?

Examples:

Seattle Public Library,   **Seattle, Washington**

We intend to become the best public library in the world by being so tuned in to the people we serve and so supportive of each other's efforts that we are able to provide highly responsive service.

Queens Borough Public Library,   **Jamaica, New York**

The Queens Borough Public Library represents a fundamental public good in our democracy. It assures the right, the privilege and the ability of individuals to choose and pursue any direction of thought, study or action they wish.

The Library provides the capital necessary for us to understand the past and plan for the future. It is also our collective memory, since history and human experience are best preserved in writing.

As Queens Library enters its second century, it will be universally recognized as the most dynamic public library in the nation. This recognition will arise from: the Library's dedication to the needs of its diverse communities; its advocacy and support of appropriate technology; the excellence of its collections; the commitment of its staff to its customers and the very highest ideals of library service.

We at Queens Library believe deeply in equity and that libraries are fundamental in empowering people to take charge of their lives, their governments and their communities. In this way, Queens Library has an essential role to play in the new millennium. The collections we build, the access we provide and the technologies we embrace will carry the people of Queens into a productive and creative future. Please join the Library in this quest.

Fullerton Public Library,   **Fullerton, California**

The Fullerton Public Library will be integral to the City's intellectual and cultural life, deeply rooted in and responsive to our diverse community. The Library will provide free and equal access to information, knowledge and ideas; promote personal enrichment and life-long learning; encourage literacy and the love of reading in all age groups; and foster cultural and educational programs and partnerships. The Library will ensure quality service through positive human connections and an inviting environment.

Douglas County Library System,   **Douglas County, Colorado**

The Douglas County Library System is a source of community pride and lifelong learning. Knowledgeable and friendly personnel provide intellectual capital, showcase art and culture, and highlight local history through evolving collections and programs.

Write a vision statement for your library:

Prioritize the ideas generated using the previous worksheets. Write them into sentences with an overarching theme. Remember to be vibrant. The more motivated your stakeholders and staff, the more passionate they will be about accomplishing these goals.

_____

_____

_____

_____

_____

_____

_____

Define Your Values

A values statement expresses the desirability and commitment your library places on key qualities. It will become a snapshot of the core priorities of your library. A values statement should complement your mission and vision statements, and like them, there is no one correct length. They are often expressed in short phrases.

BRAINSTORMING 1.15 WHAT STANDS OUT?

- What questions did you answer unanimously?
- What questions sparked debate?
- What answers are most emblematic of your library?
- What answers make you proud?
- What answers make you embarrassed?

BRAINSTORMING 1.16 WHAT GOES FORWARD?

- What are the two or three values that best describe your library today?
- What are the two or three values that you want to describe your library in the future?

BRAINSTORMING 1.17 WHAT ARE THE VALUES OF YOUR LIBRARY?

Examples:

Richmond Public Library,   **Richmond, British Columbia, Canada**

The Library Board and staff are committed to:

- Providing free, equal and uncensored access to sources of knowledge, information, programs and services that are responsive to the needs of the community;
- Reaching out directly to the community into homes, schools, businesses and institutions;
- Serving those members of our community with special needs by providing specialized materials, equipment and services;
- Recognizing and managing change in a positive way and using technology to maximum advantage.

Queens Borough Public Library,   **Jamaica, New York**

Service

- We believe that library and information service is essential to a learning society because information and knowledge are

14

indispensable to the development of human potential, the advancement of civilization, and the continuance of enlightened self-government.

Customers

- We believe that meeting the needs of our diverse customer base is first and foremost.

Quality

- We value the importance of providing rapid and comprehensive access to knowledge and information and strive to constantly improve the services we provide to our customers.

Technology

- We believe that Queens Library must be an active partner in the development and implementation of technology to ensure that access to knowledge and information will be equitably available to all.

Individuality

- We respect the individuality and integrity of each customer and each employee and foster an environment in which creativity, productivity and individual responsibility are encouraged, recognized and rewarded.

Teamwork

- We believe that each individual is a member of the team, working together to serve our customers.

Technology

- We believe the Queens Library must be an active partner in the development and implementation of technology to ensure that access to knowledge and information will be equitably available to all.

Write your values statement:

1. List ten values you and your staff hold for your library.

    Example: teamwork, customer service, patience, creativity

2. Now prioritize the values you have listed for your library.

    1.

    2.

    3.

    4.

    5.

    6.

    7.

    8.

    9.

  10.

3. Compile the essential values you have listed into one statement. This can be as complex, or as simple, as you deem necessary and may involve multiple paragraphs, bulleted points, or levels.

_____

_____

_____

_____

_____

_____

_____

_____

BRAINSTORMING 1.18 MERGE YOUR FINAL MISSION, VISION, AND VALUES STATEMENTS INTO ONE DOCUMENT.

_____

_____

_____

_____

_____

_____

_____

_____

CHAPTER 2

Use a SWOT Analysis to Plan Your Marketing Strategy

Building Your Strategic Plan Using Your Strengths, Weaknesses, Opportunities, and Threats (SWOT)

For many readers, just the ideas generated and areas illuminated in writing a mission, vision, or values statement will be enough to move you right into launching a marketing effort. After all, you now know what your institution is all about, what it treasures, and where it wants to go. It is helpful to proceed beyond the mission, vision, and values by conducting a more in-depth analysis and evaluation, to create a set of goals and objectives. Your strategic plan becomes a reality through these goals.

Carry Out a SWOT Analysis

With newly written, or rewritten mission, vision, and values statements, you now know what is best about your library today, where you want it go, and the qualities that will sustain the journey from the present to the future. The statements have established a general set of goals that the board, the administration, the foundation, and the staff have all agreed upon.

Throughout creating the statements process, the emphasis was solely on a positive, almost idealized, model of your institution. You clarified your mission and set a vision for which you will reach. Now you need to take a clear-headed, realistic look at the library's present situation. A SWOT (Strengths, Weaknesses, Opportunities, and Threats) analysis will help survey the positive and negative forces at work.

First, begin with a general examination of the environment in which your library operates. You can find much of this information in resources in your own reference department, through local government agencies and through the local chamber of commerce. These brainstorming sessions are meant to help you understand your library's position in relation to the changing population, finances, politics, and technology of your community.

☀ BRAINSTORMING 2.1 WHERE IS YOUR LIBRARY'S POPULATION?

- What population changes alter the demographics of your library's customers?

  Examples: more families, fewer professionals, same number of children and teens

- Is your area's population increasing or decreasing?

  Examples: larger families, more single-person homes, new family apartment complex

- Is the cultural/ethnic makeup of your population changing?

  Examples: larger African American populations, fewer Asian Americans, more Hispanic seniors

- What special groups are increasing/decreasing in number?

  Examples: seniors, children under 10, teens

☀ BRAINSTORMING 2.2 WHERE IS YOUR LIBRARY FINANCIALLY?

- What are the sources of income for your library?

  Examples: endowment, municipal, county, or state funds, Friends groups

- What is the average income of your library's area?

  Examples: fixed income seniors, wealthy families, working-class singles

- Is your library's budget increasing or decreasing?

- Are your library's costs increasing or decreasing?

☀ BRAINSTORMING 2.3 WHERE IS YOUR LIBRARY POLITICALLY?

- What is your library's relationship with elected officials?

- Are staff members involved in local or state politics?

- Is the library involved in elections?
- Is the library affected by potential legislation?
- Is the library prominent in the mind of voters?

☼ BRAINSTORMING 2.4 WHERE IS YOUR LIBRARY TECHNOLOGICALLY?

- What technological challenges does your library face?
- Is your library keeping up with technological advances?
- Are you successfully managing the technology you have today?
- How is the staff affected by technology?
- How is the public responding to the changes in technology?
- How is the public utilizing technology in the library?

✎ BRAINSTORMING 2.5 EXAMINE THE STRENGTHS AND WEAKNESSES IN KEY AREAS OF YOUR LIBRARY.

Using some of the ideas in the general examination as a springboard to examine the weaknesses and strengths of vital areas in a more detailed method.

Internal Analysis of Strengths and Weaknesses in Specific Categories

Area	Strength	Weakness
Administration/Board		
Staffing		
Facilities		
Collections		
Financial Resources		
Support Groups		
Customer Service		
Customer Database		
Technical Service		
Technology		
Hours of Operation		
Reputation		
Other		

After looking at these areas of operation in more detail, break down the categories into more precise parts. What are the specific strengths and weaknesses of each? You may not have ready answers for every category; in that case you may just want to write, "Needs reviewing."

Example:

Technology	Strength	Weakness
Catalog	New catalog online	Need more
Web Sites	We have one	Interactivity
Computer Access	We have 20	Needs better design
Database Usage	We have some accurate stats.	We need more! No way to update records.

Compose similar charts for each of the categories, broken down into their respective parts for your library.

 BRAINSTORMING 2.6 EXAMINE YOUR LIBRARY'S OPPORTUNITIES AND THREATS.

After you determine your strengths and weaknesses, you will need to do similar brainstorming about your opportunities and threats. Opportunities might include new programs or offerings currently unavailable to customers. Threats might include competition from outside sources or inability to handle an issue. Do not minimize or be discouraged by threats: you are likely to find what first seems like a threat may turn out to be an opportunity.

Opportunities and Threats

Factor	Opportunities	Threats
Senior Citizens	Teach Programs on computer use.	Lack of competent teachers of technology.
Children		
Young Adults		
Businesses		
Special Interest Groups		
Prospective Customers		
Competition		
Technology		
Political Climate		
Government and Regulatory Bodies		
Economic Environment		
Legal Environment		

✎ BRAINSTORMING 2.7 SUMMARIZE AND PRIORITIZE YOUR SWOT ANALYSIS.

Now that you have listed your library's strengths, weaknesses, opportunities, and threats, you need to summarize your findings. List your library's strengths and weaknesses.

- Rank the strengths and weaknesses. Which are your greatest strengths? Which are your most vulnerable weaknesses? By ranking these elements, you are getting closer to developing a concrete plan for your library. These are the areas you will concentrate on when you develop the goals of your marketing plan. Limit both lists to ten items.

- Write a SWOT Summary
  A sample SWOT summary might look like the following:

Our most important strengths and best opportunities are:

1. Reputation, position within the community;
2. Service to children;
3. Serving as a community center;
4. Being aware of customers needs and quick enough to meet those needs;
5. Staff expertise;
6. Collection of materials;
7. Serving as a center of life-long learning.

Our most dangerous weaknesses and threats are:

1. Having the necessary financial resources to meet future needs;
2. Continued change brought by technology;
3. Continue economic downturn, which affects financial resources.

Your Library's SWOT Summary:

Our most important strengths and best opportunities are:

1. _____

2. _____

3. _____

4. _____

5. _____

Our most dangerous weaknesses and threats are:

1. _____

2. _____

3. _____

4. _____

5. _____

Develop Long-Term Goals

Now, you need to combine parts of all the information discovered in the writing your mission, values, and visions statements with the priorities you established in the SWOT analysis. It is time to turn these ideas into strategic planning goals.

The goals of your strategic plan should be precise statements of the results you hope to achieve in the next five years. Your goals should be believable, measurable, and achievable by a set deadline, with a specific person in charge. Fuzzy goals like "we are going to raise more money" are not especially stimulating. No one knows when the goal has been met. On the other hand, "we will raise $1.5 million in two years, and Ms. Doe is in charge" will be very clear to everyone involved. People must believe the goals are actually achievable, or they won't even try to work toward them.

Your statements and your SWOT analysis have examined many areas, including:

- The impact of technology;

- Funding, including diversification of funding;

- Collection development;

- Technical services;

- Services to various segments (children, adults, ethnic groups, young adults, seniors, businesses, researchers, students, and organizations.;

- Auxiliary groups;

- Programs;
- Hours;
- Locations, facilities.

  This list can be grouped into four broad categories:

- Financials and Facilities;
- Customer service;
- Technology and delivery systems;
- Administrative and staffing structure.

✎ BRAINSTORMING 2.8 PRIORITY GOALS SHEET

1. Financials and Facilities

Analysis: _____

Goal 1: _____

Due date: _____

Person Responsible: _____

Analysis: _____

Goal 2: _____

Due Date: _____

Person Responsible: _____

Analysis: _____

Goal 3: _____

Due Date: _____

Person Responsible: _____

2. Customer Service

Analysis: _____

Goal 1: _____

Due date: _____

Person Responsible: _____

Analysis: _____

Goal 2: _____

Due Date: _____

Person Responsible: _____

Analysis: _____

Goal 3: _____

Due Date: _____

Person Responsible: _____

3. Technology/Delivery Systems

Analysis: _____

Goal 1: _____

Due date: _____

Person Responsible: _____

Analysis: _____

Goal 2: _____

Due Date: _____

Person Responsible: _____

Analysis: _____

Goal 3: _____

Due Date: _____

Person Responsible: _____

4. Administrative/Staffing

Analysis: _____

Goal 1: _____

Due date: _____

Person Responsible: _____

Analysis: _____

Goal 2: _____

Due Date: _____

Person Responsible: _____

Analysis: _____

Goal 3: _____

Due Date: _____

Person Responsible: _____

Prioritize: select the top four goals from the previous exercise.

1. _____

2. _____

3. _____

4. _____

☼ BRAINSTORMING 2.9 ORGANIZE YOUR STAFF TO CONDUCT YOUR STRATEGIC PLAN.

Who should be involved in the planning?

- The library director and the board chairman must be involved.

- Establish guidelines for selecting members of the committee. Those guidelines will identify who should be involved, who will provide information, and who will review the plan document and who will authorize the document.

- The board's responsibility is to provide leadership for the organization. Therefore, insist that the board be heavily involved in the planning, including participation on committees.

- Ensure that as many stakeholders as possible are involved in the planning process.

- Involve someone to administer the process. That person needs to arrange meetings, help record information, and monitor status of prework.

- Consider having the above administrator develop a planning process with dates and schedules outlined in advance for the participants.

- Encourage representation from each area of library's services in the planning process. Front-line staff can provide incredible insight into daily operations.

- Develop guidelines that help ensure that the plan is implemented.

Do you need an outside facilitator or consultant?

You may need help from a consultant or facilitator, especially:

- if your library has not done a strategic plan in the past;

- if there is a wide range of ideas, or concerns within the library;

- if there is no one in the library with good facilitation skills;

- if the library director believes an inside facilitator will inhibit participation;

- if you are new at strategic planning and would feel more assured of success with outside professional help.

Summary

Now that you know where you are and where you want to be, you will be able to develop a marketing plan to take you in that direction. Let's summarize the tasks covered thus far:

- You have identified the essence of your business.

- You have developed a mission statement, as well as values and vision statements.

- You have performed a SWOT analysis to determine the strengths and weaknesses of your library. In addition, you have identified what opportunities and threats your library will face in the next five years.

- You have chosen a general strategy based on the SWOT analysis. You have turned that strategy into a set of goals and used those goals to establish a set of objectives to be accomplished over the next few years.

- You have involved the board, the administration, the employees, the foundation, and the Friends group in the process of developing a mission, a SWOT analysis, and a strategic plan for the library. The objectives of your strategic plan will form the basis of your marketing plan.

Part 2:
Marketing
Planning Processes

CHAPTER 3

Know Your Customers

The first two chapters were designed to help you develop a strategic plan, but this is just a foundation for marketing. You now have a direction, a vision, and a set of objectives for your library. Marketing takes each objective and develops a plan or plans around it.

A marketing plan is designed to guide the process of marketing. Marketing is both an art and a science. It involves planning, analyzing, and understanding customers. It is creative and offers insight through the analysis process that would never have been obtained otherwise. The process of developing a plan will reveal an incredible amount of information about what your library can offer customers. By using the step-by-step process of market research and analysis, you will reach a far more targeted understanding of existing and potential customers. As a result, you will be positioned to implement more successful, targeted programs that hit the bull's-eye. You will maximize your funding; have the tools to think outside of the box, with the analysis skills to evaluate your thinking. Marketing makes your efforts more targeted, directed, and successful, and it is built by implementing the planning process routinely.

Identifying Your Customers

Customers are as diverse as the populations that libraries serve. Individuals can differ on many characteristics, including age, sex, interests, needs, ethnic origin, economic origin, and lifestyles, to name a few. You need to discover which customers you serve the best, and which you hope to serve better in the future. The environmental analysis is designed to help you identify your customers.

The Pareto Principle, also known as the 80/20 Rule, helps explain why you are trying to learn more about your customers. In 1895, Italian

33

economist Vilfredo Pareto observed that 80 percent of the land in Italy was owned by 20 percent of the population. He soon realized that this ratio seemed to apply to other parts of life, even the peas in his garden: 20 percent of the peapods produced 80 percent of the peas. For libraries, this means that 20 percent of your customers account for 80 percent of the business. It also tells you that 20 percent of your products and services account for 80 percent of the use, and that 80 percent of visitors use only 20 percent of your Web site pages. You study your customers to identify which 20 percent of them represent the majority of your business. They are known as the "vital few." If you focus your efforts to attract more customers like the 20 percent, you will increase business and the return on your investment will be much greater. You will also see a real improvement in efficiency, morale, and productivity.

To study your customers, you will need to focus on four areas:

- Segmentation: the process of differentiating your customers by their characteristics. It is the art and science of identifying your target market.

- Demand: the actual desire to use your services coupled with the power to do so. How many people will use your services?

- Customer decision-making process: the behavior or incentives that make your customers decide to use your product or service.

- Competition: the tangible and intangible rivalry that exists for programs and services.

Segmentation

Segmentation is the process of classifying customers into groups with different needs, characteristics or behavior. A market segment consists of customers who respond in a similar way to a given set of stimuli. Market segmentation describes the division of a market into homogeneous groups, each of which responds differently to promotions, communications, and advertising.

Reasons for Segmentation

There are good reasons for dividing the market into smaller segments.

1. Ease. It is easier to address the needs of a smaller group of customers with many characteristics in common.

2. Efficiency. You can use marketing resources more effectively by focusing on the best segments of the population for your programs.

3. Niches. You can identify underserved markets and target special groups or niches. It also helps us take the mature library products and seek new consumers.

Use yourself as an example of segmentation. How many catalogues do you receive at home? Are they different from your neighbor's catalogues? You receive those catalogues based on your purchases in the past. Your neighbor may receive a totally different group of catalogues, based on his interests.

Better yet, think of the automobile market. When Henry Ford built the Model T, there was only one automobile. That situation did not last long. The automobile industry has since studied every kind of segmentation—demographic, geographic, psychographic, and behavioral. As a result, you have economy cars, luxury cars, four wheel drive cars, electric cars, sedans, station wagons, minivans, and SUVs.

Many libraries target their services very broadly. They segment the market demographically, but give little thought to a more sophisticated approach. Your library may already divide its offerings into children's services, young adult services, research services, and business services, but you can see that there are still various segments within each of those areas. Take children's services, for example. There are children of various ages, ethnic origins, gender, geographical locations, and socioeconomic groups—each of these segments may have different needs and interests.

Classification Variables

The most common form of market segmentation uses what are called *classification variables*.

* *Demographic variables*: qualities such as age, gender, income, ethnicity, education, and occupation;

* *Geographical variables*: information like city, state, zip code, census tract, county, region, population density;

* *Psychographic variables*: items like attitudes, lifestyle, hobbies, interests;

* *Behavioral variables*: usage level, distribution means;

For further examples, see figure 3-1.

FIGURE 3-1 Basic Market Segmentation Criteria

Use these categories as criteria to describe your customers. Look for clusters of people described by these criteria.

Demographic
Age range
Gender
Income level
Occupation
Religion
Race/ethnic group
Education
Social class

Geographic
Country
Region
State
County
City/town
Size of population
Climate
Population density

Psychographic
Leader or follower
Extrovert or introvert
Achievement-oriented or content with the status quo
Independent or dependent
Conservative or liberal
Traditional or experimental
Societally-conscious or self-centered

Consumer/Behavioral
Rate of usage
Benefits sought
Method of usage
Frequency of usage
Frequency of purchase

Business Markets
Type of business (manufacturer, retail, wholesale, service)
Standard Industrial Classification (SIC) Code
Size of business
Financial strength
Number of employees
Location
Structure
Sales level
Special requirements
Distribution patterns

Demographic Variables

The following two worksheets will walk you through the process of demographic and geographic segmentation. You already have some of the information from your strategic planning; the rest you can find through your local Chamber of Commerce or county government offices.

✎ BRAINSTORMING 3.1 SEGMENTATION BY DEMOGRAPHIC VARIABLES

1. Estimate the percentage of your customers in each age group.

0–4: _____

5–9: _____

10–12: _____

13–18: _____

19–22: _____

23–30: _____

31–40: _____

41–50: _____

51–60: _____

61–70: _____

71+: _____

2. What percentage of your customers is male/female?
    _____%male _____%female
    Do these percentages vary by age?

3. What is the average income of your customers?
    Economically challenged: _____
    Moderate:_____
    Affluent: _____

4. What is the education level of your customers over the age of 25?
    High school: _____
    College: _____
    Graduate school: _____

5. What are the ethnic origins of your customers?
    White: _____
    Hispanic:_____
    African-American: _____
    Asian: _____

Geographic Variables

✎ BRAINSTORMING 3.2 SEGMENTATION BY GEOGRAPHIC VARIABLES

1. In which zip codes do your customers reside?

   _____

   _____

2. What does the Census of Population say about the area around your library?

   _____

   _____

3. Can you describe the population density around your library?

   _____

   _____

4. What is the geographical situation of your library?

   _____

   _____

Psychographic Variables

You can also differentiate groups of people by their psychographic or lifestyle characteristics. Some of your customers may enjoy local history, some may enjoy books on tape, while others spend hours studying genealogy. You can practice segmentation by lifestyle with Brainstorming 3.3. This is set up to study seniors, but you can substitute any other group.

Behavioral Variables

Behavioral methods of segmentation are easily recognized when you consider the ways different customers contact the library. Think about your customers who use the Internet to access the library. Electronic delivery certainly attracts a different segment of people than regular delivery.

Segmentation Studies

As you can see, you can "slice and dice" groups of people in many different ways. Still, it is easier to acquire more people like the ones you are currently serving well than to develop a whole new segment. Brainstorming 3.4 asks you to pick one segment of your market and create a profile.

☼ BRAINSTORMING 3.3 IDENTIFY A SEGMENT OF THE POPULATION.

Pick a broad segment of the population that is important to your library. Examples: children, Hispanics, urban residents

How can you break this large group into finer segments?

a) Are you going to describe them with demographic considerations such as age, sex, ethnic origin (don't forget you can break many ethnic groups like Hispanics or Asians into more refined national groups), economic conditions?

b) Are you going to describe them geographically in a certain area?

c) Are you going to describe them by psychographic characteristics including interests or lifestyles?

d) How about behavioral characteristics? How do they access the library? Electronically? In person?

Create a more specific segment of the population based on the ways that you broke down your broader segment.

• How many members of this population segment reside in your vicinity?

• What do you think will be their actual demand for services?

• Is there competition for the services? Think of any direct form of competition as well as any intangible form of competition, like the weather, language barriers, parental supervision.

• What will make this group want to use the library?

• Are they the primary decision maker? What role do their parents or preschool, Head Start, or other school play in the decision-making process? Example: Perhaps you have decided to target economically deprived children between the ages of 4–6. There is a significant demand by this group, especially through Head Start programs. But while the program is designed to meet the needs of four to six-year-old children, the decision making is in the hands of the administrator of the Head Start program. How can you meet the needs of the segment, at the same time you target the decision maker?

☼ BRAINSTORMING 3.4 IDENTIFY THE SERVICES IMPORTANT TO YOUR SEGMENT.

• What products and services does your segment currently receive?

• What products and services does your segment need?

- How do your services currently reach this group?

- How can new services reach this group?

- What are the costs involved with your current and new services?

- How can you get information to better serve your segment?

- How can you get the word out to your segment?

Libraries throughout the United States have used segmentation successfully to develop their programs. One outstanding example is the Queens Borough Public Library in New York. Queens Borough is an area populated with immigrants from many different parts of the world. The library has used some basic demographic segmentation to identify potential markets. They have also listened to their potential customers to develop programs that appeal to their target markets.

Success Story 3.1
Using Segmentation to Develop an Outstanding Library Program

Queens Borough Public Library,   **Jamaica, New York**

On any afternoon the Central Library of the Queens Borough Public Library is bustling. There are people of every color and nationality working earnestly at the computers and reading material. School kids cluster around the tables with textbooks. The library is a virtual activity center, continuing with programming of all kinds into the evening. The library has boasted one of the highest circulation rates for a public library system in the country. In 2003, cardholders checked out 16.9 million books, videotapes, CDs and other items.

The Queens Borough Public Library traces much of its success to creating services that are inclusive of the borough's large population of recent immigrants. The staff recognized that their target markets spoke many different languages, that there was a desire and a need for information and bestsellers in English, Bengali, Hindi, Malayalam, Punjabi, Urdu, Chinese, Gujarati, Spanish, Korean, Russian, French, and Greek. Now, materials have been collected in 68 different languages, and the online catalogue is searchable and viewable in English, Spanish, Chinese, Korean, and French. A community service database offers details of 1,200 programs on health and human services. Free Internet access is also available to non-English speaking customers through WorldLinQ™ (www.worldlinq.org), an electronic information delivery system developed through a partial grant from AT&T. Links are provided to Spanish, Korean, Chinese, Russian, and French language sites, which have been vetted by a team of multilingual librarians as being informative and authoritative.

The library further appealed to the local immigrant population through their New Americans Program. In 2003, 7,822 students from 88 countries and representing 50 languages attended English for Speakers of Other Languages (ESOL) classes at the library. In addition, the library offers free lectures and workshops in the most widely spoken of the immigrant languages, on topics ranging from citizenship and job training to children's programs and social services. Free readings, concerts, and workshops are open to the public. These offerings celebrate the folk, performing, and the literary arts of their immigrant populations whether from Asia, Africa, Europe, Latin America, or the Caribbean.

But the Queens Borough Public Library faces at least one challenge most libraries do not: many of the library's customers come from places where public libraries either do not exist, or are not available for the average person. To work with individuals outside of the library setting and eliminate barriers to service, the library must closely study the needs of their customers and develop outreach programs. They personally invite people to their facility and provide them with orientation services and networking programs. By focusing their programs on various segments of the market, they have become an integral part of the community. Still the library thrives by emphasizing the common touch, offering a welcoming arm to immigrants in a strange new world. In 2003, the Queens Borough Public Library received the first-ever National Award for Library Service from the Institute of Museum and Library Services in Washington, D.C.

Success Story 3.2
Creating the African American Research Library

Denver Public Library, Blair-Caldwell African American Research Library,   **Denver, Colorado**

The Denver Public Library is showcasing the contributions of African Americans to the Rocky Mountain West, by building a new facility, the Blair-Caldwell African American Research Library. Officially opened on April 26, 2003, the library is not only a fully functional branch of the Denver system, but a research facility and a community program area. The project was originally the vision of former Mayor Wellington E. Webb and now has the full enthusiasm of the African American Community.

The mission of the Blair-Caldwell Library is to serve as an educational and cultural resource for the people of Denver, Colorado and the world. It focuses on the history, literature, art, music, religion, and politics of African American people in Colorado and throughout the Rocky Mountain region. The library will collect, preserve, and present documents and artifacts spotlighting the contributions of African Americans of the American West, but inherent in the collection are archival materials representative of persons across all walks of life. The goal of this project is to celebrate, discover, and recognize the varied and tremendous stories of the people that help build contemporary western American life and culture. Exhibits, research by students and scholars, educational and cultural programs, and community outreach are all critical elements.

The Blair-Caldwell African American Research Library themes respond to audience research from four focus groups of over 100 community people, who articulated community needs. The participants were asked to identify the particular areas of interest that they had for preservation. The data collected from the focus groups indicated an interest in knowledge about the history and heritage of African Americans in relation to Denver and the surrounding areas.

Taking a cue from the results of the research, the facility was designed to focus on African American history and the exploration of the West. It includes documentation of the collaboration of the Asian and Hispanic populations, as they all moved through this region of the country. The settlement of the West brought ethnic populations to this area as they worked on the railroad and in the mines of the western frontier. Located on the second floor of the library, this archival research center has closed storage areas for archival materials and a staff workroom. The archives include a wide range of primary sources: photographs, manuscript collections, letters, scrapbooks, and diaries to audio and video oral histories, showcasing the stories of African American musicians, politicians, educators, artists, business owners, religious leaders, scholars, and the everyday, hard-working pioneers.

Still, the research facility only represents one part of the project. The library's circulation collection contains more than 32,000 items including books, magazines, videos, DVDs, CD-ROMs, and 40 Web-enabled public computers. Available in English and Spanish, the library's circulating collection is certain to offer materials to suit all tastes. The first floor features a gallery, a conference center, meeting rooms, and a coffee bar. Meanwhile, up on the third floor, "Western Legacy" offers 7,000 square feet of gallery and exhibition space. Exhibits will highlight historical periods, notable individuals, and local Denver history.

The Blair-Caldwell Library is a significant part of the re-gentrification of a historic area of the community. In fact, the groundbreaking ceremony attracted twice as many individuals as the library had anticipated. This new facility brings with it pride and ownership to the city, the community, and to the Denver Public Library. It certainly helps to position the Denver Public Library within this community.

Identify The Demand For Your Services

You have identified various segments, but now you need to know about the level of demand of every segment. In marketing, the word *demand* refers to the total number of potential customers in a particular segment. For each segment you have identified, you must now determine the number of individuals in that segment. For example, if you looked at the segment called "children," you would begin by identifying the numbers of children. Of course, the numbers of children would vary according to certain criteria, such as age, neighborhood, ethnicity, gender, or educational and economic levels of parents. The criteria force us to continue to segment this market and target our market even more specifically, and you begin to identify the actual demand for a product or service by segment.

Look at Brainstorming 3.5 and identify the demand for children in each segment. You can find the information you need through census reports of the area, government offices, and at the local Chamber of Commerce. Of course, this worksheet can be adapted to any of the population segments in your library.

BRAINSTORMING 3.5 CROSS SEGMENTS TO REALIZE AND TARGET PROGRAMS.

This is an opportunity to develop effective programs and effective targeting strategies. Crossing two segment factors will help your library develop effective new programs, and help you identify the core market for your programs.

- List one set of related segments horizontally across the top of a paper.

  Example: Age groups (toddlers, children, teens); economic status (poor, middle class, wealthy)

- List a second set of related segments vertically down the same piece of paper.

  Example: ethnicities (Latino, Caucasian, Asian, African Americans); family type (single parent, two parent, families with stepparents)

- List the varying demands of each cross section.

- To add weight to your decisions, include census statistics for your area when available.

Example: This table considers the needs of different ethnic groups and different age groups.

	Children 0–3 2% of population	Children 3–6 4% of population	Children 7–10 5% of population	Children 10–13 7% of population
Caucasian (31%)	-Motor Skills -Storytime	-Reading skills -Tutor time	-Technology skills -Tutor time -After school programs	-Research skills -Arts programs -Social programs
African American (25%)	-Motor Skills -Storytime	-Reading skills -Tutor time -After school programs	-Technology skills -Tutor time -After school programs	-Research skills -Arts programs -After school programs -Discussion groups
Latino (30%)	-Motor Skills -Storytime -Bilingual Early Language skills	-Reading skills -Tutor time -Second Language skills Health Programs	-Technology skills -Tutor time -After school programs -Second Language skills	-Research skills -Tutor time After school programs -Arts programs
Asian American (10%	-Motor Skills Story time -Bilingual Language skills	-Reading skills -Tutor time -After school programs Health Programs	-Reading skills -Tutor time -After school programs Health Programs	-Research skills -Tutor time -After school programs
Native American (4%)	-Motor Skills -Storytime -Bilingual Language skills	-Reading skills -After school programs	-Technology skills -After school programs	-Research skills -Tutor time -Discussion groups

You may find one particular group with large enough numbers to warrant a single program. Maybe a bilingual, reading, and technology after school program should be targeted at Hispanics age 4–8. You may also discover that you need to develop a smaller program to meet very specific needs of discrete populations.

Chart 3.6 should help you in two ways. First, you can identify key needs for individual programs. Second, in tight times or with limited staff, you can develop programs of broad appeal by looking at shared needs of many segments and market a broad scope program to multiple clients.

BRAINSTORMING 3.6 IDENTIFY THE DEMANDS ON YOUR LIBRARY.

These questions will help you identify demand for the library as a whole.

- List a few of the segments you are currently serving in the library (be both broad and specific). It may help to list these across the top of a large piece of paper.

- Can you identify the key demands for those segments? These can be listed under each segment. Use information such as *Census of Population*, current circulation data, or other information to estimate the demand.

- Identify current programs that answer the demands of each segment and their needs.

- Suggest potential solutions to needs that are not met.

Forecasting and Building Demand

Sometimes you may like to *forecast* how demand will be built in the future. There are many examples of demand building in the private sector. Disney started out by making animated films, only to expand into theme parks. They continue to expand through retail sales and stores, resorts, and vacation property, increasing demand for their products. Libraries experience a growth in demand when they open a new facility. Studies show that new buildings bring a substantial group of new customers.

Still, you want to understand the market well enough to determine which segments offer the best chance to achieve your objectives. You base that decision on past use of the library and on market research. (You will learn about market research in Chapter 5). In marketing, a key concept is *market penetration*. This term refers to the set of customers, who already use a product or service. Of necessity, you must distinguish the total available market and the percentage of market penetration you have achieved in that market. The *potential market* represents the total number of people who could use a particular product or service.

Understanding the Customer's Decision Making

When a customer buys something on sale at the grocery store, he has made a decision. When he chooses a gasoline station because of convenience, price, or service, he has made a decision. Understanding the customer's decision-making process is just as important for libraries as for any other company. The process begins with a *need* on the part of the customer. He or she begins to *desire* the service or product that can meet this need, and evaluates whether or not to use the product.

Sometimes, it is difficult to identify what exactly motivates a customer's decision making. What makes a customer decide to use a library's services? Is it the price? The collection or availability of materials? Staff assistance? The hours of operation? Parking? Convenience? A drive-up window? Electronic checkout? If you do not pay careful attention to your customer's decision making, your program will fail. Look, for example, at the Queens Borough Library in New York. Many of their customers come from foreign countries and are not familiar with library services in the United States. The library realized they had to provide personalized outreach programs to encourage these customers to use their services.

When working with children, librarians may forget that it is the parent who decides to use the service. What will convince the parents to provide their children with the opportunity to participate in a particular program or service? For example, circulation statistics were low at one inner-city library, until market research revealed that parents told their children not to check out materials, because they could not afford the fines.

Librarians can also learn by paying more attention to their own decision making. How do you decide to purchase or participate in a service? Look at your response to the various catalogues and advertisements that come to you. Merchandisers try in many ways to *create* the need and desire for a product. You may discover a need you never knew you had.

Brainstorming 3.7 is designed to help you understand your customers' decision-making process. Don't be limited by the worksheet—add any segments or influences that are appropriate for your library.

☼ BRAINSTORMING 3.7 IDENTIFY DECISION-MAKING FACTORS.

This exercise will help you to become aware of how different market segments make decisions.

- List several population segments important to your library across the top of a piece of paper.

  Examples: Professionals, Seniors, Latinos

- Who or what influences the customer decision-making process?

  Example

Latinos	Children	Seniors	Professionals
Language	Parents	Mobility	Time of day
Cultural interest	School	Time of day	Location

- Consider more specific populations and combine their influences.

  Example: Latino Professionals are influenced by language, cultural interest, time of day and the location.

  Brainstorming 3.8 draws on segmentation, demand, and customer decision making to help you plan the marketing of a new product.

BRAINSTORMING 3.8 DETERMINE PROGRAMMING BY USING SEGMENTATION, DEMAND, AND CUSTOMER DECISION-MAKING PROCESS.

- What is your idea for a product or service?

- What segment of the audience is this product designed to serve?

- What additional segments might it serve?

- What is the demand for each segment that you have identified?

- How did you determine demand?

- What or who will influence members of each segment to use this product?

- Who will, or how will you, influence each segment to use this product?

Looking at the Competition

"Competition is everywhere," says Joyce Mestis of the Tattered Cover Bookstore. "Each Saturday morning I pray for rain. We compete even with the weather. People have time, leisure activity, and some money. The choices are myriad in our culture. You can go hiking, skiing, watch television, or punch a keyboard. Competition never lets you relax! However, rain makes a huge difference!"

Many libraries may not feel they have competition, but in many ways they do. They compete for funding resources within a community, university, or corporation. They compete for private funding with individuals, foundations, and corporations. They compete for volunteers and staff. They compete with other institutions for bond elections. They compete with the Internet, television, and leisure activities.

To understand your competition, go to the source. Visit bookstores, museums, universities, and zoos, as well as other libraries. Each of these institutions is positioning itself within the community. Examine the programs that work for them. Visit their Web sites. Participate in their programs. Watch their annual fund programs, as well as capital campaigns. Use Brainstorming 3.9 to see how you measure up to your competitors. Below, bookstores is the example used to illustrate the key points.

☼ BRAINSTORMING 3.9 COMPARE YOUR LIBRARY TO A COMPETITOR.

- Discuss several areas in which you compete with similar institutions or stores.

    Examples: Cost, Hours of Operation, Location

- Rate your competitor in each of the categories and rate your library in each of the categories.

    Example: The example chart rates a library against a bookstore

Issue	Competitor-Bookstore	How does the library stack up?
Cost	High	No Price
Merchandizing	High	Limited
Quality	High	High
Customer Service	High	Improving
Location	Shopping Mall	Neighborhood
Hours of Operation	Open daily/evening	Limited hours in library
Delivery Service	Excellent	Limited in the library
Retrieve Unknown Works	Good	Excellent

Seeing the Intangible Competition

While some competition, like bookstores or museums, may be obvious, there is a less obvious form of competition called *intangible competition*. Dealing with intangible competition means understanding change and the resistance to change, understanding the well-educated customer, reading the customer's mind, and understanding the benign mentality.

1. Understanding Change and the Resistance to Change

Our society is in a perpetual state of change. Companies change, libraries change, industries change. Some of the major companies today did not even exist one or two decades ago. One of the biggest changes for libraries is the influence of new technology. Technology raises customers' expectations. People expect you to have a Web site, they expect to do things electronically that would not have been possible ten years ago.

Sometimes it is hard to recognize the changes occurring in the environment. Resisting change or being oblivious to change can be damaging. What makes libraries resistant to change? Sometimes libraries are simply too busy with the day-to-day activities to pay serious attention. Sometimes you might not really understand the changes or their implications. Maybe you are hesitant about trying something new. If you understand why you are resisting change, however, you may find it easier to recognize and accept some of the changes in your environment.

2. Understanding the Well-Educated Customer

Libraries serve a variety of customers, from those restricted to computer access in the library, to the more technologically savvy, with higher expectations of computer service. For example, online databases make it possible to sort through large amounts of information. Computers have become a decision-making tool, not just tools for obtaining information. As library customers become more sophisticated, databases become more critical. Libraries must be responsive to customer needs, or their customers will meet their needs elsewhere.

3. Reading the Customer's Mind

Winning the customer's mind is a central challenge of marketing. Decisions to use the library are based on perceptions of quality, image, support, and leadership. Those perceptions do not form through a single event, rather a customer's attitudes develop gradually; they are constantly changing and evolving. If your library is going to be competitive, you will not only have to recognize these attitudes, but also recognize that these attitudes are continually changing.

4. Beware the Complacent Mentality

Libraries are often reluctant to take risks. The same problem occurs in corporations. Libraries exist in a political environment. It seems like everything that they do is visible. How do they maintain a risk-taking, entrepreneurial attitude in such a fish bowl? The answer is to retain small, entrepreneurial groups within the library, avoid department loyalty, promote greater interaction and build teams.

Doing Market Research with Secondary Information

Libraries traditionally contain vast storehouses of secondary information, also called historical data, information that is already available. This information might exist in reference materials, periodicals, online databases, business and financial information, or census and demographic data.

FIGURE 3-2 Primary and Secondary information	
PRIMARY RESEARCH	
Quantitative	**Qualitative**
• Questionnaires	• Focus groups
• Telephone surveys	• Feasibility studies
• Polling	• Interviews
SECONDARY RESEARCH	
• Research reports	• Case studies in textbooks
• Census information	
• Standard & Poor's Reports	

Libraries can make good use of all this secondary information for their own market research. For example, computerized information from the online catalogue can be used to learn more about your customers. You can identify which books have the highest turnover or which periodicals and databases have the highest demand. You can use the computerized cardholder database system to identify the geographic areas from which your customers come to the library. You can identify what is called "marketing penetration"; that is, your customers come from specific situations.

As an individual, you have had experience with this kind of database market analysis. Every time you use a supermarket card or a credit card, your purchases are tracked. Ever wonder how you got on all of those mailing lists? The World Wide Web has added another dimension to market research. Web sites provide customers with remote use, and those Web sites can keep track of "hits." Technological advances have spurred the development of information systems, and those systems are at your fingertips.

BRAINSTORMING 3.10 ASSESS SECONDARY INFORMATION SOURCES IN YOUR LIBRARY.

Before starting detailed marketing research, you may want to take stock of what you have in your own library. List the types of secondary information in your library.

Examples:

- Government documents

- Reference materials

- Genealogy information

- Local history information

- Case studies

- Other sources within your library

Primary Research Methodologies

Data that you obtain through your own research efforts is called *primary information*. There is an extensive methodology for designing primary research.

Researchers distinguish two types of primary information—*qualitative and quantitative*. Qualitative research is conducted to examine how our customers feel about the library or any other product or service. There are several ways to obtain this qualitative information, including focus groups and personal interviews. Through these efforts, you can understand customer perceptions and behaviors. Libraries sometimes think that they know their customers, but hard data can produce some real surprises. Quantitative information gives us statistical data about our customer's behaviors. You obtain quantitative information through polling, surveys, and specific studies. Qualitative information focuses on particular characteristics of customer behavior, aside from the number of customers associated with each feature. Often researchers utilize qualitative information to refine the questions to ask on the quantitative studies. You can occasionally use both types of research together, while at other times one or the other gives us enough information.

Directional Research: Surveys

Being close to the customer is very important in the marketing process, because customers will tell you what direction you should take. One way of gaining customer input is simply to make it a rule to talk to three customers every day. Ask them if they found what they came in for; ask how you can serve them better. The responses will provide you with surprising direction-al information. The directional information you receive is not quantitative, but it is specific, timely, and certainly can alert you to new trends.

Another form of directional research is short, written surveys, which provide quick and accurate insight into customer issues. The questionnaire must be designed carefully, including the number of questions to be asked. A good survey can be an excellent research tool. However, many surveys are ineffective, because they are poorly designed or improperly adminis-tered. There can be errors in the sampling process, the interview process, the data processing, and coding.

Although designing a questionnaire is not a simple task, it is the key to obtaining accurate survey results. The language should be simple. Question sequence is very important. Even the layout of a mail question-naire can affect the response.

Brainstorming worksheets 3.11 through 3.14 are example surveys that you might use, if you want to understand customers' attitudes and feelings about products and services. Customize them for use with your library cus-tomers, or adapt them to gather directional information on products and serv-ices you are particularly interested in. Hand these surveys out to customers over a period of one week. They are designed to provide directional informa-tion, to give you an indication of a customer service problem. Additional research will provide more in-depth and specific information about a problem.

BRAINSTORMING 3.11 ASSESS LIBRARY CUSTOMER ATTITUDES.

Please place a check in the box that best describes your opinion of library services.

Question	Strongly Agree	Agree	Disagree	Strongly Disagree
The library has the materials I need				
It is easy to find the materials				
Staff are helpful and knowledgeable				
The computer catalogue is easy to use				
It is easy to renew books and materials				

Question	Strongly Agree	Agree	Disagree	Strongly Disagree
The hours of service are convenient				
Buildings are clean				
It is easy to find a place to read and study				

Please circle your gender: Male   Female

Please indicate today's date: _____ and time:_____

✎ BRAINSTORMING 3.12 SCALE-BASED SAMPLE EVALUATION

Please place a check mark at the appropriate location to indicate how you feel about library services. The plus side (left side) of the scale represents the highest mark. The minus side (right side) represents the lowest. For example, if the library has everything you need, place an "x" on the "+2"

Statement:	Evaluation
The library has what I need	+2 ....0 ....-2
Reference services provided the answer I needed	+2 ....0 ....-2
The automated catalogue is easy to use	+2 ....0 ....-2
Materials are easy to find.	+2 ....0 ....-2
Signage and directions are helpful	+2 ....0 ....-2
Access to computers is provided	+2 ....0 ....-2

Your Age: _____

Please circle: Male   Female

Today's date: _____

✎ BRAINSTORMING 3.13 COMPUTER ASSESSMENT SURVEY

Please place a check in the box that best describes your opinion of the library's computer services.

Question	Strongly Agree	Agree	Disagree	Strongly Disagree
The automated catalogue is easy to use				
Directions for use are easy to understand				

Question	Strongly Agree	Agree	Disagree	Strongly Disagree
The computer service is complex				
I would like to print information directly from the computer				
I would like to check out materials directly from the computer				
I would like to renew books directly from the computer				

Your Age: _____

Please circle: Male   Female

Today's date: _____

✎ BRAINSTORMING 3.14 LIBRARY USER SURVEY

Your ideas and opinions are important to our Library and will help us provide you the best library service possible. Please circle your responses:

1. What types of materials/services do you use most often or would like to use?

(AA) Children's materials	(BB) Bestseller books	(CC) Information
(a) Books	(b) Large print books	(c) Books on audio tape
(d) Magazines	(e) E-mail access	(f) Video tapes (VCR)
(g) CDs music	(h) CD computer software	(i) Internet access
(j) Laser discs	(k) Computer databases with complete articles	
(l) Copier	(m) Computer databases with citations only	
(n) Newspapers	(o) Out-of-town newspapers (specify) _____	

(p) Public computer with software applications (example: MS Word) (specify) _____

(q) Quiet study space	(r) Reference information	(s) Space for children's programs
(t) Coffee bar	(u) Used book sale area	(v) Gift shop
(w) Leisure reading area	(x) Exhibit area	(y) Young adult area
(z) Meeting room/auditorium		

2. When do you prefer to use the library?

(a) Morning (9 am-noon)	(b) Afternoon (noon-5pm)
(c) Evening (6 pm-8 pm)	(d) Later than 8 pm (specify)_____

(e)   Mon   Tues   Wed   Thurs   Fri   Sat   Sun.

3. Do you see a need for library service in any of the following areas?

(a) Basic Literacy	(b) Business and Career Information
(c) Public Meeting Place	(d) Community Information and Referral
(e) Consumer information	(f) Cultural Awareness

(g) Current Topics and Titles (h) Formal Learning Support

(i) General Information   (j) Government Information

(k) Lifelong Learning   (l) Information Literacy

(m) Local History and Genealogy

(n) Other_____

4. Your Zip Code: _____

How often do you use the library? _____

Do you use more than one library?

No_____ Yes_____ (specify locations) _____

Would you use library materials in language(s) other than English?

No_____ Yes_____

(specify language) _____

5. How do you learn about library programs?

(a) Bookings   (b) local library   (c) library Web site

(d) newspaper   (e) television   (f) radio

(g) other (specify) _____

Thank you for completing this survey.

Your Comments:

_____

_____

_____

Your Age: _____

Please circle: Male   Female

Today's date: _____

Focus Groups

Focused group discussions, or focus groups, as they are more popularly known, are an exploratory form of market research that libraries can use to provide insight into problems, opportunities, or issues facing managers. They can help librarians to understand various needs, beliefs, attitudes, and sensitivities of the targeted audiences (both current and potential), for example, business users, senior citizens, young adults, and ethnic groups. The information gathered from focus groups is qualitative in that it provides directional information and incredible insight. If necessary, you can validate the insight and direction gained from the focus group with a quantitative process.

There are four essential elements of a successful focus group:

- **Choice of Participants**: A focus group usually consists of 8–12 participants chosen for their homogeneity on characteristics related to the subject matter to be discussed.

- **Facility**: Groups discussions can be held in meeting or conference rooms, as well as in traditional market research facilities. Official focus group facilities include a conference room facility with a two-way glass. An observation room on the other side of the glass allows administrators and market research staff to observe. The sessions are usually recorded, either on audio or video. The normal session lasts approximately one and one-half to two hours.

- **Moderator**: It is wise to use an outside moderator specifically trained in focus group methodology. They have no opinion about the issue and can allow the conversation to be free-flowing and yet, provide direction to keep the group on target. Moderators generally come from professional market research firms, or university marketing departments.

- **Discussion Outline:** Staff working with the moderator develop a discussion outline called the protocol. The discussion itself is still relatively free-flowing, encouraging a kind of "snowballing" effect. The basic philosophy of the focus group methodology is that the dynamics of a group process will generate useful information on a cost-effective basis. Most people feel more comfortable talking about almost any subject when they are involved in a group. Group dynamics provide insight into how peer pressure plays a role in the degree of overall acceptance of a concept, product, or idea.

After the session, the moderator and market research staff listen to tapes, review notes, and develop careful analysis and reports. This is a lengthy process used to summarize results and requires significant time if done properly.

Success Story 3.3
Using Focus Groups to Identify Specific Customer Needs

Sweetwater County Library System,   **Sweetwater, Wyoming**

The Sweetwater County Library System in Wyoming conducted a series of focus groups on the needs of teachers, senior citizens, young adults, Spanish-speaking people, as well as other individuals in their remote branches. This information helped them develop a strategic plan for library services in the future. Staff members recruited participants for each group including people to help translate Spanish to English. Library facilities and city and county offices were used for the research. Screens were provided to the observers so they could watch and listen to the focus groups without being seen by them.

Standard protocols were developed specifically for each group. For example, the following protocol was developed for the Spanish-speaking group:

Objectives:

To determine:

1. Barriers of library use.

2. Incentives for library use.

3. Collection and staff needs.

4. Communication channels.

5. Effectiveness of an advisory committee.

Protocol:

Participants were asked:

- To state their name.

- Why they have chosen to live in this community.

- How long they have lived here.

Next, they were invited to discuss:

- The role of the library in the community. Did they use the library? Why or why not? Were there particular barriers that prevented their use of the library?

- The collection material including books, music, books on tape, and videos. What did they need?

- Facilities and staff. Was it important to have Spanish-speaking staff?

- Children's story hours. Should they be conducted in Spanish? Should they be bilingual in format?

- Computer literacy. Should the catalogue be available in Spanish as well as English?

- Communication programs. What was the best way to reach this demographic group?

Note: The final discussion item was of potentially hiring an advisory committee to work with library staff to maximize communication and library service.

Results of the focus group discussions:

The local chairman of the Hispanic Coalition coordinated the focus group discussion composed of Spanish-speaking individuals. The participants were originally from Columbia, Mexico and the Basque region of Spain.

They wanted music from South America and Mexico and more videos in Spanish in the collection. They requested children's literature, such as Spanish lullabies, young children's books, and bilingual books. They asked for Spanish auto manuals, computer manuals, driver's license manuals as well as legal information. They also wanted doctor and dentist referrals. Bilingual or Spanish story hours, welcome brochures, and catalogues were all requests made by the group, and they were most enthusiastic about the prospect of a "Spanish Advisory Group." When asked about the best way to contact them, they recommended advertising through the church or Spanish-speaking radio stations.

There were also two focus groups of young adults, aged 11 to 14. They confirmed that the majority of them had access to computers at home and that their use of the library has changed in the last few years. Although they like books, they use the computer for information more than they use the library. In fact, they showed that their use of computers and technology was very sophisticated. At the library, they wanted online access for homework research projects and more computer facilities. They also requested their own space with a lounge so they could read and snack, stating that now they feel the library is only for "little kids and old people." They were enthusiastic about forming a "teen advisory" council that would meet once a month to advise the library on activities and collections. They wanted "cool" things in the collection, such as books on four-wheeling and Seventeen Magazine. Social events like a "Halloween Party" also generated great enthusiasm. They also wanted listening stations for CDs.

Senior citizens also voiced their opinions in focus groups. They stated they would like to see the library catalogue the computer at the senior center and would also like to have the library's computer classes in a more personal environment. They were interested in the library's programs, especially Wyoming Authors, a series of presentations from local writers. For a small, remote population, Wyoming has produced some wonderful authors.

The information the library acquired was a valuable tool in improving the library for all age groups and the results of these focus groups are being used in the Sweetwater County Library System strategic planning process. Young Adult services have already seen changes because of the focus groups. "The work has lead to positive changes, and that is always good news," according to Paul Holland, Director. The use of focus groups is a very effective tool libraries can use to assess the varied needs of their customers.

Brainstorming exercise 3.15 guides you through the steps of planning your own focus group.

☼ BRAINSTORMING 3.15 STEPS TO CONDUCTING A FOCUS GROUP DISCUSSION

1. Determine that focus group methodology is appropriate for the issue of group. Develop objectives for the focus group.

2. Determine the number of groups. Focus groups are usually done in pairs if possible.

3. Develop a budget. Expenses include the following:

    a. moderator who will develop the protocol, facilitate the discussions, listen to the recordings, analyze the results and produce the reports
    b. the facility
    c. incentives to encourage individuals to participate (refreshments)

    A focus group can cost between $3,000 and $45,000, but those expenses may be minimized in several ways. The library can be used as a facility. Incentives to encourage participation can include items that have been donated to the library (e.g., grocery gift certificates, movie passes, fast food restaurant certificates). One can also develop partnerships with local universities to provide market research.

4. Enlist a moderator or market research firm.

5. Develop a timeline of activities.

6. Enlist participants.

    Library staff are generally pretty knowledgeable about individuals who would make good participants. Each focus group consists of 6–12 individuals, who are homogeneous. They are called by library staff members. They are also sent a post card to remind them. In addition, library staff members should call each one the day before the group discussion. After they have come and participated with the focus group, their participation is followed by a thank you note.

7. Develop the protocol. The moderator develops the protocol and it is reviewed by the administrator or staff involved. Additions, changes, or corrections are made.

8. Locate recording equipment. Each focus group should be individually recorded.

9. When the group convenes, welcome each participant. Show the participants to places at a large table and place cards with their names. Introduce them to the moderator. When all of the members of the group are present, proceed with introductions.

If the group discussion is being held in a meeting room, library staff should sit behind a screen. The optimum arrangement is in a focused group facility with a one-way glass. Observers may sit behind the glass so that they may observe the reaction of participants. Participants are informed of their presence. A staff member takes notes of the discussion in addition to the tape recording. There are instances when the tape recording fails, so the back-up information is very helpful.

For the plan of a successful set of focus groups, read about the Sweetwater County Library System, in Sweetwater County, Wyoming (Success Story 3.3) and their use of focus groups for developing a strategic plan for library services in the future. They wanted more information on the needs of groups, including teachers, senior citizens, young adults, Spanish-speaking people, as well as individuals in their remote branches.

Personal Interviews

Market research professionals find that personal interviews offer many advantages. One of the most important is the opportunity for feedback. Sensitive information can be given in confidence to the interviewer. (An outside source is preferable, because library employees can become defensive.) The interviewer can probe for answers that are more complex and can provide visual aids. You can conduct them in the library or even a shopping mall. The location of the interview influences your customer participation rate.

There are disadvantages, though. For example, there is the possibility that the interviewer may exert influence, knowingly or unintentionally. Personal interviews are also an expensive methodology.

Telephone Interviews

Telephone interviews have the advantage of speed. The data can be entered directly into a computerized system and analyzed quickly. The telephone interview is a common methodology for "polling" at election time. Costs are certainly less than face-to-face interviews. Also, telephone interviews are more impersonal than face-to-face interviews. Often people will answer confidential questions more willingly on the telephone. It is a better medium for gathering sensitive information.

Research Design

Before you actually start your research, review the steps for conducting effective research.

1. **Determine research objectives**. What are you trying to learn about or understand? Can you express those items as research objectives? Be specific.

2. **Plan the research design**. First of all, determine what is available in secondary information that will help; then select a basic research methodology to gather your primary information. You can use surveys, experiments, test markets, secondary data, or observation. You can choose to contact individuals through the mail, in person, or by telephone.

   Personal interviews are expensive, but they are valuable, because you can use visual aids and make personal observations. If you want to know how people feel about something, you might want to use focus groups. Focus groups allow you to explore and to learn about why people feel the way they do. If you want to have statistical information, consider using a telephone or written survey. However, if you are dealing with certain populations, a written or telephone survey will be ineffective (e.g., populations with a limited command of English).

   Often you will decide to use a combination of research methods. For example, a series of focus groups will help you understand the issues and how people feel. You can then verify this information by doing a quantitative study, such as a telephone or written survey.

3. **Conduct a pilot study**. A pilot study is a test designed to check the assumptions of your study before you present it to a target group. There are various forms of pilot studies. For example, if you give a few people your questionnaire, they will help you identify flaws in the questionnaire before you give it to a large number of people. A focus group, meanwhile, might provide qualitative information to guide a subsequent quantitative study.

4. **Plan the sample**. A sample is a subset of a larger population. Define the target population. Define the sampling size and how you are going to select the sample population.

5. **Gather Data**. Implement the surveys or experiments to gather the data. You may want to gather information in person at the library. You may want to use the telephone or a written survey. Each method will have pluses or minuses in reaching targeted groups.

1. Describe the problem:

    _____

    _____

2. Make a hypothesis:

    _____

    _____

3. Choose a research technique:

    _____

    _____

4. Select a sample:

    _____

    _____

5. Collect and analyze the data:

    _____

    _____

Develop Your Market Goals and Objectives

Be general on your goals at first. In the process, you will reexamine and refocus these goals. The objectives of a marketing plan involve specific numbers and periods. Figures 3-3 and 3-4 (page 69) review the planning process. Beginning to set goals for the marketing plan can be difficult.

You begin to set goals and objectives after you have completed gathering information. You have identified the SWOT analysis including the strengths, weaknesses, threats, and opportunities. You have analyzed all of the information concerning market segmentation, demand, consumer decision-making process, and competition.

You begin to think of marketing goals and objectives. How do you begin to estimate the results in attendance at an event, or in the use of a new product? What results would you have if everything went wrong? Then how would that estimate change if everything goes perfectly. It is probably that neither one of these two alternatives would happen. However, an in-between result will probably be an accurate forecast.

Do not be surprised if you rethink and revise your goals and objectives. A marketing plan is valuable, because it makes us think and rethink. In strategic planning, goals are succinct; whereas in marketing, goals are

62

6. **Process and analyze data.** The information obtained needs to be tabulated and entered into a computer for analysis. You may want to link one part of the information to another. For example, if you want to know whether people with certain demographic characteristics share motivational characteristics, you will want to code certain responses so you can analyze the data in such a way.

7. **Produce an analysis and report.** The analysis and report summarize and interpret the data so it can be used for management decisions. The analysis will also point out relevant links and details found in the investigation. Use Brainstorming Worksheet 3.16 to plan a research project for your library.

8. **Assess the cost.** How do you determine what to spend on market research? Focus groups usually cost $3,500 or more per group. Costs vary depending on the incentives that are offered to encourage people to participate, the location, and the facilitator. Quantitative studies vary in price depending on methodology and difficulty of study. Maybe a better question is, what is the cost of a mistake? Market research saves millions of dollars for corporations planning new products and services. If you are contemplating a major bond election, a few thousand dollars in market research is well worth the investment. Market research can determine the direction and communication strategies for a successful campaign. It can help you design a building that will meet customer needs. When planning specific programs, look at the cost of a mistake.

9. **Get the help you need:** You can look for qualified market research professionals to assist you in every area. Specialists in election campaigns are excellent in "polling." Many corporations have market research departments. Their employees may work with you on a voluntary basis. Local universities often have marketing departments. Close partnerships with marketing professors, their students, and the library can provide a wealth of information.

10. **Select the "best" research design.** There are no hard and fast rules for good marketing research. This means that you can choose between alternatives. Cost of acquiring the data often plays a role in the decision-making process. The ability to select the best research design comes with experience.

BRAINSTORMING 3.16 DEVELOPING A RESEARCH PROJECT

Use this worksheet to map your own research project. Before making a final decision, you might want to look at the next section, Develop Your Market Goals and Objectives.

broad. You should base marketing goals on information gathered through your situation/environmental analysis. You should have a separate goal and set of objectives for each segment, or niche, of the marketplace you have decided to target for your services. The objectives in this case need to be specific. If you are at a loss for readily quantifiable objectives, think of market penetration, ticket sales, and number of people in attendance, circulation measurements, and increased card registration.

Establishing specific goals and objectives provides very specific targets at which to aim. Having specific goals and objectives forces you to use data effectively, helps set priorities for activities, and gives you an idea of the resources needed to attain them. It also forces you to realize that some of your goals are unrealistic. Goals that encounter too many obstacles should be eliminated.

Example of a goal with objectives:

Goal: to develop a comprehensive library program for the Latino population

Objective 1: to reach 5,000 adult Latino customers

Objective 2: to reach 2,000 Latino children

Objective 3: to raise $50,000 to support this program

 BRAINSTORMING 3.17 MARKETING OBJECTIVES

Writing goals and objectives can be difficult and require some practice. This worksheet is designed so that you can begin to write goals and objectives.

Objectives must be measurable and quantifiable. Identify target markets, promotional costs and funding sources within each objective. Below, list your objectives for each goal category.

1. Service Goal:

Objectives:

A.

B.

C.

D.

2. Funding Goal:

Objectives:

A.

B.

C.

D.

3. Positioning/Promotion Goals:

Objectives:

A.

B.

C.

D.

4. Facilities Goals:

Objectives:

A.

B.

C.

D.

5. Technology Goals:

Objectives:

A.

B.

C.

D.

6. Customer Goals:

Objectives:

A.

B.

C.

D.

7. New Product Service Goals:

Objectives:

A.

B.

C.

D.

Identifying Problems

For libraries, as for families and companies, challenges are an ever-present reality. Issues exist with staffing levels, developing the collection, and customer service. Costs of books and materials are always on the increase along with the need to diversify the collection with electronic subscriptions. The expenses for computers, electronic subscriptions, printers and networks continue to rise. Along with the expanded need for technology comes the need for staff training, as well as staff expertise to manage systems.

In addition, problems of declining economics affect libraries in every location. The situation forces you to look closely at the mission and services that you should be providing. It also requires you to be creative in finding solutions.

Take the time to analyze. First, think about a problem as a situation that needs to be corrected. Remember that the presence of a problem often leads to the discovery of an opportunity.

People often talk about "the window of opportunity." Before you develop goals and objectives, you must examine and state your assumptions. Those assumptions provide guidelines and rationale for constructing your goals. Assumptions are important, because they describe how you feel about certain economic or environmental conditions, which are beyond your control, but with which you must contend as you carry out your plan. You cannot prove assumptions. They are based on the best information you have.

For example, if your community is facing a declining economy and increased unemployment, these factors can create an opportunity for libraries. When unemployment goes up, this produces a specific group of individuals in the community that needs information on career searches, job retraining, and resume development. In this circumstance, the library has an "opportunity" to respond to a problem. There may also be opportunities for additional funding through foundation grants, LSTA funds, or corporate funds to support this opportunity.

Do creative sessions with a small group of staff brought together to discuss problems and opportunities produce results? Those sessions build a team, involve staff in the marketing process and develop consensus and understanding. As you begin to discuss problems, look for opportunities.

When you hear: "We've never done it that way before."
Ask: "Why haven't we?"
When you hear: "We can't do it because of a lack of funds."
Examine alternative funding sources.
When you hear: "We have tried that before and it did not work"
Ask: "What made it not work? What is different this time? What part of the project didn't work?"
When you hear: "We don't have time."

Ask: "How important is this project or service? What can be delegated to other individuals?"

In this worksheet, you will try to put the elements of the environmental analysis together. Again, it will clarify your thinking to write it out.

✎ BRAINSTORMING 3.18 SUMMARY OF ENVIRONMENTAL ANALYSIS, MARKET RESEARCH, AND MARKETING GOALS AND OBJECTIVES

1. Name the segment of individuals you wish to focus on:

    _____

    _____

2. Identify the demographic, geographic, pyschographic, and behavioral characteristics that you have used to identify this segment.

    _____

    _____

3. What is the estimated demand by this segment? How have you estimated the demand?

    _____

    _____

4. What is the competition for this segment? Identify both tangible and intangible competition.

    _____

    _____

5. What factors will influence the customer decision making process?

    _____

    _____

6. How will you get the information you need on this segment? Is it from Secondary Information?

    _____

    _____

7. Is it from Primary Market Research that you create yourself?

   _____

   _____

8. Is the Market Research you are using quantitative? Can you make statistical predictions from the research? What methods are you using? Telephone or written surveys? Other?

   _____

   _____

9. Are you using qualitative or directional market research such as a focus group or interviews?

   _____

   _____

10. What have you learned about this particular market segment from your analysis and market research?

    _____

    _____

11. Can you now develop specific goals and objectives for this particular segment?

    _____

    _____

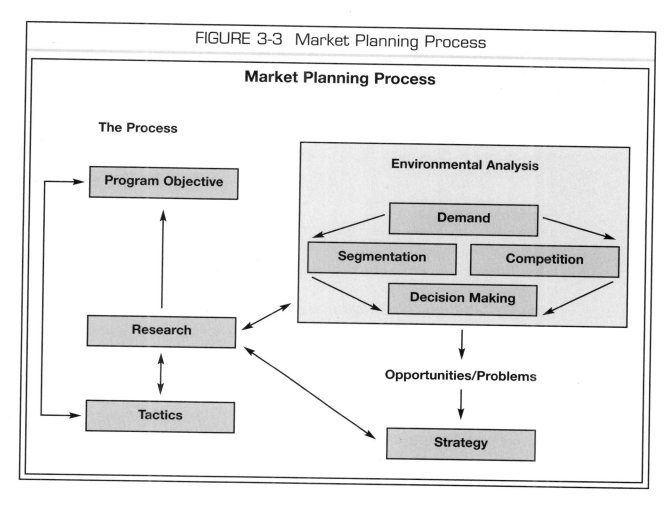

FIGURE 3-3 Market Planning Process

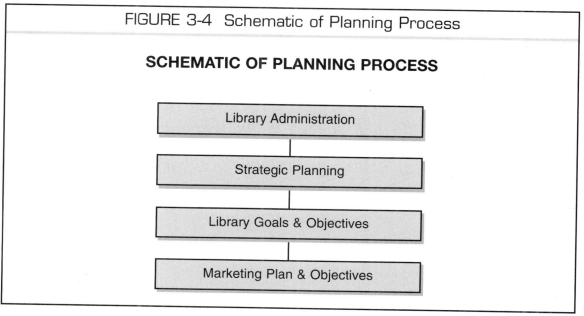

FIGURE 3-4 Schematic of Planning Process

Summary

This chapter contains many new terms. The first phase in marketing is a very time-consuming part of marketing. It is full of detail. You can easily understand the amount of analysis that goes into marketing. When you do a careful environmental analysis, you come to understand what makes your customers react to your services. The environmental analysis forces you to think about your customers in new ways. The guesswork is removed through market research. When all of the data is in hand, you can develop specific marketing goals and objectives.

1. You have studied the various stages in the environmental analysis. Those include segmentation, demand, customer decision-making process, and competition. You know that there is both tangible and intangible competition.

2. You understand that customers use many different variables to make a decision to use your products and services. You now understand how to target our markets.

3. Market research is called primary or secondary. Primary research is research you create, while secondary research is information that already exists. As for primary research, you have looked at telephone surveys and written surveys. You have examined directional research, which allows you flexibility to understand how your customers feel about a service, although it does not provide quantitative information. You also examined focus groups as a form of directional research.

4. All of this information provides you with the data to develop specific marketing goals and objectives. Marketing goals are broad, while objectives are finite.

5. This area of marketing is invisible. The more information you acquire about your customers, the more successful you will be later as the marketing plan unfolds. It will guide communication programs, as well as the products and services themselves. It will influence where and when you offer programs and services.

CHAPTER 4

Marketing Goals Using the Six Ps Strategy

Product, Place, Price, Promotion, Positioning, and Politics

The first step in the development of a marketing plan is to determine who your customers are and what they want. You have developed the goals and objectives. Now you have to develop specific strategies that will provide a "road map." These strategies together are called the *marketing mix*, also known as the four Ps of marketing: product, price, place, and promotion. In addition to the traditional four Ps, libraries need to consider two additional Ps: positioning and politics.

Each of these strategies require careful consideration and planning. You will quickly learn that navigating the Ps is complicated. For example, products differ from services, and, yet, they both fall under the first P of marketing. If you make mistakes in our planning in any one of our strategies, it will affect everything you do. Take your time. There are no shortcuts.

You want to understand your customers in depth. Customer demands are changing all of the time. Remember that the best products or services can fail if the marketing strategies are not addressed successfully. The effectiveness of each of your products or service will be determined by the diligence you apply in the understanding, as well as the creativity you employ to implement the marketing strategies.

The First P: Products and Services

Products are tangible items. In the library, they might be books, CDs, DVDs, or books on tape. However, libraries deal mainly with services. Both products and services fall under the first P in the marketing mix.

Although you are treating products and services together in developing your plan, there are significant differences. Products are tangible, services are intangible. Products can be inventoried, services cannot. Products require no customer service; services require a high degree of customer interaction. A customer cannot see, feel, smell, hear, or taste a service before they agree to use it. Services cannot be separated from their providers. The customer believes that the library employee brings something special to the process. Service marketing is a field of marketing unto itself and requires special consideration.

Take a rental car business, for example. If you rent a car, it is not enough that the car works. The process of getting the car also shapes your feelings about the service. If you have to wait in a long line, if your reservations are lost, or if you have to put up with inexperienced or rude help, those experiences influence your feelings about the service.

At the library, reference services require a high level of customer-staff interaction. Your service cannot be mass-produced, and librarians use a high degree of personal judgment when they perform the service. Reference services are labor intensive and are subject to quality control issues.

Products, on the other hand, are tangible. They can be mass-produced. They have distribution channels, wholesalers, and retailers. Look at books, for example. What channels do you go through to buy books?

When customers use the library's products and services, they are really seeking the benefits of those products and services. Perhaps they are seeking information or material for recreation. People "buy" the *benefits*. They buy solutions to their problems.

Perhaps you have never thought of "benefits" when designing your programs. Some of the benefits are so obvious that they may not occur to you. Take, for example, the benefit of creating "a gathering place." While the library staff may not have it foremost in their minds, customers may seek it as a benefit. Another example is that of the Internet. While you were developing Internet services to serve your regular customers, you probably were unaware that you were developing "benefits" for travelers away from home. You were providing them with connection when they are not in your vicinity.

For each product or service that you provide, ask, "What is its purpose? What needs does it satisfy? What are the benefits? Some common benefits that may apply to your programs or services include the following.

• Convenience	• Self-expression
• Knowledge	• Dependability
• Information	• Price
• Comfort	• Delivery
• Curiosity	• Availability
• Pleasure	• Gathering place
• Self-actualization	• Reliability
• Saves money	• Satisfaction of the senses
• Awakens the intellect	

Understanding Features and Benefits

Although you may be able to see the benefit of a service, your customer may not. How will the customer benefit from using the services? How can you communicate those benefits to your customer? To be successful, each product or service offered by the library must share six elements of quality. Together these elements produce the benefits that the customer desires. Those qualities include performance, features, reliability, durability, esthetics, and perceived quality.

1. **Performance:** Federal Express says, "We deliver, we deliver." They guarantee performance within 24 hours. Fee-based document delivery services in libraries also promise that documents will be delivered in a specific time.

2. **Features:** In a library fee-based information delivery service, features would include the different services and their features. They might offer a "super rush" feature, or a standard feature of offering the service in 3–5 days. This is analogous to the "bells and whistles" of commercial products, which are discussed below. You could also use such features as automatic check out, reserve, and renewal services as features.

3. **Reliability:** High levels of customer satisfaction and high levels of contract renewals indicate that the service is reliable. Never miss a scheduled deadline. If you promise to deliver information or materials within a certain time, be reliable about delivery. Libraries are known for their reliability in reference services.

4. **Durability:** A product should stand the test of time and consumer usage. Timex watches and Maytag washing machines remind you of the durability of their products. The library buildings provide a sense of the durability of their services.

5. **Esthetics:** Esthetics refers to a pleasant atmosphere in which your customers can use the service. In the example of a fee-based service, a highly qualified professional staff is an "esthetic" feature, packaging a report in an attractive/pleasant format is an esthetic feature. How are the books and materials displayed in the library?

6. **Perceived quality:** When customers view a service as being of high quality, they will recommend it to other potential customers. For example, if you deliver excellent service in providing genealogical information, customers will tell others who are interested in genealogy.

Understanding the "Bells and Whistles"

If you were buying a camera, you would want to know if it had a zoom lens or panoramic capability. Perhaps you want a camera that is waterproof or small enough to fit in your pocket. These are the different special features, or "bells and whistles," of the camera.

In a library setting, examine the copy machines that you provide for customer use. The "bells and whistles" may include the different sizes of paper that can be used, the speed of the machine, the ability to collate and staple.

Consider the products of your library and its services, as well as the benefits that they offer your customers. Take the automated catalog, for example. Think of the features that are included with that catalog. Attributes include public access terminals, printers, remote access, and information concerning other collections, digital photographs, and online databases. The benefits to the customer include easy access to up-to-date information from their home, office, or in the library. Automation means that it is easier and more accurate for the customer to find information about the materials he/she wants and faster to get them.

☼ BRAINSTORMING 4.1 ASSESS YOUR LIBRARY'S PRODUCTS AND SERVICES.

- List the products and the services your library offers.

  Examples: Interlibrary loan, photocopy center, new fiction center, ready reference collections.

- Think of several applications for each service or product.

  Examples: New fiction center provides rotating list of current titles, multiple copies for high-demand books, compiles the latest titles for readers; Interlibrary loan provides thousands of titles for local residents, makes journals and periodicals available, helps researchers; ready reference collections puts the most used sources in clearly defined area for customers to browse, offers a starting point for research, helps with homework and quick answers.

- Think of the wants and needs that these products and services satisfy and several applications for each product and service.

  Examples: New fiction collection satisfies fiction readers eager for new titles, undecided readers looking for something new; Interlibrary loan satisfies customers who need titles the library does not carry; ready reference satisfies users who need a quick answer or additional information to start a search.

74

- Think of possible users of your products.

  Examples: Interlibrary Loan made available on the Web and marketed to professionals; ready reference marketed to students completing homework at the library.

- Think of specific benefits to make your product desirable to each of your possible users.

  Example: Interlibrary Loan is information for professionals from libraries near and far; ready reference is quick answers to homework's tough questions.

  If you can communicate the benefits, as well as how these products satisfy customer needs and wants, you will increase the appeal for the products. Making a list of target users will help you evaluate your library's current marketing of these products and what else your library can do to increase your product's usage.

BRAINSTORMING 4.2 HOW DO YOU CONDUCT A PRODUCT/SERVICE EVALUATION?

An important part of developing your library's products and services is to conduct an evaluation of those very things.

- Compose a chart that lists your library's products and services.

- Rate each product and service against a scale of excellent, very good, average, below average or poor.

Service	Excellent	Very Good	Average	Below Average	Poor
• Service to young adults			X		
• Trademark/ logo search capability		X			
• Services to children	X				

- Provide honest evaluations and throughout the process, try to justify your answers with facts and observations.

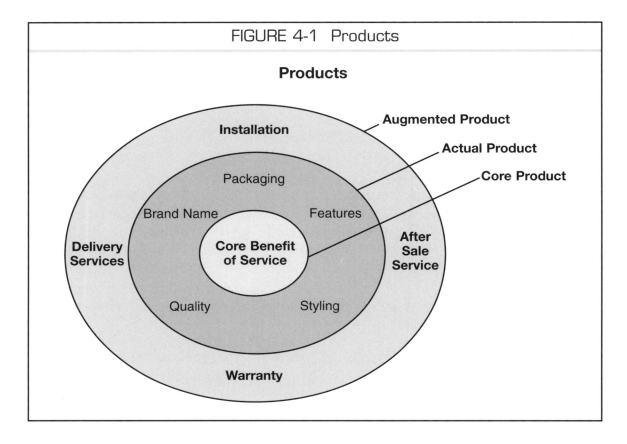

FIGURE 4-1 Products

Products

Augmented Product
Actual Product
Core Product

Installation

Packaging

Brand Name   Features

Core Benefit
of Service

Delivery
Services   After
Sale
Service

Quality   Styling

Warranty

Figure 4-1 illustrates that products or services have multiple layers. To appeal to customers, each layer should be exposed. To the basic product or service you can entice clients with packaging, brand names, quality, styling or features. These are parts of the actual product. The augmented product entices by highlighting the long-term or lasting benefits once the product has been accepted—warranty, life improvement, delivery, etc. Products and services should be marketed using the core product, actual product and augmented product feature to maximize appeal.

Acknowledging the Product Life Cycle

Libraries need a mix of new and growing products along with the old and staple ones. Yesterday they wanted books. Today they want books-on-tape, CDs, DVDs, and videos. The products continue to expand. Each product and service you introduce goes through a four-stage "product life cycle." The cyclical manner in which these products and services are accepted is demonstrated in Figure 4-2.

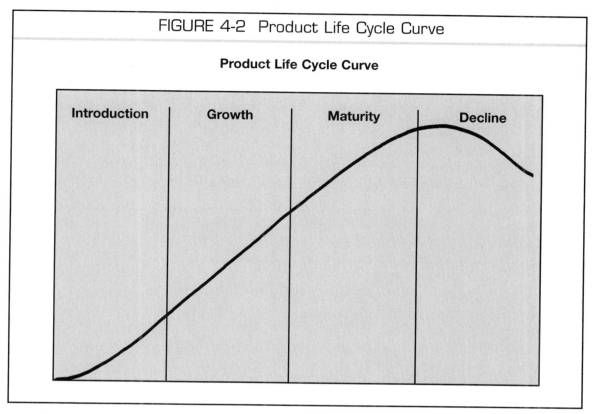

FIGURE 4-2 Product Life Cycle Curve

Product Life Cycle Curve

Introduction | Growth | Maturity | Decline

- **Introductory stage** is when a product first appears in the market place. The product may not have any competitors. It requires a great deal of investment in its development and loses money at this stage.

- **Growth stage** is when the product or service begins to grow. It is successful. At that time competitors begin to copy the product or service. Those competitors can even make improvements.

- **Maturity stage** is when the product or service is most highly utilized. In the profit world, it is at the most profitable stage of a product.

- **Decline stage** is indicated when the market shrinks and profitability falls.

Marketing-oriented businesses constantly monitor the life cycle of their products and services. Some products, like Ivory Soap and Arm and Hammer Baking Soda, have been at the mature point in their product life cycle for years. Both of these products have had a very long product life cycle. However, when sales begin to slip, a new advertising program appears to remind the customer of the benefits of these products.

Libraries, too, need to remind customers of their products. In the high-tech area, a product life cycle of 18 months is considered long. The computer hardware and software industries must constantly be updating and renewing products. Libraries as a whole have had long product life cycles. They are in the mature stage of their product life cycle. Libraries are in danger of slipping into the decline stage of their product life cycle unless they are attentive.

All consumer-oriented businesses realize that they must constantly introduce new products and services to remain viable in the marketplace. The volumes of new products must not surprise libraries.

FIGURE 4-3 Cash Cow/Rising Stars

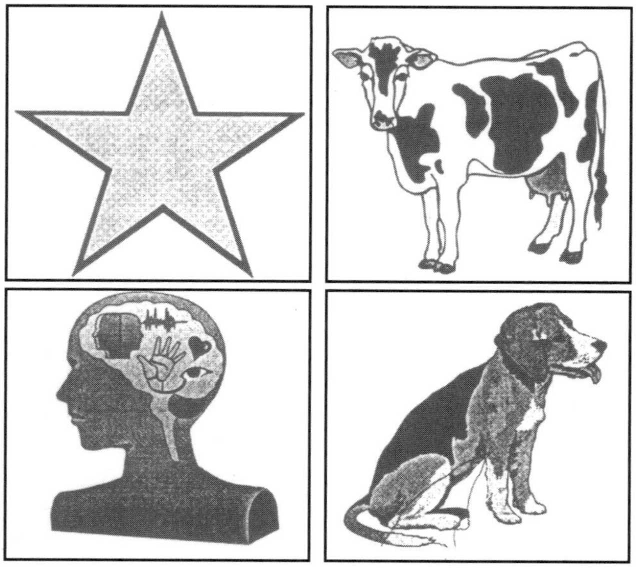

Label your product and services as cash cows (which provide lots of profits, sales or activities), rising stars (which are tomorrow's cash cows), dogs (which are just plain dogs) and investments in the owner's ego (which are those things you just can't give up…these are tomorrow's dogs).

In Figure 4-3, you can see how many business people describe their products. Some new products become "rising stars," while others are "dogs." Others are "cash cows." They keep attracting customers. Can you identify some "cash cows" for the library? Is the use of Web sites and the Internet a "rising star?" Do you have any dogs?

Understanding the Customer Adoption Curve

Customers do not just jump out and buy every new product or service, even when you introduce it. They study and examine before they participate in the adoption process, a process that takes place for every product or service. Customers adopt a product or service in increments.

The first people to adopt a new product, service, or technology are called the *innovators*. They take the risk of being the first to sample a new product. *Early adopters* participate in a new product or service after it has been established, but before it is common place. The *early majority* adopts the product or service as it is becoming established. The *late majority* participates in the program; product or service only after it has been widely accepted. *The laggards* come in as the products or service is mature.

Every product or service has an adoption curve. Although librarians often expect an immediate reaction by customers to a new product or service, you should be aware that acceptance of a new product or service is normally more gradual. You use promotional efforts to shorten the length of this curve. However something new is introduced, you must take into consideration the adoption curve when you develop a new program or service. Often, you tend to try something without regard to the customer adoption curve.

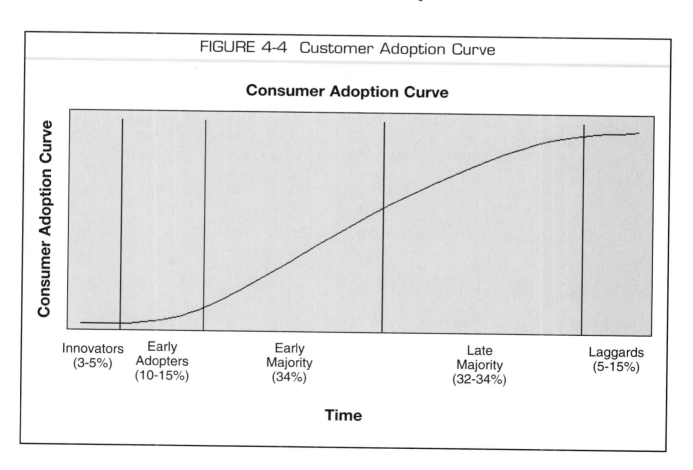

FIGURE 4-4 Customer Adoption Curve

✎ BRAINSTORMING 4.3 WHERE ARE YOUR SERVICES ON THE ADOPTION CURVE?

- List several of your libraries products and services.
- Rate your adoption of those products and services.

  Here is a chance to examine your timing for adopting some new products.

Products	Innovators	Early Adopters	Early Majority	Late Majority	Laggard
• Online Catalog					
• Self Checkout					
• Food/Café Areas					
• Internet					

- Using a similar chart, rate the adoption of those services by your users to identify how quickly your users take to your services.

- If you want to explore further, rate the adoption of services by different customer segments. This may help you to develop new programs or schedule additional instruction for certain groups.

  Examples: seniors and self-checkout; Hispanics and the Web; teens and interlibrary loan

- Estimate the potential adoption of new services.

Does a Brand Name Matter?

When you make a trip to the grocery store, you often make a choice between two products. Perhaps, you need to buy a bottle of ketchup. Do you choose a name brand such as Heinz, or do you choose a cheaper, generic brand? What about facial tissues. Will you pay a little more and choose Kleenex? You know you can count on name brands for consistent quality. You are not always sure about generic brands.

If you are attempting to establish a brand identify with a product or service, you try to build a rich set of positive associations for the brand. There are five dimensions that you can use to communicate a meaning.

- **The attributes:** for example, the Energizer Bunny that "just keeps going."

- **The benefits:** a strong brand suggests consistent benefits. For example, a Hershey bar indicates good taste consistently.

- **Company values:** A strong brand communicates the values that the organization holds.

- **Personality:** A strong brand exhibits some personality traits.

- **Users:** a strong brand suggests the kind of people who use the brand.

A strong brand name should trigger another word to people. A good brand stands out from the crowd. It is distinctive and easy to remember. For example, when you talk about Xerox, it signifies the word documents, Volvo stands for safety, Kodak means film, Kleenex means tissue, and Federal Express triggers overnight delivery. What does the name of your library signify?

Success Story 4.1
Branding Youth Services

Brooklyn Public Library,   **Brooklyn, New York**

The staff of the Brooklyn Public Library has set a new standard for library professionals, developing a unique marketing strategy to strengthen ties to the local community. Currently the nation's fifth largest library system, the Brooklyn Public Library serves 2.5 million people with 60 branches in all. "Libraries are being pulled and sometimes pushed into the hyper-speed, celebrity-driven, information-overloaded world," said Director of Marketing and Communications Beth D. Weinstein. Weinstein and her staff have responded to these new challenges with one of the most sophisticated marketing and communication programs in the country, "branding individual services...within the library."

With the Internet making virtually every library across the country accessible to anyone, branding has become more of a concern for libraries. Brooklyn Public Library has answered that call and in return has received much needed funding, both public and private for new and innovative programs. Just as you can recognize the Coca-Cola brand through their cursive signature, you can recognize the Brooklyn Public Library through its illustrations. Aaron Meshon, a well-known illustrator, developed the images and logos for use system-wide on the library Web site, annual reports, television commercials, postcards, pencils, booklists, and many other communications.

The branding of the Brooklyn Library's youth services division is a key example of this strategy, a new way to face what Weinstein considers an important challenge,"positioning libraries as important community centers."Public Libraries throughout the country focus on programs and products for youth, from toddlers to teens. The staff at the Brooklyn Public Library realized that they could make their total program more effective increasing awareness, participation, circulation, and funding by creating one solid, dynamic image.

From the beginning, Weinstein and her staff recognized youth services as a key component of the Brooklyn Public Library brand. In the information clutter of New York, they sought to establish their leadership in programs for kids from toddlers to teens. At the center of this effort would be the new Youth Wing, a 10,500 sq. ft. space opened in 2000, at the program's center. A flagship fusion of high-tech wizardry and carefully constructed human touch, the Youth Wing embodies the future of the Brooklyn Public Library, combining the best in traditional library service with the new possibilities of the digital age. The state-of-the-art facility contains a technology loft with almost 40 computers, as well as age specific areas for toddlers, children and teens. The collection was expanded through the addition of new books, CD's and other materials, while specialized Web sites KidZone and InfoZone were developed to reach out to children and teens, who were more likely to access the library online than on foot.

But while the Brooklyn Public Library added the facility, the marketing staff created the promotional campaigns to establish the brand image in the eyes of the community, the young people, the parents, the politicians, the staff, the donors, and the stakeholders."Brand reinforcement is vital to maintain 'product' identity and differentiation," said Beth Weinstein. "After identifying and building a brand, effective marketing requires continuous reinforcement of the message, as well as the development of new promotions to keep the brand fresh and exciting."They created and developed print materials, pens, mugs, maps, and T-shirts with a strong visual identity and used the brand image around events for press, donors, public officials, and other key persons. At the Youth Wing grand opening, all information sheets, promotional key rings and other materials used the illustrations designed by Aaron Meshon. In exchange for free advertising, they found media partners for sponsorship, offering the media credit on signage, the calendar of events and other collateral program material. The staff also developed partnerships with community organizations to increase awareness, and to build audience and brand value. These innovative techniques have helped the Brooklyn Public Library secure its place as a leader in the youth services department in Brooklyn and beyond. As Beth Weinstein summarizes it, "The Library users and funders now associate

Brooklyn Public Library with an image, an image encompassing their programs, graphics, logos and customer service that says if you are in need of anything having to deal with children or teens, Brooklyn Public Library is your first and last stop, the *411* on everything."

The effort, creativity, and participation that made the $2.5 million renovation a success since its opening day are the same qualities found throughout the Brooklyn Public Library. An additional $4 million allowed the library to focus on new programs like After School Assistance, which brought reading specialists to all 58 branches of the Brooklyn Public Library system, and Connecting Libraries and School Projects (CLASP), which helped the library reach out to the community's youth. "Kidsmobile" provided visibility throughout the borough, offering a rotating collection of 2,000 books in a vehicle the size of a small motor home. There are special festivities around Hispanic Heritage Month and Black Heritage Month.

The youth program continues today with the "Get the Card!" campaign. The first part of that campaign was an internal effort to educate library staff members throughout the library system with fliers and e-mails featuring images of the new library card. The public campaign in summer 2003 targeted new readers through collaborations with other great destinations including the New York Aquarium, Coney Island's Astroland Amusement Park, and Cyclones' baseball games, signing on 75,000 new cardholders. Branding and marketing strategies like this one have powered the reinvention of the Brooklyn Public Library, leading the way for other libraries across the countries.

Success Story 4.2
Branding through a Unified Newsletter

Laramie County Library System,   Cheyenne, Wyoming

The Laramie County Library System in Cheyenne, Wyoming is small as libraries go, but it has a strong heart and a strong image. Laramie County has a population of 81,958 in a state with only 494,423 residents and great distances between communities. In 1998, the library foundation became a separate entity with its own director and agenda, but, as former board president Vanda Edington observed, "While donations came in, the Foundation lacked momentum and direction. It functioned as a conduit for...donations but did little more." Gradually, the board members recognized that the Foundation and the library would both be stronger if the board presented one unified, dynamic image to the public.

A unified newsletter was the board's greatest innovation, serving as a vehicle for telling the community about the Laramie County Library and Foundation, while establishing the library brand. Months of work went into developing the look of the newsletter and letterhead, including the "bird and book" logo based upon the "Literacy Equals Freedom" sculpture donated to the library in 1998. The quarterly newsletter would contain information on awards, special projects and grants, donors and volunteers, and a wide range of activities from the Tuesday Night Book Club to the Booklovers Barbecue. There would be columns like Behind the Scenes at Your Library and special articles to appeal to Hispanic readers. The Foundation section, Edington adds, "deals with what has been funded through donations…what needs to be funded, and how the reader can help."

The development of the mailing list for the newsletter has been focused and planned. The list contains approximately 7,000 names including all donors, current or previous, people who have participated in a library focus group, served on a committee, or made a comment on library programs, as well as members of various civic organizations, private grant-making organizations, and all elected officials from city to state-level. Though the newsletter has a broad distribution, the Foundation wants it to reach as many activists as possible. Through the newsletter, the communities, civic leaders, library donors and supporters, business leaders and elected officials are all presented with one image, one view, and one brand of the library, and the results are beginning to show. The building of a new central library and the renovation of current branches all depend on the next election, and due to the branding achieved through the library foundation's newsletter, the Laramie County Library System is more likely than ever to have this significant vote go in its favor.

The Laramie County Library Foundation's newsletters are available at www.lclsonline.org/library_foundation/news_events.html

How powerful is branding in libraries? Can you establish an identity for your library? Do people think of children's programs when they think of the library? Do you give consistent benefits to our customers? If establishing a brand signifies strength in the community; you need to be aware of the practice.

In the case of libraries, you are branding intangible services. It is a little more difficult than branding tangible products, but it can be done. You want to give your service a memorable image through consistent graphics, logo, and design. You want your brand image to be so strong that the library is the first place people think of when thinking about children's programs or information. Branding reassures your customers that this is "my kind of product or service." They match up their image of themselves with the image you have given your service.

Libraries are just becoming conscious of "branding" and its importance. Libraries are beginning to understand that they must put one image forward, that they must present a strong, dependable image to the public. In this section, there are examples of three large libraries that have developed branding programs: the Brooklyn Public Library (Success Story 4.1); the San Francisco Public Library Friends and Foundation (Success Story 4.3), which created one brand that conveyed one image to the community, and the Friends of the St. Paul Library (Success Story 4.4), who also wanted to convey one image to the community. There is also a story (Success Story 4.2) about a smaller library system (Laramie County Library System, Cheyenne, Wyoming) and its foundation that presents one image to the community through its newsletter. "After all," says Foundation Director Susan Vittilow, "we wouldn't be in business without the library."

Success Story 4.3
Presenting One Image to the Community through a Friends Group

Friends and Foundation of the San Francisco Public Library,   **San Francisco, California**

The people of San Francisco actively support their library system through their votes and their generosity. Over the years, two strong non-profit library support organizations emerged. The Friends of the San Francisco Public Library, formed in the 1960s, provided support for the San Francisco Public Library through advocacy, outreach and financial support. The Library Foundation of San Francisco was created two decades later to lead a $34 million capital campaign that would furnish and equip San Francisco's beautiful new Main Library, which opened in 1996. The campaign used a unique and inclusive fund-raising and "branding" strategy that encouraged participation from many segments of San Francisco in this important civic project. Groups active in the development efforts include the Gay, Lesbian, Bisexual, and Transgender community, the Latino-Hispanic community, the Chinese-American community, and the Filipino American community. Each of these groups raised funds to create an "Affinity Center." These affinity centers house special collections, services and programs for the individual communities.

After that successful campaign, the Friends of the Library continued to support the San Francisco Public Library, although they found themselves approaching the same donors for funds, which created some confusion. With encouragement from the City Librarian Regina Minudri, and then her successor, Susan Hildreth, members of both boards discussed the possibility of working together. Finally, they decided to merge. They hired a consultant experienced in nonprofit mergers and explored the benefits of putting the organizations together to create one "brand" that would represent the broad support for the San Francisco Public Library. They wanted this brand to embody the spirit of the Friends group—its dedication to advocacy, grassroots organization, and support in programming—combined with the fund-raising efforts of the Library Foundation. This unified organization is proving to be an effective community building tool, developing capital campaigns for two branch libraries.

The new organization has been strengthened even more with the recent arrival of a new Executive Director, Martin Gómez, formerly of the Brooklyn Public Library. His missions are to create a new "brand" for the new organization, to nurture stakeholders, and to promote the "Affinity Centers" within the library.

Creating one brand, one identity is very important as the Friends and Foundation launch their capital campaign to benefit the 26 branch libraries of the San Francisco Public Library system. "Branding is effective and powerful," says Deborah Doyle, Board Chairman. "We look forward to using it again successfully on behalf of the San Francisco Public Library."

Success Story 4.4
Strengthening the Public Image

Friends of the Saint Paul Public Library,   **Saint Paul, Minnesota**

The Friends of the Saint Paul Public Library have experienced a transition into a sophisticated organization that truly acts as a public "brand" for the library. In 1975, the organization became a Foundation when it received an endowment of two million dollars from a private donor, who left his entire estate to the library. With that gift, they began to take on the additional responsibilities required of a Foundation. Serving as the major cultivator of the renaissance of the Saint Paul Public Library, the Friends organization makes sure they are unified and in step with the library. This is their way of presenting one view, or "one brand," to the public.

The library, with help from the Friends organization, recently raised over $6 million in private support. The City of Saint Paul matched that campaign with $15.9 million. In addition to helping provide monetary support, the Friends have acted as guarantor in the sale of bonds for construction, playing a crucial role in the central library's renovation plans.

The Friends annual fund-raising and financial efforts provide critical support to the Saint Paul Public Library, for children's programs, outreach activities, purchase of crucial materials and staff training. The cultural programming department brings in over 150 performances, which more than 24,000 people attend. The Friends cultural programming efforts bring 6,000 people into the library for nearly 60 events each year, including author, theatre, and music events. The Friends cosponsor the Minnesota Book Awards, which honor the best of the state's literary talent. The events increase awareness of the library's rich resources, which range from great fiction and labor history to music CDs and videos. The Friends hold events at every library branch in Saint Paul, as well as numerous other sites in the community.

The Friends continue to build on past success and work to insure adequate public funding of the Saint Paul Public Library system. They actively lobby the City Council, and the City Council positively responds to their requests. The City Council approved a biennial Capital Improvements Budget allocating $1.75 million in 2000 and recommending $4.2 million in 2001 to renovate the Central Library. Their advocacy efforts in the last nine years have helped restore and increase the budget of the library by over $10 million.

Since the Friends have helped create one dynamic, powerful image of the library within the community, the community has responded tenfold. With seeds planted and cultivated by the Friends, the library will continue to develop for many years to come. The patrons now view the library system as an institution with a broad outreach program, attentive to customers and widely supported by the community.

The Second P: Place

In marketing, place is not just the physical location of the central library and its branches. Place is also the ways you deliver your services—how customers access library information and materials, get assistance, and solve problems.

One central idea in understanding place is the distribution channel—the way a product gets to the library and how that product gets from the library to the customer. These distribution channels may include library wholesalers, databases, electronic connections, and online catalogues. Delivery systems to branches as well as interlibrary and intralibrary loan opportunities create a larger sense of place. All of these systems exist to make it easier for the customer to gain access to the products.

A successful place strategy addresses the following:

- **Demand:** How do you get the right quantity of the right materials in the right place? How well do you predict demand and get the inventory to where the demand is located?

- **Price:** Are you developing a distribution strategy that moves the products to the customer within the lowest possible cost?

- **Customer Service:** Are your services out of the way or too complicated for your customers?

Everyone in your distribution channel is your customer. To get that book, product, or service from the wholesaler to the customer, a great many people have to work together and make it a priority. You must ensure efficient technical service and form strategic alliances. You must develop catalogues for children and catalogues in other lanuages, like Spanish, Chinese, French, and German. A successful organization integrates planning for physical distribution and planning for marketing.

The rise of the digital marketplace has also changed the concept of place dramatically. Library leaders now see libraries as containing both digital and book collections. The way users gain access through home computers or at remote terminals located throughout a community creates an extended sense of place, with no hours of service and no limitations.

Using Place Creatively within Libraries

Libraries are creative with this idea of "place." They form partnerships with community colleges to provide public/educational facilities. There are challenges in administration and operation, but in the end, it is a "win-win" operation. The public benefits through longer hours of service, and the use of additional facilities, including language labs and business workstations.

Many libraries are creating a "Children's Place" in their facilities. This *place* is particularly attractive to preschool children and their parents. There are not only books and materials, but games and toys. Books on parenting, as well as the presence of parenting "specialists," enhance the experience for the mother, father, or adult caregiver.

In other areas, "place" means that different libraries combine their efforts. State funding joins public and school libraries. Public libraries work with universities to provide a central location.

Today's libraries position the library as an essential player in these cooperative programs. They join forces with other nonprofit institutions to contribute to the public culture. They work with public television and radio to form cooperative learning programs.

The physical library building is an intrinsic part of the public library's identity. It stands as a sense of pride and values within a community, offering scholarship and access to information. In the twenty-first century, a great library is not confined to the "place" that is the public library building.

☼ BRAINSTORMING 4.4 IDENTIFY YOUR LIBRARY'S PLACE.

How does the concept of place affect a vital marketing strategy? Answer these questions to help you develop ways of making your presence known to users in new geographic areas.

- Describe your distribution outlets or locations of your library branches.

- List changes in population growth or decline that will influence where the services of your library are placed.

- List growing areas in your community that are not currently served by libraries.

- List popular locations in your community and the closest library to each of those locations.

- Will improvements in technology/automation affect the need for physical locations in your system?

- What other changes in your environment will affect the physical location of your services?

- Describe the distribution channels used to get new materials to your library and to the customer.

- Describe the online capability of your library and how that provides access to library customers.

- What are your hours of operation for your locations? Do those hours of operation meet customer needs?

Inviting Customers into the Library through Merchandising

Now consider the "place" or "placement" of your products and services in the overall merchandizing effort of the library. How do you make the library appealing to the customer? How do you organize collections and materials, services and programs, so that the customer is stimulated to participate? When you are merchandising your service, you must consider everything in the library, including the location of library services, the hours of service, the products (books, CD's, Books On Tape, DVDs), signage, the convenience of services (getting a library card, checking out materials, paying fines, reserving a book, using the online catalogue), the level of customer service by staff, parking, promotional material and displays. Merchandising comprises all the activities that relate to the consumer.

But, as consumers become more sophisticated, they expect more of libraries. Customers expect the same level of service from libraries that they receive at commercial bookstores or other retail outlets. They expect databases, Web sites, and remote access. They want coffee shops, drive-up access, instant turn around, interlibrary loans, e-books, and other materials. With all these new demands, libraries must decide who their real customers are and what those customers need. They have to choose how to place product and service offerings. How will place serve the customer?

More specifically, how do libraries become more aware of the way they organize their "place." For years, many libraries were content to organize their collections on the Dewey system, with books lining the shelves. The customer would find the Dewey decimal number through a catalog system and match that number to the books on the shelf. These days, the same customer might go to a bookstore and find that the books are displayed in groups with their covers exposed. Large signs denote a special area and collection, attracting the customer to other items. The same types of displays can enhance a customer's experience within the library.

Another "place" factor in customer service is atmosphere. Every library has a physical layout that makes it easy or hard to get around. The color of walls, the availability of comfortable chairs, paintings, promotions, collections, availability of service personal, computers that work and are maintained all contribute to the library's "feel," whether charming or somber. The atmosphere contributes to the customer comfort and enthusiasm for returning. Signage, restrooms, the availability of customer related services as checkout services, renewal services, information services, parking services, hours all contribute to the atmosphere of the library.

The physical place of the library attracts and retains customers. Retailers and realtors in the general market boil success down to three critical factors: location, location, and location. Libraries need to be increasingly aware that site location can have a major impact on the libraries business.

How Can Libraries Employ "Place" When Merchandising?

The most recently opened branch of the Richmond, British Columbia, Public Library sets the standard for merchandising. Their Ironwood Branch has the comforts and hospitality of a bookstore, with a 20-seat computer training and learning facility, a digital reference centers for both adults and children, a fireplace lounge with refreshments, and an Internet café. There is a self-checkout program, which accounts for over 90 percent of the transactions, self pick-up for holds, self-sorting of library materials, a large collection of bestsellers, CDs, CD-ROMs and videos. This neighborhood branch is open 74 hours a week and is highly automated and cost effective. It is a prototype for branch library development.

Success Story 4.5
Setting the Standard for Merchandising

San José Public Library,   **San José, California**

Librarians may have a lot to learn from retailers. Back in 1992, the head of the San José Public Library called for a new merchandising model to promote the library's collection and make that collection more accessible to their customers. The new merchandising committee, led by Dave Genesy, began to rethink organization, merchandising, display, and maintenance. For Genesy, library patrons were just like any other shoppers—they wanted to find the book they wanted easily without assistance. The old business adage held true, "the right product, at the right time, at the right price, displayed well."

The staff at the San José Public Library considers everyone who comes in their doors a browser, even if you enter looking for a specific book. How many times do you go into the grocery store with a shopping list and come out with many extras? It is the same in libraries or bookstores. But if this is true, then librarians must rethink the way they present their collection. As the San José staff recommends, "Keep the browser in mind at all times; our collection should be displayed in as interesting and exciting a way as possible." The displays must constantly change to meet readers' changing needs and interests.

Most of all, the San José staff emphasizes creativity and adaptability: innovative displays may include "the use of paperback dumps, tables, covers, face-out books stacked face-up, floor stacks, spin racks, slat wall, and end displays, anything you can think of that will display books attractively and in the 'right' location." The collection, the floor plan, the traffic flow, special collections, displays, artistic design, functionality, signage, not to mention furniture, fixtures, lighting, and use of color—the San José staff considers all of these in their merchandising program. A lack of resources should not stand in the way: each library must do the most with what they have.

According to the staff at the San José Public Library, there are several steps to merchandising your library. They include the following:

1. **Planning:** Identify your goals, a time frame for action and evaluation techniques. Visualize what you want. Visit other libraries and bookstores.

2. **Decide what you want to achieve:** Do you want to give a positive message to your community that their library has what they want? You can start with one department at a time. Perhaps it is a display in the children's area.

3. **Examine resources:** Identify what resources are required. Do you need new fixtures? Who will design the display? What materials

do you require? What resources are available through the library? What other sources to you have at your disposal?

4. **Borrow from others:** Use ideas from retail businesses. Study your local supermarket or bookstore. Do they use racks? Slanting bookshelves?

5. **Team Effort:** Get staff involved during the planning process. It gives a varied perspective to the activity. Also, it empowers the staff and increases their support. Build a task force, have weekly meetings, use written memos as well as informal input opportunities. Communication is vital. Implement written procedures so that all staff understands the goal and the vision.

6. **Action Plan:** Write down your ideas; include what actually will be done, the steps to be taken, who will be doing it, a time frame for completion, resources used, how it will be maintained, and any evaluation measures to be used. Be sure to incorporate staff ideas. This is an ongoing plan. Look at it regularly for needed revisions.

Maintenance is another critical factor. The San José staff warns even a well-designed display may "disintegrate into disarray; book dumps not regularly refilled become ineffective, face-out books on new book shelves will get checked-out and not restocked." A planned approach to maintenance is vital. Written guidelines spell out that maintenance is a shared responsibility of both clerical and professional staff. "Maintenance takes time, and it must be ongoing. Take the attitude that your library is your home and your customers are your guests. Take responsibility and share the ongoing effort to maintain a welcoming, comfortable atmosphere."

The final part of the planning process is evaluation. Does the plan work? Is it accomplishing the goals as you stated them? Are your guidelines and procedures effective? Have you estimated the resources appropriately? There are several methods to measure your success, whether circulation, user surveys, comments by staff and users, or time saved by librarians.

☼ BRAINSTORMING 4.5 DESCRIBE PLACEMENT IN YOUR LIBRARY.

• List several rooms in your library and explain why they are where they are.

Example: The children's reading room is in a large bright, carpeted room; the map room is in the basement, because of the weight of the map cases.

- List several pieces of furniture and explain why they are where they are.

  Example: the computer terminals are in the center of the rooms to provide easy access; the desks and study tables are near the reference collection for convenience; the conference rooms are at the rear to reduce noise from entering the library.

- List several collections and explain why they are where they are.

  Example: the preschool picture books are on the bottom shelf so that children can peruse them; the reference collection is housed in a short book case so customers can leaf through them on top of the shelf.

- List several signs that are located in the library and explain their effects.

  Example: the Information Desk sign is hung from the ceiling so customers throughout the library can easily locate it; the children's reading room sign is colorful to appeal to children.

☼ BRAINSTORMING 4.6 IDENTIFY WAYS TO MERCHANDIZE YOUR LIBRARY.

These questions will help as you begin to think of where you can get merchandizing strategies and how you can implement them in your library.

- What do you like and dislike about retail outlets? Think specifically about the things you remembered or took away from your last shopping trip.

  Example: The orange aprons at Home Depot helped me identify salespeople; the small trays of lollipops, mints and gum at Starbucks worked effectively; the large signs over customer service and the cash registers at Target let me know exactly where those important stations were located.

- What can you borrow in the form of other ideas? Think of different retail spaces like bookstores or the groceries? Identify the kinds of racks and tables that they use. Examine how they build displays.

  Example: Grocery stores place their promoted items at the end of each aisle to maximize exposure to people going down that aisle, but also to people just passing by the aisle; bookstores display new titles in a way that ensures the customer sees as many covers of the book as possible, because the book influences the buyer as much as the title or the author.

- How can these ideas be implemented in libraries?

  Examples: Use an identifying marker for all employees on the floor of the library so that customers can always find someone to help them; make bookmarks, buttons or fliers for your next big event available at the circulation desk for last minute take aways; display your new fiction on a large entry table in a display that lets you expose the covers.

☼ BRAINSTORMING 4.7 DEVELOP A MERCHANDIZING PLAN.

- Identify goals you want to accomplish.

  Examples: increased circulation of nonfiction titles; promotion of annual booksale; increased use of reference services

- Identify the time-frame in which you want to accomplish your goals. Do you want a long-term plan or a quick fix?

  Examine the resources. What resources and materials do you require? Where can you find what you need? What materials and resources do you already have on hand?

- Develop several ideas for achieving your goals.

  Examples: create a new nonfiction display table at the front of the library; create fliers and posters for the annual booksale and place the fliers at the circulation desk and posters at the ends of the aisles in your library; have reference librarians or all staff wear "Ask Me" buttons as they circulate the floor.

- How are you going to get the staff involved?

- Implement an action plan and support it by circulating it to all staff.

The Third P: Price

Price goes by many names, but in the end all organizations must set prices on their products or services. You pay *tuition* for education, *fees* for professional services, *fares* for airline service, and *taxes* to help support libraries. A price is an amount of money charged for a product or service.

As a service provider, the library's highest costs are in the personnel department. Traditionally, funds for books and materials represent only 10 percent to 20 percent of a library's total budget. As a result, libraries rarely price individual programs, services, and products. However, every service does have a price. In addition to the cost of books and materials, one has to plan for the costs of space, personnel, administrative services, and other direct costs.

Andrew Carnegie provided libraries with access to millions of dollars in the early-twentieth century. He believed in free access to information and books for all, and became the great benefactor of libraries throughout this country. In the meantime, as libraries have become dependent on government funding and fund-raising, they have entered the fee-based arena by charging their customers fees for fines, copying, rental programs, and research services, among others. In each of these services you have to come up with an economic figure, or a price if you will. How do you do that?

Determining the actual costs involved in any new products or service is the first step in pricing the service. A decision must be made about whether this service should be "free" or considered a value-added service, for which there should be a charge.

In order to provide any service, the costs must be covered. There are fixed costs, also known as overhead, and there are variable costs. The fixed costs go on whether you do the program (once or one hundred times) or not, while the variable costs depend on the program.

In all of these pricing methods, costs set the floor. The price must cover all of the costs of delivering the product or services. The customer determines whether the library has set the right price. The customer weighs the price against the perceived value of using the service. Customers also compare prices of competitive products. You must entertain several pricing strategies.

Cost Plus Pricing

Cost plus pricing is the simplest kind of pricing. A standard markup is added to the cost of a product of service. You often see this kind of pricing in construction work. You also see an example of this kind of pricing in libraries, in library book sales, special events, and programs. Cost plus pricing is used when you are certain of the cost of the service.

Competitive Pricing

If the service is one of several comparable services in the market place, the service should be competitive in price. For example, copy machines, microform copiers, as well as video rental should be competitively priced.

Discount Pricing

Sometimes manufacturers put a low price on their product to encourage people to buy. This strategy often enables them to make a substantial penetration in the marketplace. An example of this type of pricing occurs when a Barnes and Noble store enters a market place. They discount their prices to encourage new customers to buy and then raise their prices over time. Another firm that has used discount pricing to entice new customers is Amazon.com. This company has lost substantial amounts of money by discounting prices to entice the consumer to shop online.

Premium Pricing

Consider this for products or services offered at the highest level. Premium pricing strategies are used in pricing luxury automobiles. The level of personal service that accompanies the purchase goes far beyond the actual purchase. In libraries, fee-based research and document delivery might be considered for a premium-pricing model. In the area of donations, the large and special gifts are primary examples of premium pricing. If your service or your product is innovative, in demand, and has little competition, a premium pricing model should be selected. The customer service that you provide to accompany this pricing model must be premium, as well.

Pricing strategies must be in keeping with your overall financial objectives. Make certain that your pricing strategies are consistent with your overall goals and financial well being. Carefully analyze the actual cost of developing a service. In determining an appropriate pricing structure, identify each component, not only the hard costs, but also the cost of staff time, physical space, administrative overhead, and other costs not easily determined. You may want to review your budget at this point to organize your cost analysis.

Above all, take heart. Pricing is not an easy strategy for retailers or for libraries.

The Fourth P: Promotion

Promotion requires careful attention if your marketing plan is to be successful. Libraries now recognize that they have to create a "product" with sales appeal. They must promote that appeal, because they are operating in a competitive and sophisticated environment and must be as visible as other cultural and educational institutions. They are entering the arena of advertising, and the trend is growing. All of the areas of promotion are complex and require a great deal of creativity and planning. These areas include public relations, promotions, incentives, paid advertising in various media, and Web site design.

Understanding Sales Promotion

Although libraries may not know it, they are in the business of sales. You think about how you can attract customers, how you can hold on to those customers. You do "merchandizing," you create "incentives," and you train at customer service so that staff can assist the customer in the best way possible. Customer loyalty is important and you measure your effectiveness with customers.

Libraries usually do not use the language of sales promotions, but they are a part of the advertising efforts made. Sales promotions are shaped by three components. They include the incentive, the means of delivering the incentive, and the way the word will get out. These choices add up to a promotional strategy.

Libraries often provide incentives. These can be a gift, a coupon, a contest, an experience, or a special event. You usually do the promoting through advertising, point of sale materials, direct mail, or in person. Think of "Summer Reading programs" and the incentives offered: free McDonald's coupons, free rides at amusement parks. Promotion comes through brochures, buttons, flyers, or cards. The point of sale material may include a banner in the library, a big poster, certificates. These promotional programs encourage trial, build awareness, and reward loyalty.

Read the story of the Houston Public Libraries Power Card™ on page 97. While this is a story of a major urban library, it can be duplicated in smaller communities. A campaign such as this one is a win-win effort for local politicians, corporations, as well as the library. It can be done on a much smaller scale in any community. Examine your community for potential partners, provide the example to your local Mayor or City official, and form a team to produce results.

Success Story 4.6

Maximizing Promotional Efforts through Partnerships with the Power Card™

Houston Public Library,   **Houston, Texas**

In his 1998 inauguration speech, Mayor Lee P. Brown made the kind of promise politicians rarely follow through on, "Books were the first rungs on the ladder I, like many others, used to climb out of poverty...Now, it's my goal to see every school age child in Houston gets a library card." Mayor Brown backed his words with the $1.5 million Power Card™ Challenge, a new program designed to double the number of juvenile cardholders to roughly 300,000 by June of 1999. The other goals of the program included:

- Give a Power Card™ application to every school age child in Houston;

- Encourage all kids to "activate" their card by visiting a Houston Public Library;

- Increase juvenile circulation at least 30 percent from July 1998-June, 1999;

- Enhance services to youth by increasing popular materials, programming and community outreach.

To promote the program, the Library built over 250 partnerships in the community with schools, corporations, clubs, and media, not only ensuring the success of the Power Card™, but also laying a foundation upon which the library could build.

One of the first and most important companies to join the Power Card™ program was the company that knew the most about power in the area, Reliant Energy, the city's electricity and natural gas provider. Andrea Lapsley, Assistant Director of Marketing and Development, approached the company, because it had such broad community ties. Soon, Robert Gibbs, Director of Corporate Community Relations at Reliant Energy, committed the support of his staff members to assist the library.

Together, the library and Reliant Energy developed a marketing plan to create, promote and "sell" the library card as if it were a new product. The library card was transformed into the Power Card™, the product and brand name of library services. Reliant Energy created the Power Critter logo and the graphic design—a swirl of bright colors giving the appearance of energy—providing a strong and exciting brand to identify the Houston Public Library in an instant. The company also helped prepare and pay for bilingual Power Card™ applications, bright colorful posters, and still brighter orange T-shirts with the slogan "packing the power." Reliant Energy's contribution cannot be emphasized enough. They even included information about the Power Card™ in their monthly utility bills.

The program quickly became so massive that it called for even more partners. The library began working with public, private, and charter schools, Head Start programs, juvenile detention facilities, and day care centers, distributing applications by mail and staff visits. Teachers, school librarians, principals, and administrators, soon became the program's biggest boosters, working for 100 percent sign-up in their schools. The program offered a great opportunity for the public library and the schools to work together on similar goals. Staff members from every library branch became part of the "sales force," visiting schools, making presentations, and conducting sign-ups. Those schools that achieved 90 percent sign-up were rewarded with a colorful banner funded by Reliant Energy proclaiming, "Our school packs the Power."

To raise more money, the library charged a $40 annual nonresidency fee for customers living within unincorporated areas of Houston. This was no small feat, but it needed to be done so those corporate sponsors could offer their promotions to the whole city. The library director approached the mayor and each council member to discuss waiving the nonresidency fee for children under 18 years of age, an idea met with great enthusiasm, so much so that the mayor and council approved the waiver for seven contiguous counties. The waiver really allowed the library to market and achieve such high results for the first year.

The library also formed partnerships with a variety of youth organizations. Agencies such as Girl Scouts, Boy Scouts, Boys and Girls Clubs, Big Brothers and Big Sisters, and the mayor's After School Initiative program, all helped by distributing applications and promoting the Power Card™ in their publications.

Other city departments got involved, as well. The fire department provided top personnel as special story-time guest readers. The parks department distributed and collected Power Card™ applications at its thirty-five community centers. Sign-ups occurred at "Fundays in the Park" across the city as well as the zoo. Applications were distributed at city health clinics. A presiding judge of the municipal courts required every youth offender to register for a Power Card™.

The cultural arts community also provided support. The Children's Museum created a Parent Resource Center, while staff at the Museum of Fine Arts began allowing free Saturday and Sunday admission to any child with a card. Reliant Energy sponsored three Power Card™ Sundays, at the museum where any child with a Power Card™ received free admission. Dr. Peter Marzio, the innovative director of the Museum of Finea Arts, allowed any child free entrance to the museum on Saturdays and Sundays throughout the year. Museum staff were trained to take library card applications on site thus giving a child immediate free admission. Other museums provided registrations during Museum Open House Day, and promoted the library in newsletters to their institutions and members.

Signing people up off-site turned out to be one of the most successful strategies in pursuit of the Power Card™ goals. The library made a commitment to take the Power Card™ Program to more than 500 outreach events. Citywide festivals like the Power of Houston, Houston Rodeo and Livestock Show, the Children's Festival, and the International Festival each netted more than 1,000 completed applications. The library did off site registration at educational conferences, community meetings, political functions, neighborhood festivals, little league sign up, career days, job fairs, town hall meetings, malls, department stores, and health fairs. Reliant Energy again helped by arranging registration at the offices of various corporations. A person could fill out a simple form, and Reliant Energy would issue them the card right on the spot.

The library also worked with local media to promote the Power Card™

program. The library's public information officer, Sheryl Berger, developed a far-reaching strategy to ensure that every Houstonian heard about the Power Card™.

A kickoff press conference featured the High Impact Squad, a group of performers dressed in superhero costumes performing death-defying basketball dunks. Video footage of the High Impact Squad along with a group of young people in orange T-shirts became the central images for a public service announcement (PSA) produced by Warner Cable. There was coverage by most Houston TV stations as well as editorials and news articles by the local newspaper. Eller Media donated 200 billboards placed in strategic locations around the city, while local radio and television stations donated airtime to run the PSAs. Staff was interviewed on local TV and radio stations, including those of Spanish language media. Billboards appeared all over the city.

Another essential element of the Power Card™ program was a Power Card™ event at each library. The events increased registration and circulation, developed partnerships within the community and strengthened teamwork among the staff. Those events included puppet shows to musical performances.

The visual aspect of the Power Card™ was an important part of the promotion strategy. The Power Card™ "brand" was strong, vital, exciting and easily recognized, finding its way to all kinds of products. Photos from the press conference were quickly transformed into a series of promotional products, including a PowerPoint presentation, display boards for use at outreach events, and the Power Card™ Web page (www.hpl.lib.tx.us/powercard), a focal point in promoting the program. The library purchased disposable cameras for each branch to use to document their activities. The Power Card™ Page is loaded with pictures of kids holding up their Power Cards™, of staff out in the community, of staff rallying around "The Power Tower," which documents sign-ups as the Power Critter moves up a stack of books each month.

The enthusiasm of the Power Card™ program is contagious. Once a month, all library staff dons their orange T-shirts on Power Card™ Dress Up Days, while some wear white or gray polo shirts to recognize outstanding individual achievements. The library was awarded the prestigious John Cotton Dana Library Public Relations Award for the program. In addition, the library was honored when the Texas Library Association named the Power Card™ Challenge the program of the year. Meanwhile, Library Journal named Mayor Lee P. Brown "Politician of the Year" and one of the "Six Politicians Who Made A Difference." In August 2003, the Library won the first-ever IFLA 3M Library Marketing Award for the Power Card Challenge. The partnerships built during the program have also been sustained, proving the Power Card™ a powerful tool of cooperation, communication, promotion, and improvement.

Brainstorming 4.8 lists the questions that you have to answer if your promotional campaign is going to be successful. Try using this for a promotion that you are thinking of, and continue to use these questions whenever you are planning a promotional campaign.

☼ BRAINSTORMING 4.8 DEVELOP A PROMOTION STRATEGY USING THE QUESTIONS WHO, WHAT, WHEN, WHERE, WHY, AND HOW.

- Who? Who are your current customers? Who are the new customers you are trying to reach? Who is the promotion aimed at?

- What? What specific product or service are you trying to promote? What will get your customers interested? What do you want them to do?

- When? Timing is important. The best work you can do will fall flat if the timing is off. When should you start promoting? When are you planning the event or product in relation to the rest of the community schedule? When can you expect returns?

- Where? Where should you place your ads? Where will your customers be sure to look or listen?

- Why? Why are you providing this product or service? Why should your customers know about this?

- How? How are you going to do this? This question incorporates all of your other answers into one comprehensive plan.

(Professional people can help with the where and how. Otherwise, be sure and think of these things.)

The Fifth P: Positioning (and Repositioning)

Positioning is often called "the battle for your mind." It is not what you do to the product. It is how you position your product in the mind of the audience. Why would you want to position or reposition your library? To respond to changes in the information industry or to correct a damaged or weakened posture. Reputation or image is more important than any specific feature when it comes to selling a product.

Corporations develop a "positioning" strategy when introducing a new product. Should that new candy bar be positioned next to Hershey's and Snickers or could it be positioned next to the health food bars? How should that new car be positioned? Libraries, too, are "positioned," whether that positioning is done intentionally or not. Companies behind consumer products give a great deal of thought to positioning strategies, as those strategies will influence how customers perceive their products. Think of the way Xerox owns the copying business. They have positioned themselves as the "document" company. Sabena Airlines has "positioned" the country of Belgium as a beautiful country in order to attract more people to their airlines. How about ski areas? Are they positioned to appeal to a local audience or are they determined to be one of the top 10 in the country?

How is your library perceived in your community? As a leading cultural institution? As providing important service to the community? Libraries must be aware of their own positions in the market place. Those audiences for whom a library must be positioned include the following:

1. Elected officials who determine the library budget;

2. Parents and children;

3. The business community;

4. Neighborhood associations;

5. Senior citizens;

6. Donors;

7. Customers seeking popular materials;

8. Customers seeking reference and research materials;

9. Customers from a variety of ethnic groups and cultures;

10. Students.

In an academic library, audiences would include:

1. Administrators who determine the budget;

2. Departments (engineering, geology, history, literature, business to name a few);

3. Faculty members (individual faculty members as well as department groups);

4. Graduate students (students at a distance, students in different disciplines);

5. Undergraduate students (in different disciplines, different requirements such as students at a distance, employed students);

6. Graduated students (alumni);

7. Business and Industries that provide support the university.

In addition to positioning the library as a whole, you can position individual products and services. For example, providing an automated circulation system in various languages, as well as online services and services from remote locations, offers an opportunity to reposition the library. However, in promoting this new service, remember that it is not the automation that customers will think is important, but the benefits of that automation—such as faster and easier access to information, books, and materials.

Each segment will require separate positioning strategies. An outstanding summer reading program can be used to position the library to parents and children. Some libraries provide special services for elected officials, and these targeted services serve as positioning strategies for that segment of the market. Services designed to meet the needs of the business community position the library to that community.

The keys to position are communication, advertising, and promotion. If you establish a strong business department, but do not let the business community know, your positioning strategy will be ineffective.

BRAINSTORMING 4.9 ASK THE RIGHT QUESTIONS TO POSITION FOR POWER.

When positioning your product, service, or library, ask how various audiences perceive you now.

- Mayor, city council, county officials, other elected officials

- Business leaders

- Parents and children

- The community

- Students

How do you find out how they feel about you? You can do some formal market research including surveys and focus groups. You can invite small groups of each constituency in to talk to you about how they feel. If you invite people in to talk to you, do not get defensive when they tell you things that you did not want to hear.

What programs/services will enhance the position of the library in the eyes of your audience? You have many different audiences, so what works for one will not necessarily work for another. Each one of the following items helps to position your library in the eyes of the audience. Ask your customers about the following areas.

- Leadership in technology.

- Improved service to special groups within the community.

- Merchandizing your library.

- Improved customer service.

- Amenities such as a coffee shop.

- Special events.

- Collaboration with other institutions.

- Philanthropic programs.

- Special collections or exhibits.

- Programs, book clubs, activities.

A solid, strong position in your community is not achieved over-night or through a single program. It comes through constant good customer service, quality products, continued visibility, and leadership. Remember to use all forms of media to communicate your position. The objective of public relations, publicity, Web sites and advertising is not only visibility, but also positioning. Communication through the media offers an opportunity to reinforce how the customer sees your library.

If you work in a public library, you will want to use Worksheet 4-10 to detail your customers' perceptions of you and how you might change them. Worksheet 4-11 is the same exercise adapted specifically to an academic library.

 BRAINSTORMING 4.10 HOW DO YOU POSITION YOUR LIBRARY?

After completing your answers, ask what you did to discover how people feel about your library. Did you discover their feelings through focus groups, interviews or surveys? Other ways?

How is your library perceived by:	What would change that perception:	What will you do to change their perception:
• Elected officials (Mayor, county or city commissioners		
• Community as a whole		
• Parents and children		
• Neighborhood associations		

How is your library perceived by:	What would change that perception:	What will you do to change their perception:
• Senior citizens		
• Donors		
• Customers seeking popular materials		
• Customers from ethnic groups		
• Customers seeking reference and research materials		
• Young adults and students		

BRAINSTORMING 4.11 HOW DO YOU POSITION YOUR LIBRARY IN AN ACADEMIC SITUATION?

How is your library perceived by:	What would change that perception:	What will you do to change their perception:
• **Administrators** There are several levels of administrators. There is the President of the University, the academic Deans, the Board of Trustees.		
• **Faculty** Divided the faculty into disciplines. The faculty in the business school may feel differently than those in the engineering school.		
• **Undergraduate students** Undergraduate students come in many different varieties. Perhaps you want to know how you are positioned to older students, to minority or ethnic students, or students in various disciplines. Perhaps it is students at a distance. Identify students in various groups.		

How is your library perceived by:	What would change that perception:	What will you do to change their perception:
• **Graduate students** The needs of graduate students are very precise and demanding. The position of the library depends greatly on how those needs are met. Divide your graduate students into various segments to determine your position.		
• **Community** Do various members of the community have access to the library? Can you break the community group down into sub groups?		
• **Donors** How is the library positioned to donors?		
• **Auxiliary organizations** Do auxiliary organizations include alumni of the University? Are there other groups who use the resources of the library?		

Success Story 4.7
Repositioning for Success

Douglas County Libraries,   **Castle Rock, Colorado**

Douglas County, Colorado is a beautiful area graced with rolling hills, open space and a panoramic view of the Rocky Mountains, from Pike's Peak to Long's Peak. Fifteen years ago the Denver Technological Center was built south of the city, and Douglas County soon became one of the fastest growing counties in the country. The people moving into the county were well-educated and had high expectations, but by 1990, the Douglas County Libraries were facing a fiscal crisis. Then, new Executive Director Jamie LaRue came to the Library Board with a brash idea: separate the library from the county and form an independent library district. He knew that if he went straight to the voters for an increase in the mill levy to 2.5 mills, he could deliver services and products to win the voters support.

Mr. LaRue's first step as the new Director was to ask two local newspapers for weekly columns. While there were no local TV or radio stations, the newspapers were free and delivered to every home. The library would focus each week on information that was vital for the communities to hear before the election: the small size of the library buildings; the inadequate number of books for such an upscale audience; and a lack of children's programs. In addition, the library was open too few hours and days a week, and while the county had been charging the library $86,000 for automation services, that price was escalating to $110,000.

Market research was also used to determine what customers wanted, to discover and verify what the library staff believed were the best selling points of the Library. The library hired a professional agency to assist them in developing a telephone survey, testing people at random out of the phone book. As LaRue suspected, people wanted more hours, books, and children's programs.

The library also built voter support through more personal appeals. They built on local pride asking, "Don't we deserve better?" But when business leaders proved unresponsive, LaRue tried a new strategy: he realized the constituency was 80 percent women and women with children, so he began talking to babysitting cooperatives. "When I went back to the usual group of business leaders," LaRue said, "they told me that their wives had already told them how to vote on the library issue."

The next step was to penetrate the market in certain areas. Comparing census and patron information, the library realized, as LaRue said, "if we carried the essential precincts, we could carry the election." They soon began targeting specific elementary schools to encourage students to sign up for library cards, requiring parents come to the library with their children to sign the card.

In the end, the Douglas County Library System won the election by a 2–1 margin, but this was only the first step in repositioning the library system. Now, the library had to keep the promises made during the election.

As expected, the libraries opened seven days a week, and a period of "smart growth" began. Since 1991, the district has built or renovated a library a year and opened satellite libraries in rural elementary schools. External changes have been accompanied by internal ones. The product mix of the library includes adult literacy, homebound delivery of books, online book discussion groups, children's programming, Shakespeare at the Rock, local history collections, Web site, Internet classes, family programs and events. The Library increased also their contact with customers by sending out monthly newsletters via e-mail, continuing to build trust by keeping their promises on schedule and within budget. In 1995, that trust was sufficient for the community to vote for another mill levy increase by one and a half mills.

As a manager, Jamie LaRue encourages staff to take risks, make mistakes, be creative, and provide excellent customer service. "People want to be associated with success." Their positioning statement is "We're not just building libraries, we are building community." "The purpose of the public library is pretty clear," LaRue said. "It is our job to gather, organize and provide public access to the intellectual capital of our culture. We take that job very seriously."

LaRue believes that there are seven strategic directions for the future of the library:

1. Building a Web site that should be everyone's favorite bookmark;

2. Showcasing art and culture;

3. Continue to develop an institution that is educational, friendly and knowledgeable;

4. Building a library that is the dynamic center of the community including the local history collector;

5. Providing marketing and promotion to bring people in business and government to the Library;

6. Provide lifelong learning;

7. Provide current and deep collections.

In 1990, the Douglas County Library had 14 employees and a budget of $668,00. Now, it has grown to over 225 employees and an annual budget of $10 million. "Seventy-five percent of the households in Douglas County have library cards," LaRue notes. The Douglas County Library System earned the Colorado Public Library Excellence Award, and in 1998, the Colorado Library Association honored Jamie LaRue as librarian of the year. He and the staff of the Douglas County Public Library have listened to their customers, developing the programs and collections, building the libraries and assuming leadership on technology programs. They have truly repositioned library service within Douglas County.

Success Story 4.8
Repositioning by Taking a Leadership Role

Richmond Public Library,   **Richmond, British Columbia, Canada**

Like other libraries, the Richmond Public Library, BC, Canada sees the risk that the public library and the profession of the librarian may become marginalized by the tools and products of the digital age. Acting aggressively to change its roles and responsibilities, the library has taken an active role in developing its technology. It has created an award winning, community based Web site (www.yourlibrary.ca) and sells technology services to businesses and organizations in the community.

The library's strategic plan lists one of its values as "the extension of information services beyond the Library's walls with digital media and communications technology." The library needed to adopt an aggressive campaign for digital technology. They train the community in the use of technology, provide new services based on this new technology, and, in the process, carve out new roles for the staff.

The staff of the Richmond Public Library has taken on three roles. They include:

1. Teacher. They provide leadership and education for a variety of audiences, including the general public, schools and teachers, city staff, and businesses.

2. Creator. Through the development of their dynamic, interactive and award-winning Web site.

3. Marketer of information technology. The library markets a variety of Internet services to secure its position in a changing world.

Through these roles the library began to understand their customer's needs and could thereby take a leadership role with its technology and with its customers. They developed Internet sessions for individuals, students, and seniors, given for a small fee. They continue to offer more specialized training and programs for teens, businesspeople, parents, teachers, teacher-librarians, members of the local Chamber of Commerce and the City of Richmond. Teaching has become a rewarding part of the Richmond librarian's work. They are recognized as being leaders in the area of technology course development and consequently, have gained increased status in the community and with other libraries.

The second part of their strategy is to communicate with the community about the benefits and attributes of the Internet. The public relations department writes a column for the local newspaper, the *Richmond Review*, entitled "New on the Net." These articles send the message that the Internet is exciting and relevant, with the library at the core of this communication.

The third part of this strategy to reposition the Richmond Public Library in the digital age is the creation of a unique Web site. This Web site is an essential source for library information and act "as a platform on which to further develop and market staff skills." Local businesses also use the Web site to provide new and interactive services. The World Wide Web provides the library another opportunity to market itself and serve its customers in better ways. A complete description of the Richmond Public Library's Web site is available in Chapter 7.

The success of the Richmond Public Library's marketing plan ensures the presence of library services in the community. Service to the public is constantly improving. The library staff is continuously developing new skills and partnerships form between the library and the community. The Richmond Public Library has not let the past dominate the future. They have taken risks and developed an entrepreneurial behavior. Taking advantage of every opportunity, they have generated funds by maximizing sales opportunities. As a result, the Richmond Public Library has assumed a role as leader and repositioned their library to be a dominant force in their community.

USING MARKETING POSITION STRATEGIES

Strategies to improve the position of the library might include

- Positioning on good customer service

- Positioning on leadership in the technology age

- Positioning on driver product attributes. Federal Express and the U.S. Post Office both position on delivery of their service. Do libraries position themselves by delivery? Access? Availability?

Successful positioning strategies must possess two important attributes. They must be unique and they must be credible. The purpose of a positioning strategy is to create distinction in the minds of your customers between the product/service of your library and other similar products/services. Unsupported claims to distinction do not work when promoting your service to intelligent voters, customers and politicians. You should promote only what you can deliver. A positioning strategy must have credibility.

DEVELOPING THE POSITIONING STATEMENT

Why do you need to find a succinct statement that reflects our position? In this country you have an excessive use of communication. You can see it everywhere. There is television, radio, newspapers, magazines, billboards, trucks, street cars, buses and taxi cabs, electric lights, subways, even grocery carts with advertisements. There are hundreds of advertising campaigns calling for your attention.

How do you cut through the communication explosion to get our message through to you? How do you find that window in your mind? You do it by developing what you call as "the unique selling proposition." What do you do as a library that is unique? That no one else can do? What do you do better?

People do not change their minds easily. They file away in their minds the way they perceive you to be. When it comes to libraries, most people have already made up their minds. Libraries have been around since their childhood. "But," you say, "libraries have changed! "Even though libraries have changed, you have to change the perception in the mind of the customer. If you want to change customer's perceptions, it really doesn't work to slowly build up a favorable opinion over a period of time. Instead, you really have to make a big impression or a big blast into their mind.

Therefore, you develop advertising and communication programs to do just that. Those advertising and communication programs must be consistent, dynamic and blast through the mind of the customer.

You start with the positioning statement. This statement is short, direct, dynamic and to the point. It clearly states the important message in 25 words or less. For example, the positioning statement for the Post Office overnight delivery service is "We deliver, we deliver" Nordstrom's retail stores say, "No problems at Nordstrom's." The Seattle Public Library in their recent bond election and private campaign said "A library isn't a library without you!" The Denver Public Library said, "A Great City Deserves a Great Library" during their bond election.

Try writing your own positioning statement with members of some of the groups that have been involved in your marketing process.

✎ BRAINSTORMING 4.12 DEVELOP YOUR POSITIONING STATEMENT.

Develop your positioning statement. Remember that you want it to be short, direct, dynamic, to the point, and no longer than 25 words.

_____

_____

_____

_____

_____

_____

_____

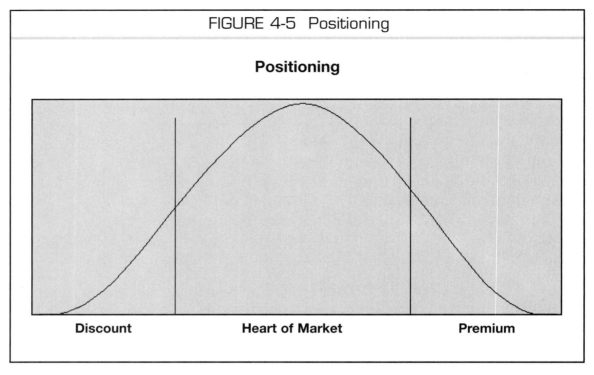

FIGURE 4-5 Positioning

Positioning

Discount   Heart of Market   Premium

Figure 4-5 illustrates positioning as it relates to the market place. The majority of products or services are positioned to appeal to the "heart of the market," for example, discount stores like Walmart, Target, Dollar Stores, as opposed to premium products like a Mercedes or Lexus. Libraries, for the most part, fit into the "heart of the market," though some special libraries and special collections fit into the premium section of the market place.

Paying Attention to Our Nonverbal Communications

Consider your library's brochures, letterhead stationery, and business cards. Are they consistent? Do they present the kind of image you desire? Do you have a logo that conveys the mission of the library? Are there graphic standards for the use of that logo and the design of your stationery, signage and other elements of communication?

How about the signage at your library? Does it provide clear direction? Is it easily understood? Do you have handmade directional signs?

What image do your facilities, furniture and fixtures present to your customers? Are they cluttered, disorganized?

All of these elements reflect the position of your institution in your community. They reinforce the image you project.

Success Story 4.9
Repositioning the School Library

Dewitt Wallace-Reader's Digest Fund,   **New York, New York**

As recently as a decade ago, libraries in many of the country's public elementary and middle schools were not considered essential to a quality education. That may partly explain why school libraries by the thousands fell victim to budget shortages during the 1960s, 1970s, and 1980s. Those that survived usually had to make do with outdated collections, part-time staffing and lack of support from school administrators.

Things began to change in 1988. That is when the DeWitt Wallace-Reader's Digest Fund launched its Library Power Program, the beginning of a ten-year $40 million investment to revitalize public elementary and middle school libraries across the country. Developed and tested for two years in New York City where libraries in many schools had been eliminated completely, Library Power began expanding nationally in 1991. It spread to other urban East Coast locations experiencing problem similar to New York's and to Southern, Midwestern and Western states where outdated libraries desperately needed refurbishing.

Since the inception of the campaign, 37 state associations, including the school library media associations and 20 state library agencies have participated in the campaign. Although the data collection is not complete, early evidence suggests that schools that have fully implemented Library Power are seeing results. The combination of renovated facilities, expanded resources, flexible scheduling and collaboration among education professionals is beginning to change the role of public school libraries. Once considered not vital to the teaching and learning process, they are now thriving, essential centers of activity for entire schools."

The Library Power: Building Partnerships for Learning program is "repositioning" libraries within public schools.

The Sixth P: Public Policy and Politics

Libraries often have to consider a final P in their marketing mix: public policy and politics. Libraries in every sector must work with city councils, county commissioners, universities and research institutions, organizations, state and federal governments to obtain their budgets. They form library districts, raise money through bond elections, and raise private dollars to enhance programs and building. Political strategies become a key to success.

When developing political strategies, careful attention must be paid to individual politicians, who play important roles in the decision-making process. Apply the first steps in the marketing planning process to identify who they are (segmentation) and what will encourage them to support the library (customer decision-making process).

In many locations, there are public policies that influence the development of programs and services within the library. These policies may include city ordinances, legal requirements, and legal operating structures. For example, your library may need to comply with a policy that states that money received from customers' payment of library fines goes directly to the city's general fund and cannot be used specifically for library purposes. Marketing planning must take these issues into account.

Figure 4-6 provides a quick visual reference for the 4 Ps that appeal to customers and influence their opinions. The next figure (fig 4-7) places the 4 Ps and their customer influence in the context of the larger environment from which customers make their decisions.

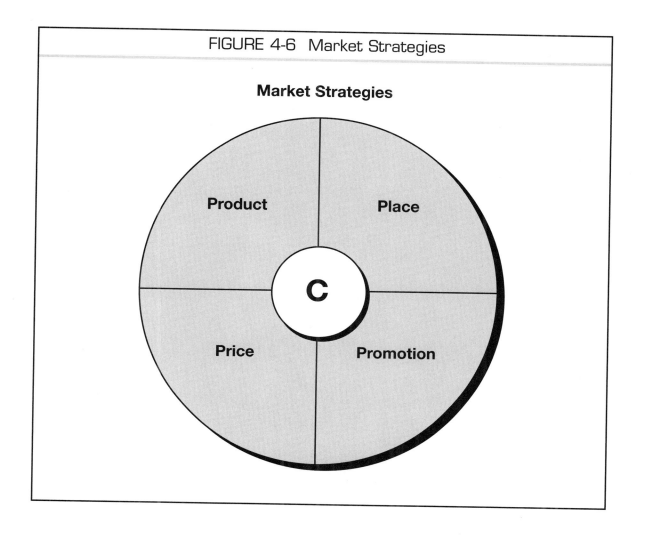

FIGURE 4-6 Market Strategies

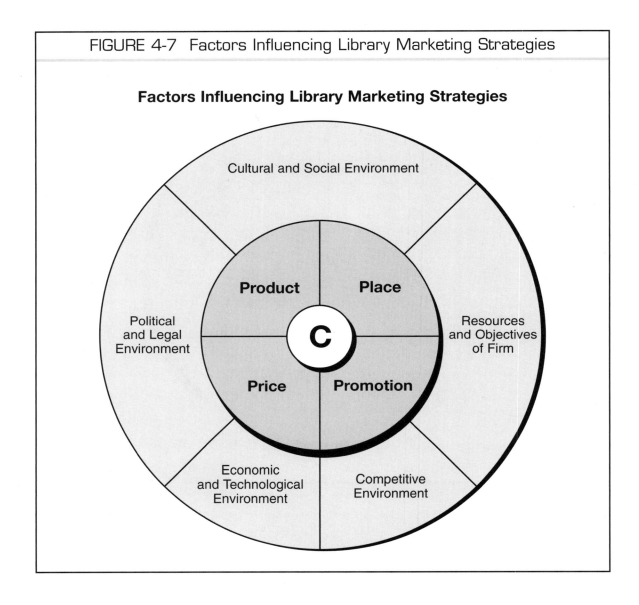

FIGURE 4-7 Factors Influencing Library Marketing Strategies

Factors Influencing Library Marketing Strategies

CHAPTER 5

Combine Smart Marketing Tactics with the Right Action Steps

Marketing tactics include all of the advertising, promotion, sales, and public relations that are the visible part of marketing and occur in all areas of communication. Some of those tactics are paid advertising, public relations, promotions, direct mail, Web sites, and the Internet. Each of these areas is an avenue to communication. They need to be targeted, planned, coordinated, and executed in a timely manner for success.

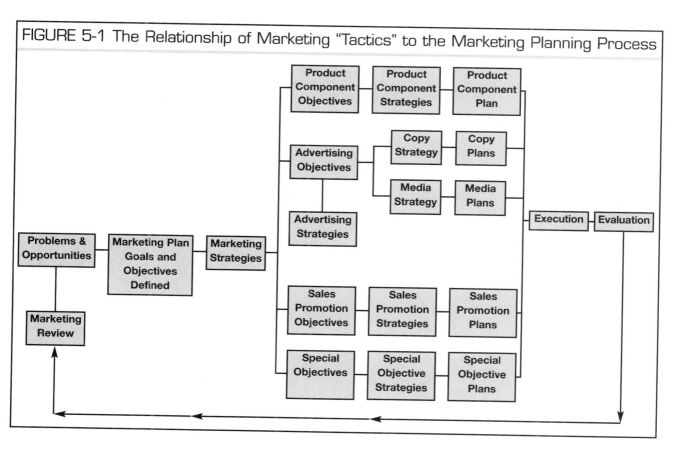

FIGURE 5-1 The Relationship of Marketing "Tactics" to the Marketing Planning Process

Figure 5-1 also illustrates another view of the marketing planning process. You can see that the marketing review process as well as the identification of problems and opportunities, the Marketing plan goals and objectives have been defined. The Marketing strategies (product, price, place, positioning have been reduced. We are seeing in this diagram the role of advertising and promotion. Once again, we see various strategies and action steps. As you look at this diagram, it becomes apparent how many strategies and action steps must be coordinated. Timing becomes very important. If there is a delay in the development of copy strategies or media strategies, you will miss the "window of opportunity." The various steps in the marketing planning process demonstrate how well the planning must be coordinated, timely and accurate.

Developing Effective Public Relations

Good public relations help to maintain the reputation of your library, to win understanding and influence opinions. It involves excellent customer care, effective communication, and responsibility to the local community and the environment. It requires planning, executing, and sustaining activities, and often anticipating tomorrow's issues. Good public relations can build better awareness and relationships with every element of the community (see chart on the next page).

According to Philip Kotler in his book, *Kotler on Marketing*, public relations consist of a set of tools that can be classified under the acronym of "PENCILS."

P = *Publications* (company magazines, annual reports, helpful customer brochures)

E = *Events* (sponsoring art events, seminars, informational events)

N = *News* (favorable stories about the library, its people and products and services)

C = *Community involvement activities* (community needs, library fundraising events)

I = *Identity media* (stationery, business cards, corporate dress codes)

L = *Lobbying activity* (efforts to influence favorable legislation)

S = *Social responsibility activities* (building a good reputation for the library)

Employees	Library Customers

• Managers
• Clerical Staff
• New employees
• Employee Families
• Profession Staff
• Retired Employees
• Outstanding Employees
	• Satisfied
	• Dissatisfied
	• New
	• Old
	• Potential
	• Special Segments
	   - Children
	   - Ethnic groups
	   - Senior Citizens
	   - Special Interest Groups
	   - Neighborhoods
	   - Students
	   - Educators
	   - Community Groups

Library Stakeholder • Board Members • Foundation Members • Friends	
Library Funders—Public Sources • City Council • County Commissioners • Mayor • City Budget Office • Angry Politicians • Campaigning Politicians • City Manager • Elected Officials • State Legislators • Politicians with a "stake" • The Electorate	**Library Funders—Private Sources** • Corporations • Foundations • Individuals • Community Groups
The Media • General Press • Business Press • Library Press • Wire Services • Hostile Journalists	• Local Weekly Publications • Business Newsletters • Electronic Media • Friendly Journalists • Outstanding Journalists

Understanding a Public Relations Strategy

A strategic approach to public relations creates an effective outcome. Many libraries employ a public relations specialist and staff, to create press releases, editorials, provide background information, and create events.

Your strategy must be linked to marketing goals, objectives, and strategies while supporting the overall goals of the library. Again, set objectives that represent the goals you want to achieve. They may focus on building better relationships with essential groups or maximizing your library's position in the community. Clear objectives will help you set a target, chart your progress, measure results, and be effective.

Identifying other Public Relations Skills

Communicating with the Staff

Too often, you do not communicate well with the staff; you assume that the entire staff knows what the library is doing. What do employees need to know on a regular basis? By what means do they prefer to communicate? What new things are you doing? How can you improve communication? How can you build a team? A well-informed staff becomes your first priority.

Communicating with the Community

Here again, you need to build an action plan. It is an opportunity to look at those strengths and weaknesses that you developed in Chapter 1. Public relations staff can concentrate on building up weak positions and capitalizing on strengths. It can take years to build a good image. You want to work hard to maintain and protect that image.

Using Events to Carry a Message

Libraries are famous for book sales, as well as a myriad of other events. How can the book sale become a more targeted event? How can you use the book sale to create publicity? Events are a wonderful way to bring people into your family. Events help to establish a feeling of community with the library. If you are going to do an event, you must do it well. Target the audience that you hope will participate, do the planning necessary to make the event successful, involve volunteers, consider partnerships with other nonprofit organizations. Give the proper amount of timing and planning to events. Do not take on more than you can do well. Read about the community center created through the library at Ruidosa, New Mexico (see Success Story 5.3).

Handling a Crisis

One of the times when public relations of any organization are put to the test is a time of crisis. A crisis can be any story, event, or rumor that has the potential of affecting your reputation, image, or credibility in a negative way. There are objections to censorship policies, a theft, or a fire, natural disasters, safety issues, legal issues, and occasionally staff misconduct. A strong public relations staff skilled in handling a crisis can assist the organization. A well-managed crisis can often enhance the image of a library rather than damage it. There are some rules for handling a crisis. They include the following:

- Always tell the truth.
- Be as forthright as possible.
- Have a communication plan in place in advance.

- Convey that you care.

- Move quickly. Do not act confused and stunned.

- Do not utter just any comment. If you do not know what to say indicate that you do not know at this time—but get answers quickly.

- Do not avoid the press. Seek opportunities to get in from of the press to tell your story.

- Make every effort to gather the pertinent facts.

- Enact the necessary measures to resolve the situation.

- Appoint staff members to act as a crisis communication team, if necessary.

- Educate staff members about your crisis procedure.

- Be as objective as possible.

- As the crisis passes, do an analysis and summary report. Evaluate your response and identify suggested improvements.

- Work to restore your image.

Creating a Consistent Image

You can create something of value for your customers. One of the first steps is to create a consistent image for the library that is reflected where people see the following:

- logo;

- stationery;

- Web site;

- signage;

- bookmobiles:

- vans, delivery trucks;

- other visible entities of the library.

The image has character and a quality that makes it unique and irreplaceable.

Whether or not you have a marketing or public relations office in your library, someone in the organization is responsible for creating newsletters, signage, press releases, annual reports, and other forms of communication to your publics. Just as any public business with stockholders, libraries must keep in touch with their stakeholders. That communication reinforces the value of the investment, the vote, the donation and the use of the library.

Success Story 5.1
Providing a Unique Service through the Tool Lending Library

Berkeley Public Library,   **Berkeley, California**

The Berkeley Tool Lending Library is a unique place. It opened in 1979, funded by a $30,000 Community Development Block Grant from HUD and was designed to meet the community's need for projects to rehabilitate low income housing. While the project began with 500 tools, it now has over 5,000 tools for loan. The tool library is a service of the Berkeley Public Library, a system which consists of a central library and four branches. It is housed in the South Branch and is staffed by four individuals. The library funds all of the materials, equipment, services, and salaries within the tool library.

The original objective of the Tool Lending Project (as it was first known) was to provide a service to the residents of South and West Berkeley, an area of the city where low-income families resided. Tools were loaned free of charge for residents of South and West Berkeley, while a nominal fee was charged to patrons in the higher income areas of Berkeley. After several years the tool library became funded by a library property tax and all fees were removed. The original tool library operated out of a tool-mobile, but after several years the library constructed a facility to house the equipment and tools. This facility resembles a storage shed, rather than a traditional library.

The purpose of the Tool Library was so that patrons could have access to the tools to improve their homes. The benefits of the service were

- personalized instruction and advice, especially to women and the elderly,

- low income families were able to borrow tools that they could not easily afford to buy,

- improvements in the neighborhood and community built community pride and self-esteem.

With access to home improvement books, videos and advice, patrons would be able to initiate projects themselves, rather than having to hire a professional. Community forums were originally conducted to determine what services, tools, videos and books were most needed.

Tool Lending Specialist Pete McElligott initiated the grant process that started the Tool Library and ran it for 22 years. Two staff members, who continue to order, repair, and circulate tools, assisted him. In addition to the original three employees, a fourth was added to offer construction expertise and to help around the library once the demand from the public increased.

The collection has now grown to include several thousand home repair and gardening tools such as weed-eaters, hedge trimmers and demolition hammers. In addition, there are a variety of hand tools available for gardening and pruning. Frequently requested tools include cement mixers, hand trucks and dollies, wheelbarrows, and post hole diggers. For those with renovation projects, there are skillsaws, sawzalls, drills, and tools to install and repair electrical and plumbing systems. Earthquake retrofitting is a major need in the City of Berkeley, and the Tool Lending Library stocks the tools needed to complete this project, including a number of rotary hammers. How-to books and videos are available at the South Branch next door.

The Berkeley Public Library maintains a Web site that contains information about the Tool Lending Library (www.infopeople.org/bpl/tool/index.html) including its hours, regulations and tools available. The tools can even be renewed online.

Success Story 5.2
Servicing the Business Community with the Business Resource Center

Aurora Public Library,
                                           Aurora, Colorado

Public libraries play a major role in supporting businesses in their community. The Aurora Public Library recognized the needs of businesses to have access to information available in book, CD-ROM, or online database form. They decided to develop a program that would help them raise the funds they needed to collect these necessary materials. Aurora, Colorado has been named as the fastest growing city of its size in the country. This growth mandated a support for the fast growing business world within the community.

Cost has always been a major factor in providing information. New and sophisticated electronic products are expensive. To tackle the project, the library developed a partnership with the Aurora Chamber of Commerce, the City of Aurora, and the Aurora Community College. Business leaders from the community assisted the library in raising the required funds and promoting the program. The Aurora Public Library provides a "niche" market to the business community, which distinguishes them in their city.

The library recognized that managers, when introduced to a new line of business products, would want access to valuable information from remote locations. They placed importance on the accessibility and quality of information as well as the depth and breadth of their print and virtual collections. Many of the library's databases are available remotely through the Web-based catalog of the library.

Focus groups provided invaluable insight into the needs of business customers of the library. In addition, they performed competitive analyses of information services from nearby sources, which included both private and public sector competition. Once the study was done, the staff of the library knew they had to gain that competitive edge and that promotion was the key to their success. As promotional efforts, they produced a video, held informal "breakfasts" for business leaders, and made brochures. They also developed a "product mix" that was targeted for their customers' need for information. They hired and trained staff to assist customers in their search for information, provided essential hardware and software, installed direct telephone lines, and provided access to fax and copy machines—all to meet their customers' needs. Office furniture was added to the center, and a thorough electronic media and hard copy reference collection was developed. Thus, the Business Resource Center of the Aurora Public Library was up and running.

The original vision for the service is credited to their Director of Libraries and Television Services, Mr. Thomas Nicholas. The funding came from the City of Aurora, the library budget and private donors. By creating this dynamic "niche," the Aurora Public Library has established a "position" within the City of Aurora and the business community.

Success Story 5.3
Creating Community through Special Events

Ruidoso Public Library,   **Ruidoso, New Mexico**

Ruidoso, New Mexico is a small community of approximately 14,000 residents located 138 miles north of El Paso, Texas. The feeling at the library is that the taxpayers provide the buildings and the use of the buildings needs to be maximized. In order to do this, the library has formed many partnerships with the community. The Library is the place to be in Ruidoso.

Phyllis Reed, Library Director, provides the leadership for this community centered library. She makes community partnerships with the library a top priority, as she develops her staff positions. The library events are a function of Diane Thorgeson, a reference librarian and exhibits management specialist. As Diane says, "When one show is moving out of the library, and the other exhibitors have not yet arrived, it is blah. Huge white walls with nothing on them, empty display cabinets, and vacant shelf tops! The new exhibit arrives, and the environment comes alive again...Every show is different. We have had a local dance conservatory perform, puppeteers, singers, classical groups, potters, painters, quilters, photographers, carvers, and paper cutting artists, to name a few." Diane works with the many community partners to make the events a success, while the entire library staff participates and supports Diane, and all of the partnership activities.

September 11 Commemorative Show

Artists expressed what they felt in all mediums and displayed their works at the library. Over 100 people were involved in this event. The mayor opened the show; fire trucks sounded their sirens in the library's parking lot at 11 minutes after the hour, then everyone observed one minute of silence. There was standing room only in the 15,000 sq. ft. building. It was an extremely memorable moment shared by many community members and library patrons.

International Literacy Day

A day proclaimed by the library to celebrate literacy, the library involved and invited the mayor, the governor, and mayors of nearby communities to highlight International Literacy Day. Mayor Leon Engleston, issued a proclamation claiming this to be International Literacy Day. The superintendents of local schools, as well as superintendents of area schools, including the Mescalero Indian Reservation attended.

Several Literacy organizations were invited to participate. They developed booths, passed out literature and basked in the publicity and recognition of their efforts. Joining the library was the Lincoln County Literacy Council, the Hispanic and Indian representation, and the Sierra Dove Global Association, which promotes literacy to the undeserved using the Alpha Model. Alpha stands for Arts, Love of language, Phonetic, Hands on, Auditory training. They use equipment for auditory training. Also included was the Region 9 Cooperative program, which provides an outreach to community schools, helping schools with their EPSS programs (Educationally Planned Student Success). This program concentrates on reaching children before they start to school.

All of the organizations felt honored to be included in the day's activities. At the same time, politicians had an opportunity to be recognized. The Library was able to create an event, which emphasized their value to the community. Becoming a part of the community is not only a library goal, but also a goal of the Ruidoso Public Library Library Board.

ART EXHIBIT

The library works with the Regional Arts Council to host monthly exhibits of artists in the community. The library is one of three buildings that features "Art in public places." Ruidoso is an artist's community with many artists of different disciplines. There are performing artists, writers, potters, and singers.

In the current art show, the library is featuring the Southwest Designers Guild, which is a floral design membership organization. The art show will be a judged event, bringing in judges from surrounding areas. The various floral designers are creating 15 large designs and placing them throughout the library. Some of the designs are geared to children while others carry out different themes.

At the same time, an artist name Elizabeth Arigo is exhibiting her work in turned wood throughout the library. She uses different varieties of wood to create beautiful works.

A third artist, Vicky Mauldin, has watercolors displayed on the walls. Next door, at Ruidoso Village Hall, more artists are displaying their work.

While artists donate work to show, the works are also for sale. When an artist sells a piece of work, 10 percent of the sale is given as a donation to the Arts Council to build a future cultural arts center.

The first Friday of every month, the Ruidoso Public Library sponsors an Art Show Opening and Reception. This event features musical entertainment in the form of a band or single musician, and food donated by the artists themselves. The Arts Council helps promote the reception by providing $25 to the library to provide for paper plates, ice, napkins and punch. This is a "happening," the place to be on the first Friday of every month. In addition, the art on display brings a great deal of public recognition to the library. The Arts and Entertainment section of the newspaper features the art shows and displays at the library, bringing the library significant recognition.

Ruidoso is a tourist town. The library puts themselves on the map by being the center of activity. Many people are attracted to the library through the various events. The library contributes significantly to the quality of life of the community through these extended programs. These events create visibility, and enthusiasm by getting the mayor and local politicians to participate. Because we have a wonderful newspaper and get extensive coverage; many people come into the library for one exhibit or event, and become hooked on what our library has to offer. The Library, and the Arts Council, in turn, receive support from the community in the form of adequate budgets, volunteers, and community partnerships. The library has established itself as a community center within the city of Ruidoso, New Mexico. As the Web site states, "The library is a center for lifelong learning in the mountains."

Promotion

Promoting services to one segment of customers is important. Many libraries focus their promotions to the entire customer base rather than "the sum of the parts." Strengths of the library and special programs can best reach customers if you target an identified group of the population.

Niche Markets

Niche markets are those segments of the market that you have identified and decided you are uniquely able to serve. Libraries often try to be all things to all people. However, often the strength is in serving one particular group of customers well. Serving one particular "niche" well often creates uniqueness to the library system. The library is recognized because of its niche. Every library should find a niche, and then serve that niche better than anyone else in the market.

A library should target its marketing efforts for two primary reasons. First, a library that targets its products has less competition. Therefore, it has a better chance of providing a leadership role in the market segment that it chooses. Second, when a library focuses on a particular segment, it can do a better job of understanding its customers and meeting their needs. That puts the library in a better place to succeed.

The ideal niche is big enough to be "worth it" and to have growth potential. It is one that the library can serve effectively. The library can build unique skills and customer goodwill as the niche grows and becomes more attractive.

The key idea in developing a niche market is specialization. There are several different ways to specialize:

- End-use specialist. This library serves one type of end-use customer.

- Geographic specialist. The library would serve only a certain locality.

- Product specialist. Perhaps the Church of Jesus Christ of Latter Day Saints and their genealogy library would be an example.

In this section, you read the stories of libraries that have developed special niches: the Berkeley Tool Lending Library, which actually does lend out tools (Success Story 5.1) and the business resource center of the Aurora, Colorado, Public Library, which has made delivering service to the business community its priority (Success Story 5.2).

Using Advertising

Most marketing plans eventually lead to advertising and promotion. In the world of business, this can take you to advertising agencies and consultants, but few libraries have a budget for substantial advertising. Instead, many libraries are developing strategic partnerships through which they are implementing sophisticated advertising and promotion programs.

Developing a Media Strategy

To initiate a successful, targeted advertising and promotion program, you must develop a *media strategy*. This media strategy is a part of the communication or promotional plan for the marketing plan. It consists of:

- a goal statement;
- a media calendar;
- a budget.

The goal statement should identify the target audience and the scope of the advertisement, for example, to achieve 80 percent awareness of the summer reading program among mothers in the 20–35 ages in the greater metro area within two months. The media calendar outlines when and where each advertisement or promotion will be placed. The final calendar allows you to compare scenarios, timing, and proposed effectiveness, and choose among the various outlets. The budget identifies the costs associated with the plan.

A written media strategy can be a great tool. Advertising is driven by deadlines, and those deadlines can be easily compromised because of a mistake. By keeping a written diary of your promotion and advertising activity, you can learn from past mistakes and create a more efficient process for the future. A written strategy can also help you to plan the timing of your promotional and advertising activities well. Timing is everything, and you probably cannot afford to be advertising and promoting everywhere.

Choosing Advertising Media

A variety of sources should be considered when creating media plans, including print media, electronic media, broadcast media, and television media. Each will vary in *reach* and *frequency*. *Reach* refers to the total number of people in your target market who are exposed to your ad at least once. *Frequency* refers to the average number of times that a person in your target market is exposed to your ad.

Electronic Media Web Sites

In a split second, new visitors to your Web site will form a lasting impression of your library. The design and architecture of the Web site creates an experience that your customers have with the library. They will make judgments on how easy or difficult it is to find the information they want on your site. You can also use the Web to extend your "brand."

The home page can serve as a strong advertising tool, inviting customers to your many services. Placing advertisements on the Web is easier for libraries than buying print ads or commercial time on radio. It is an excellent way of getting information cheaply and quickly to your customers. It can also help you keep communications moving up and down the distribution channel. You can have people reserve books, sign up for library cards, take care of their fines, and check the status of materials.

Remember that the Web site is never completely finished. If you are going to build a relationship with your customers via the Web site, you have to keep in touch. You must keep your site current and interesting. The site must be monitored, evaluated, refreshed, and renewed. At the Douglas Public Library District, they are committed making their Web site "everyone's favorite bookmark." Web sites receive more thorough coverage in chapter 7.

Print Media

This form of media refers to everything that is in print, including newspapers, magazines, brochures, directories, direct mail, yellow pages, point of purchase gimmicks, outdoor and transit advertising, and billboards. Each form of print advertising has a shelf life, as well as a reach. Newspapers have a very short shelf life, while yellow pages have a much longer shelf life.

Direct Mail

Direct mail is used to sell a person something or to convince a person to support an organization. Electronic databases offer libraries opportunities to use their customer databases to provide direct mail service by segments. Direct-mail solicitation is used frequently to develop a membership program. Again, segmentation is of the utmost importance. Women tend to be more responsive to a direct mail solicitation in membership mailings.

The "normal" response rate is one percent. Therefore, this type of promotional activity can seem quite expensive. The key to success is repetition. Consider mailing up to three times per year to increase the response rate.

When developing a direct mail appeal or promotion, you must consider many variables . They include:

- **Timing**. When will your mailing arrive?

- **Packaging**. What does the mailing look like? Subtleties like the choice of a postage stamp and the color and shape of the piece will affect the response rate.

- **Letter or appeal**. People read the postscript and special quotes first.

- **Ease of response**. Have you enclosed an envelope for quick response? Do you provide postage?

- **Get through the clutter**. Be creative in your appeal. How will your piece of direct mail stand out?

Telemarketing

A direct mail appeal combined with a telemarketing effort will increase the response rate. Telemarketing is a disciplined, planned effort to reach customers through the telephone. Telemarketing is very helpful in renewing Friends memberships, enlisting volunteers, and building audiences.

Libraries tend to shy away from telemarketing. None of us likes to be called by sales people at dinnertime. However, telephone calls coming from library staff and volunteers are usually well received. They are the only time that library customers hear directly and personally from the library. The telephone calls asking for support of a membership program or special event will provide a unique opportunity to learn how your customers perceive the library.

A training session should be held for volunteers. Your success depends heavily on both a predeveloped script and the individuals who do the telephoning. Make the training and actual telemarketing sessions fun. Provide food and drink.

Ask a local real estate company or bank to donate their offices and telephone system to be used in a telemarketing campaign.

Taking Steps in Creating Advertising

1. **Identify one program or service you want to promote.** This is your first step. Then develop your "unique selling proposition." This statement makes a person want to use your library. It can be the same as your positioning statement.

2. **Develop a creative plan with details of both your public relations and advertising program.** This plan will also identify your mix of creative products, including direct mail, signs, telephone book advertisements, open houses, news events, and newspaper and radio ads. Place a budget around this program. Calculate how much staff time will be required, and decide which one of these programs is the most important to you.

3. **Develop quantitative objectives.** How many people will be drawn to your program or service by each form of advertising or public relations efforts? Marketing penetration, ticket sales, and number of people in attendance, circulation measurements, and increased card registration are examples of easily quantifiable objectives. At first, you will have to make a reasonable guess. As you gain experience with this kind of estimation and track your customers, you will find which promotion or advertising is most effective.

4. **Establish specific goals and objectives so you have targets for which to aim.** Having specific goals and objectives forces you to use data effectively and establish priorities for activities. It also gives you an idea of the

resources needed to attain them, forces you to realize that some of your goals are unrealistic, and should be eliminated.

5. **Do not spread yourself too thin**. When mistakes occur, it is usually because you have not provided sufficient time to do a good job of promotion. You mail invitations too late and do not take the time for the personal contact that is the key to success. Budget time and effort to the promotional methods that will work most successfully, and then do it well.

6. Keep the three qualities of credibility, longevity, and continuity in mind.

   Credibility: If people do not believe your advertising, they will not try the service.
   Longevity: Determine advertising strategies and keep the campaign in front of the target audience long enough to establish recognition.
   Continuity: Develop a plan and stick to it. Concentrate on a few areas of greatest effectiveness and put enough money into it to generate recognition.

Do It Yourself

Recent changes in technology allow libraries to create their own advertising. Through personal computers and specialized software, scanners, digital cameras, you can create ads for print media or make brochures, posters, and bookmarks.

- **Gather all of the facts**. Those include date, time, location, and ticket price. Ask yourself who, what, when, and where.

- **Remember your unique selling point**. Capture your message in a simple phrase.

- **Do not try to tell the whole story in a single ad**. When you design your first ad, go back and take out half the copy.

- **Put yourself in the place of the prospective client**.

- **Remember the KISS rule**: Keep it simple, stupid.

Choosing to Work with an Agency

Advertising agencies occasionally "adopt" a nonprofit organization. They will develop a full advertising campaign and call on other vendors to provide material, shoot commercials, and donate their services. They will work with the media to get placement of print and media advertisement. Advertising federations or clubs also have public service committees that will work with nonprofit organizations on a campaign.

You must be very clear on the selling points of your service before you begin to work with an agency to develop the advertisement.

- Develop your marketing goals and objectives.

- Identify your target audiences.

- Define parameters (dates) of campaign.

- Identify resources to support campaign.

- Identify prospective advertising agencies, large and small.

- Study campaigns they have done for other clients.

- Seek client recommendations.

- Choose an agency that can work well with you.

  Here are some other general guidelines to keep in mind:

- Appoint *one* individual to work with the agency. It is very confusing for an ad agency to work with a group of volunteers.

- Give your representative clear directions. Identify the scope of the program or service you want to promote.

- Define your specific target audiences. Do not try to reach everyone with one campaign.

- Develop marketing goals, objectives, and specific advertising objectives.

- Be sure that the appropriate people have an opportunity to participate in and approve of the objectives of the campaign before giving creative direction to the campaign. Make sure your group agrees on the direction, target audience, and objectives. Then *trust* the agency.

- Develop time lines.

- Agree on financial estimates before you begin the project.

- The advertising agency will develop a storyboard or outline before developing a full campaign. If desirable, this storyboard can be tested in a focus group setting to determine effectiveness of communication strategy.

- Remember that the ad agency knows the advertising business better than you do.

- Present the ad campaign to staff, board members, and Friends before it appears on television, radio or in print. Introduce the campaign in a spirit of celebration, perhaps including buttons, T-shirts, or other items.

- Develop a point-of-sale campaign to reinforce the campaign in the agency. Examples of point-of-sale items are posters, coffee mugs, and book marks.

Making News

It is easy to forget the many components of the media. Figure 5-2 reminds us that the media comprise much, much more than newspapers.

FIGURE 5-2 Media Components	
Print • Magazines • Journals • Business Press • Newspapers • Yellow Pages • Brochures • Billboards • Newsletters • Transit Ads • Direct Mail and Telemarketing	**Broadcast** • Radio • Cable TV • Broadcast TV **Electronic** • Internet • World Wide Web Sites

Making Friends with the Media

An important component of any promotional strategy is to establish effective relationships with the media. Your relationship with the media must be built on mutual respect and mutual need. Some key tips to keep in mind include:

- Get to know essential journalists and publications, and make sure they know you. Ask to meet them. Present them with a basic media kit on that first meeting. Your media kit should contain some general information on the library and any specific infor-mation about programs in which they may have a special interest. You will get more things in print if you ask them how you can help them. Do not give them extra work. Media people are always overworked and bound by deadlines.

- Build long term relationships; identify programs and outlets that will fit your library. A good relationship is mutually beneficial.

- Always be helpful to journalists, return their calls and meet deadlines. You can get specific information through local press associations. In smaller communities, you can call neighborhood publications, radio stations, and newspapers. They will usually be quite responsive and give you the name of appropriate individuals. Those good contacts often result in better media coverage when you need it.

- Be creative when it comes to news and features. In fact, be assertive. Give them material on which they can write a story. Better yet, write the story for them.

- Develop a partnership with the local newspaper. Write a weekly column for them to publish. Be sure and target the column, meet deadlines, and make the column interesting. Jamie LaRue, director of the Douglas County Public Library, writes a weekly column that appears in the *Douglas County News-Press* and the *Highlands Herald*. Figure 5-3 lists some of his column titles from 2003.

FIGURE 5-3 LaRue's Library Columns

These are the titles of columns for 2003.
Check his web site (Jlarue@jlarue.com) to read these columns.

January 2003
1- New Castle Rock Library Construction Questions
8- Literary Hoaxes
15- Phone Book Listings for the Library
22- Highlands Ranch
29- Highlands Ranch, Part 2

February 2003
5- The Columbia
12- The Pre-Overdue Notice
19- TV's
26- Russell is a Republican

March 2003
5- Mr. Rogers
12- Volunteering
19- Too Much Information
26- The Home Library

April 2003
2- JBC Decision
9- Home Library-Results
16- Library Troubles
23- You're Never too Old
30- Mistakes in Columns

May 2003
7- New Website
14- Generations at Work
21- Tile Project
28- The Patron Purge of 2003

June 2003
3- Douglas County Libraries
11- I Pledge
18- The King and I
25- Your Memories Are Safe With Us

Writing a News Release

The news or press release is used to create publicity in the newspaper about an event, program, or activity. You have no control over whether or not the media actually publish your news release, but a well written release is more likely to be published, than one poorly written. Creating a successful news release mandates that you cover the five Ws: Who, What, When, Where, and Why. *Who* will be involved in or hosting the activity? *What* will they be doing? *When* will the activity take place? *Where* will they hold the activity or event?. *Why* is the library doing it? Some other guidelines:

- Write the release on library letterhead or special library press release letterhead that clearly identifies your library.

- Include the name of the contact person in the library (usually the person writing the release) and all contact information.

- Date the release.

- Start with a headline.

- Always double-space the text.

- Keep it simple.

- Give accurate facts.

- Provide information in digital form.

A sample news release is included here (Figure 5-6). You will see that this news release answers the questions of who, what, when, where and why. It also has a strong logo identification, which makes it stand out among a pile of news releases. Photos also help to get the news release printed. Figure 5-4 gives you a sample photo release form that Douglas County Library System has customers sign, and Figure 5-5 is a request for press releases.

FIGURE 5-4 Photo Release Form - Douglas Public Library District

Douglas Public Library District

D   P   L   D

PHOTO RELEASE FORM

I hereby grant the Douglas Public Library District permission to use my photograph and/or my minor child's photograph, and/or statement for publicity, advertising, or similar purposes. I understand this may involve placing my photograph and/or my child's photograph on promotional materials within the library or in the electronic or print news media. I further understand my name or my child's name may be used to identify the photograph.

Date: _____

Name of Adult: _____

Name of Child: _____

Relationship to child (if applicable): _____

Signature of Adult: _____

(Signing on behalf of his or herself and/or signing as parent or guardian on behalf of Child, as applicable.)

Phone Number: _____

FIGURE 5-5 Press Release Request Form

Douglas Public Library District

D   P   L   D

CONTACT: Katie Klossner or Aspen Butterfield
312 Wilcox St, Suite 204
Castle Rock, CO 80104
720-733-9412
720-733-9622 (Fax)
kklossner@mail.dpld.org
abutterfield@mail.dpld.org

Press Release Request Form

If your branch and/or department has a story or topic that you feel merits an E-newsletter article, banner link on the DPLD website, and/or a press release, please fill out this form with as much description as possible, and return to Community Relations. *It is recommended that you photocopy this information and give to your Manager and/or keep at the branch.*

Today's Date: _____

Contact Name: _____ Phone #: _____

Branch: _____ Email: _____

Information for: E-newsletter   Banner Link   Press Release

Title of Event: _____

Event Date(s): _____ Time: _____

Location: _____

DETAILED description:

(Feel free to draft your own article or press release and attach it to this form for review by Community Relations):
_____
_____
_____
_____

For press releases, please circle your media preference:

ALL Media (includes Denver and TV stations)

Colorado Parent   *HR Herald only*   *The Voice only*   *DC News-Press only*
                                        (3 months advance notice)

Parker Chronicle only   *Denver Post/RMN only*   *DC8 only*

Other Media: _____

DEADLINE: 3-4 weeks PRIOR to the event date

• Please Return to Community Relations •

FIGURE 5-6 Sample Press Release - King Lear in Castle Rock

Douglas Public Library District

D P L D

CONTACT: Aspen Butterfield
720-733-9412 (office)
720-733-9622 (fax)
abutterfield@mail.dpld.org

312 Wilcox Street, Suite 204
Castle Rock, CO 80104
www.dpld.org

For Immediate Release (7/18/02):

Catch King Lear in Castle Rock!

For twenty years, Theatreworks has delighted the Colorado Springs area with award-winning productions of Shakespeare's timeless plays. Now Douglas County residents can savor the same dazzling experience at the Douglas Public Library District's *Shakespeare at the Rock*, July 24-28, under a large tent at 100 S. Wilcox in Castle Rock.

Theatreworks will bring along the entire cast, crew and set to present *The Tragedy of King Lear*, considered by many to be Shakespeare's masterpiece. The free performances of *King Lear* will start at 7:30 pm every night. Free tickets will be given away at 6 pm before each performance, on a first-come, first-serve basis. The event will also feature a Renaissance marketplace starting at 5:30 pm before each show. On July 24, 25 and 28, performers from the Colorado Renaissance Festival will entertain at the pre-show marketplace. Cast and crew "talkbacks" will be held after the July 25 and 26 performances. This production of *King Lear* is recommended for ages 10 and older.

According to Theatreworks Producing Director, Drew Martorella, "*King Lear* is an awesome demonstration of the creative imagination. Full of a terrible kind of beauty, the play tells the story of a powerful monarch who gives away his kingdom to his daughters, and then suffers the most appalling consequences. By the play's end, King Lear has lost everything: his possessions, his family, his power and his sanity. His journey through a storm into madness is a story of redemption and discovery. Lear's suffering is legendary. While he suffers as much, or more, than any other character in literature, he gains insight, wisdom and finally, love."

Murray Ross is the play's director. Bob Pinney plays the title role. Martorella relates, "Bob Pinney was the inevitable choice for the role. Long-associated with Theatreworks, he is widely regarded as the region's finest actor." Christopher Lowell, Ashley Crockett, Beth Clements, Amy Brooks, Mark Hennessy, Khris Lewin, Mel Grier and Michael Preston are cast in the play's other major roles.

Scenic Artist Christian Medovich, Costumer Lindsay Ray and the Theatreworks design team have created an ancient, tribal atmosphere for the play's setting. Susan Smith, principal cellist for the Colorado Springs Symphony, plays throughout the performance.

[*Shakespeare at the Rock*, 7/18/02, p. 1.]

Shakespeare at the Rock is the jewel in the crown of the Douglas Public Library District's first annual Shakespeare Festival. DPLD libraries across Douglas County are currently featuring a variety of events and activities relating to the Bard, including workshops on Shakespearean gardens and language. Check at your local library for details.

FIGURE 5-6 (cont.)

DPLD Shakespeare Festival Sponsors include: the Gay & Lesbian Fund of Colorado, First Bank Highlands Ranch, IREA, Fast Signs DTC, Flying Horse Catering, the Friends of the Philip S. Miller Library, L. Scott Brody D.D.S., Ash & White Construction and the Friends of Parker Library. DPLD would like to extend special thanks to the Colorado Renaissance Festival and Comfort Suites of Castle Rock. For more information about the Douglas Public Library District Shakespeare Festival and *Shakespeare at the Rock*, visit the DPLD website at www.dpld.org, call the DPLD Event Line at 720-562-9097, or visit your local library.

Highlands Ranch Library (9292 Ridgeline Blvd), 303-791-7703
Lone Tree Library (8827 Lone Tree Parkway), 303-799-4446
Louviers Library (Louviers Village Club House), 303-791-7323
Parker Library (10851 S. Crossroads Dr.), 303-841-3503
Philip S. Miller Library (961 S. Plum Creek Blvd, Castle Rock), 303-688-5157
Roxborough Bookmobile (7999 Rampart Range Rd.), 720-981-3040

# # #

Brainstorming worksheet 5.1 is an exercise in writing your own press release. You can use this as a guide for any press releases you write.

✎ BRAINSTORMING 5.1 HOW DO YOU DEVELOP A PRESS RELEASE?

Who: Provide the name of the library, and the contact people.

_____

_____

What: Provide a description of the event or news.

_____

_____

When: Provide the date of the news release as well as the date of the events?

_____

_____

Where: List the name of the facility or location of the event or program.

_____

_____

Why: Identify why you are promoting or hosting this program or event

_____

_____

Ways to Make News

Libraries must seek ways to make news. Think of "good news" events that will attract coverage. The tactics listed below will create positive awareness among your selected target audiences:

1. **Tie in with the news events of the day**. Provide news media with contacts in the library that can verify information.

2. **Tie in with media on a mutual project**. Television, newspapers, and radio stations sponsor a few events. They provide substantial publicity for the events they choose to sponsor.

3. **Conduct a poll or survey and release a summary of the results**. If you do market research studies, publish the results.

4. **Arrange an interview with a celebrity**. Ask sports figures and other celebrities to participate in children's story hours or other events.

5. **Arrange a testimonial**.

6. **Celebrate an anniversary**. Involve the community. As a local bakery to bake a large cake. Invite the mayor and other elected officials to the party. Ask local entertainers to perform.

7. **Tie in with a holiday**. Host a Christmas party or a Halloween party for kids or seniors. Again, ask local bakeries to provide refreshments and a local bank or retail store to provide invitations.

8. **Stage a debate**.

9. **Appear on radio or television talk shows**.

10. **Write a monthly book review in the local paper.** Develop lists of new books that have just arrived in the library for your column.

11. **Photographs**. Local newspapers will normally print a photo of the mayor reading stories to children.

12. **Slide shows**. Well-prepared slide shows are popular as programs for neighborhood groups and social groups.

13. **Host a local contest or tournament**. Want to reach your adults? Host a contest or tournament with a popular game. Ask the producer of the game to provide copies at no charge. Ask a local bank to sponsor the game by providing prize money and printing services. Promote the game/tournament through local schools. Everyone wins in this kind of program. The bank looks like a good citizen. The game producer gets publicity. In addition, the library appeals to young adults.

14. **Host a contest for senior citizens**. Seniors love bingo, of course. They love events and tournaments that challenge their minds. Again, a local company can work with you as a sponsor.

15. **Create seminars and workshops**. Seminars and workshops on topics like "How to do a Patent Search," "How to Get a Job," "Financial Planning," or "How to Publish a Book," can be public relations tools for libraries.

16. **Speeches**. Speeches on subjects relevant to specific organizations can create positive public relations for libraries. Community organizations and civic clubs are always in need of programs and welcome speakers, who are well prepared.

17. **Special events**. Ground-breaking, ribbon cuttings, celebrities reading stories to children, an author reading from his or her book, and book sales, are all examples of special events that create good public relations. Take time to make some of your events special by inviting a local politician to participate.

18. **Special features**. Various organizations, such as fast food restaurants, football and baseball teams, and *Sesame Street*, have created giant animal or bird mascots to attract attention. Create team spirit among the staff, while enhancing your image within the community, by creating a character to attend community events.

Choosing News Media

Newspapers

Call your local newspaper about the opportunity to use small "drop-in" ads that appear every time the paper has space. Prepare ads in specific sizes and provide copies to the newspapers. These ads can feature specific programs or services and will be printed at no charge to you.

140

Television

Television stations provide "public service" time for nonprofit organizations. However, free time usually means that ads do no appear at prime time. At some television and cable stations, public affairs department personnel will assist you in developing advertising. In addition, some of these stations sponsor events and programs, which they promote heavily.

Radio

Radio stations clearly identify their target market. If you want to consider radio advertising, ask local stations to provide you with information on their listeners. Prime advertising time on radio is "drive time." You should select radio stations whose target audience matches the segment that you are trying to reach. Many stations broadcast a community calendar that will list your program or event at no cost. Some radio stations now are accompanied by a Web site, where they list your events continually.

Phone book

Do not forget the local yellow pages. Short advertisements should be placed in many different areas of the directory. Libraries often have to make a decision on the types of media to use. As a matter of routine, they find that the yellow pages are very effective. Occasionally a bond election or a library card program will need more advertising. Consultants can assist libraries to discern the most appropriate choices to reach the library's target audience. Many times, the expense prohibits libraries from utilizing television advertising. They concentrate instead on yard signs, radio advertising during the last few weeks leading up to an event, buttons, banners, and brochures.

	Advantages	Disadvantages
Newspapers	• Your ad has size and shape, and can be as large as necessary to communicate as much of a story as you care to tell. • The distribution of your message can be limited to your geographic area. • Split-run tests are available to test your copy and your offer. • Free help is usually available to create and produce your ad. • Fast closings. The ad you decide to run today can be in your customer's hands two days from now.	• Clutter-your ad has to compete for attention against large ads run by supermarkets and department stores. • Poor photo reproduction limits creativity. • Price-oriented, medium-most ads are for sales. • Short shelf life. The day after a newspaper appears, it's history. • Waste circulation. You're paying to send your message to a lot of people who will probably never be in the market to buy from you. • A highly visible medium. Your competi-tors can quickly react to your prices.
Magazines	• High reader involvement means more attention will be paid to your advertisement. • Less waste circulation. You can place your ads in magazines read primarily by buyers of your product or service. • Better quality paper permits better photo reproduction and full color ads. • The smaller page (generally 8 x 11 inches) permits even small ads to stand out.	• Long lead times (generally 90 days) mean you have to make plans a long time in advance. • Higher space costs plus higher creative costs.
Yellow Pages	• Everyone uses the Yellow Pages. • Ads are reasonably inexpensive. • You can track responses.	• All of your competitors are listed, so you run the ad as a defensive measure. • Ads are not very creative, since they follow certain formats.
Radio	• A universal medium-enjoyed at home, at work, and while driving. Most people listen to the radio at one time or another during the day. • Permits you to target your advertising dollars to the market most likely to respond to your offer. • Permits you to create a personality for your business using only sounds and voices. • Free creative help is usually available. • Rates can generally be negotiated. Least inflated medium. During the past ten years, radio rates have gone up less than other media.	• Because radio listeners are spread over many stations, to totally saturate your market you have to advertise simultaneously on many stations. • Listeners cannot refer back to your ads to go over important points. • Ads are an interruption to the entertainment. Because of this, radio ads must be repeated to break through the listen-er's "tune-out" factor. • Radio is a background medium. Most listeners are doing something else while listening, which means your ad has to work hard to be listened to and understood • Advertising costs are based on ratings which are approximations based on diaries kept in a relatively small fraction of a region's homes.

FIGURE 5-7 Media Advantages and Disadvantages at a Glance

FIGURE 5-7 (cont.)		
	Advantages	**Disadvantages**
Television	• Permits you to reach great numbers of people on a national or regional level. • Independent stations and cable offer new opportunities to pinpoint local audiences. • Very much an image-building medium.	• Ads on network affiliates are concentrated in local news broadcasts and on station breaks. • Creative and production costs can quickly mount up. • Preferred items are often sold out far in advance. Most ads are ten or thirty seconds long, which limits the amount of information you can communicate.
Internet	• Reaches a target audience. • Highly interactive. • Can provide enormous amounts of information at a very low cost. • Very flexible: you can change your pages quickly as conditions, products, and prices change. "Links" to other sites can spread your reach.	• Reaches only the computer-literate. • Lots of Internet clutter that may make your site hard to find. • A new (albeit fast-growing) medium.
Direct Mail	• Your advertising message is targeted to those most likely to buy your product or service. Your message can be as long as necessary to fully tell your story. • You have total control over all elements of creation and production. • A "silent" medium. Your message is hidden from your competitors until it's too late for them to react.	• Long lead times required for creative printing and mailing. • Requires coordinating the services of many people: artists, photographers, printers, etc. • Each year over 20% of the population moves, meaning you must work hard to keep your mailing list up to date. • Likewise, a certain percentage of the names on a purchased mailing list is likely to be no longer useful.
Tele-marketing	• You can easily answer questions about your product/service. • It's easy to prospect and find the right person to talk to. • Cost effective compared to direct sales. • Highly measurable results. • You can get a lot of information if your script is properly structured.	• Lots of businesses use telemarketing. • Professionals should draft the script and perform the telemarketing in order for it to be effective. • Can be extremely expensive. • Most appropriate for high-ticket retail items or professional services.
Specialty Advertising balloons, sandwich boards, key charms, etc.)	• Can be attention grabbers if they are done well. • Can give top-of-mind awareness. • Gets your name in front of people.	• Difficult to target your market. • Can be an inappropriate medium for some businesses. • It's difficult to find items that are appropriate for certain businesses.

FIGURE 5-7 (cont.)		
	Advantages	**Disadvantages**
Word of Mouth	• Low cost. • Natural extension of personality of business. • Keeps customer needs in clear view. This is an important adjunct to your other marketing efforts.	• Word of mouth is very dependent on levels of quality and customer service. • Must be managed carefully. Ask for referrals. Provide collateral advertising material to your customers. • Sometimes used in lieu of any other promotional efforts, which is dangerous.
Reprinted with permission from *The Market Planning Guide* by David H. Bangs, Jr. Published by Dearborn Trade, Chicago, IL. Copyright, 1998. All rights reserved. To order, call toll free 1-(800) 621-9621.		

Advertising advantages and disadvantages

The wide range of advertising alternatives means that you must carefully determine which form best suits your specific needs. You should also be aware of your advertising outlet. Figure 5-7 gives general information on the advantages and disadvantages of different forms of advertising.

Create an Action Plan

Your action plan puts your marketing program in place. You need to establish a control system to tell you whether the marketing that you have planned for your library is being accomplished on schedule. Planning and implementing a control system tests each of the employees who perform each of the tasks. The individuals become completely committed to their portion and know how it all fits together. It demands powerful personal qualities of integrity and devotion from them.

If you are working with a group of people, involve them in setting time frames and personal commitments. The dates for individual jobs become a personal inspiration to those accomplishing the work. Controls provide clarity, direction, and feelings of achievement that can be measured. They help you build a team. They provide assistance in that every member of the team feels responsible. If you are doing this by yourself, your control system will test your own self-discipline and determination.

The following group of Brainstorming activities and worksheets will help you negotiate the promotional process. Skip any that are not appropriate for you and your library.

BRAINSTORMING 5.2 REMEMBER THE STEPS TO A SUCCESSFUL PROMOTIONAL CAMPAIGN.

- Who? Who are the customers and the prospective customers for this program or event? Have you targeted your market so that you can develop the promotional program to meet their needs?

- Why? What do you want to see as a result of this promotion? Is it a new program or service? Do you want to create or maintain an image?

- When? Timing in advertising and promotion is very important. If it is late or early, it will not be effective.

- What? What specific products or programs are you trying to promote?

- Where? What media would be the best for your campaign?

- How? If you are having a professional firm do it, leave this to them. If you are doing it yourself, identify the steps.

BRAINSTORMING 5.3 ESTABLISH PROMOTION/ADVERTISING GOALS.

These are goals that libraries set for their advertising and promotional campaigns. It is designed to make you think about these things. You will be thinking in new terms.

- Do you want to penetrate certain markets? If so which ones? What are your measures of success?

- Do you want to increase your usage by present customers? Are you trying to promote one special program or service? Which one?

- Are you trying to create "top of mind" awareness? How?

- Are you trying to expand your offerings demographically? To whom?

- Are you trying to announce a new service or a new location?

Your answers to these questions will tell you how you want to be perceived.

BRAINSTORMING 5.4 CONDUCT A PROMOTIONAL AUDIT.

Use this worksheet by yourself or with a group. It serves as a step-by-step checkpoint.

This Audit has been conducted by: _____

Date: _____

Do You:	Yes	No
Project a strong and consistent image in all Your materials, signage, logo, web site?		
Do you have a professional designed logo?		
Do you know what promotional programs have worked?		
What has not worked and why?		
Do you have a yearly public relations and promotion plan?		
Do you have strong media relationships with professionals?		
Do you assign one person to make sure your program is implemented?		
Do you have a web site?		

 BRAINSTORMING 5.5 PRODUCE A PROMOTIONAL SUMMARY.

This summary is helpful for you if you are doing a variety of promotions for an event or program. Use it so that you can coordinate your programs, make sure you have targeted the audience, coordinate the target dates and not be surprised by costs.

Type of Promotion	Target Audience	Target Date	Cost
Public Relations Press Releases Brochures			
Sponsorship			
Direct Mail, Invitations			
Web site or Internet presence			
Open house, programs			
Newsletter			
Advertising			

BRAINSTORMING 5.6 MAINTAIN A MARKETING TACTICS ACTION PLAN.

Organization of your total program gets an assist by writing down the action steps, date that those action steps will be completed, as well as the individual responsible. Writing these steps down helps to analyze if the dates and programs can be completed as scheduled.

146

By: _____

Date: _____

Action Steps	Date	Person Responsible	Results

For further instruction in constructing your own marketing plan, see the two sample plans in Appendix A.

Conducting an Evaluation Process

After you have implemented a marketing plan, you need to evaluate the process. You need to examine your decisions and make the necessary adjustments. You should approach the evaluation process like a puzzle. Ask yourself what part of the plan worked and what did not.

- Did you make an error in the plan?

- Were you clear about the original objectives?

- Did you analyze each of the strategies?

- Was sufficient time allowed for the action steps?

- Were you too optimistic in the time schedule?

- What should you do to correct the mistake?

Once you have identified the cause of the problem, rectify it. In any case, the change will require cooperation from all of the staff involved. This is not the time to say, "We tried it and it didn't work." Learn from your mistakes and create an atmosphere of change.

You should evaluate your efforts after each program or service has been introduced. Often it is beneficial to do it with a group of people, who were involved with the introduction process. Talk about your successes. Where did things really go well? Talk about the mistakes that were made and steps that could have been improved.

Mistakes can occur because you underestimate the time required to promote the services. It is better to reduce the number of strategies and tactics. That is often difficult to do. People tend to be over optimistic about the things that can be done. Remember to estimate what you think you can accomplish and then implement only half of them. The overall results will be better.

Ask if the goals that you set were valid and will they still be valid when you try to rectify the problem. Were they realistic? Remember that you set goals as a starting point. They do not have to be a final decision. You may want to revise your goals and objectives in the light of new information you uncover as you examined the marketing mix and as you develop strategies. Maybe it is time to revise your goals.

The essential section of the marketing plan is the marketing strategies. You actually talked about the four Ps, plus two additional Ps. Those include product (or service), place, price (budget, funding, revenue source), promotion, positioning and politics. You can have the best idea, product or service in the world, but if you do not have the distribution strategy or the other strategies to get the product to the customer, you will not be successful.

Each of these steps requires a judgment on your part. You will find yourself estimating the time required to do something, the resources required, the staffing level required and the budget. It is a learning process. Your judgment will improve with experience. The most common reason that strategies fail is that a library fails to follow the fundamentals of implementation. It is easy to run out of time in the implementation of actions steps.

Now you have done it. The assembled forms take shape and become your marketing plan. The marketing plan is a working document and not intended for outside review. It is a document for your use. It will guide deadlines, expenditures and expectations. You can share it with fellow employees and colleagues. Usually you write an executive summary of the plan if you want to share it with others. Mostly it is a document to keep you on track.

References

Bangs, David H., Jr. 2002. *The Market Planning Guide: Creating a Plan to Successfully Market Your Business, Product or Service, 6th ed.* Chicago: Dearborne Trade Publications.

Technical Assistance Research Programms. 1986. *Consumer Complaint Handling in America: An Update Study.* White House Office of Consumer Affairs: Washington, DC.

Part 3
New Directions in Marketing

CHAPTER 6
How Libraries Use Relationship Marketing

What is Relationship Marketing?

Libraries may have relationships with the mayor, the city council, county officials, legislators, major donors, customers, partners, individuals, families, students, parents, children, neighborhood leaders, voters, communities, foundations, and corporations. They also have collaborative relationships with each other, with state associations and state libraries, with school libraries, university libraries, and special libraries. In order to build lasting positions in the market, libraries must first build strong relationships with all these players. These relationships are built on trust, knowledge, information, benefits, and leadership.

In relationship marketing, you develop a consciousness about the relationships with your customers. Each customer, voter, stakeholder, donor becomes an integral part of your organization. You want to "own the market," to be the leader in the community, to set the standard for excellence and to dominate the field. If you do this, you deepen your relationships with the customer, donor, stakeholder, voter, and with one other. Building strong relationships develops stronger bonds with the customer, strengthens our financial role, and helps the library assert its leadership.

How does relationship marketing differ from the traditional market planning that you have learned? Traditional market planning provides you with a structure through which you can develop a product, program, or service; conduct market research; identify the strategies and tactics; and guide the product or service to the customer. Relationship marketing goes a step further. It allows us to build interactive programs directly with our customer. You build the customer into the design process so that you meet the customers' needs and personal strategies. You actually build an infrastructure of suppliers, vendors, partners, alliances, and customers whose relationships help to sustain and support the library. These close encounters with our customers, donors, and politicians give us first-hand information and experience. They allow us to take intelligent, calculated risks. It is a fundamental shift in the role of marketing. It transcends the role of understanding the customer to actually involving the customer. Instead of developing programs for the customer, you are developing programs hand-in-hand with the customer. In this way, you have a partnership with the customer. Together you can more effectively handle the dance of change.

Relationship marketing is designed to bring a greater whole to the partnership or collaboration than either side could accomplish on their own. It calls for creativity, flexibility, and sensitivity. It calls for innovation, credibility and risk taking. Libraries must think of creating new standards, rather than focusing on following existing standards.

Often I hear librarians wish for a "marketing director" within the library. Somehow that person would be responsible for identifying groups of customers and entice them into the library. In relationship marketing, *we* move to a new level. Marketing becomes part of everyone's job description, from the custodian to the librarian. It is integrated within the organization. The ultimate assignment of the marketing department is to serve customers' real needs, and to communicate the essence of the library. The real goal is to define the standards and provide the leadership for the community.

Close relationships can last a lifetime. If a library forms relationships with strong partners, that relationship makes the library stronger. Those relationships carry the message of the library in a personal way. Those individuals who carry the message of the library include the following: board members, donors, partners, and collaborators, as well as customers.

Those relationships are the key to successful bond elections and capital campaigns. They are the key to responsiveness within your community and successful growth for your organization. Building strong and lasting relationships is hard work and is difficult to sustain. The consistency of individuals is important including the library director and professional staff. Developing a clear mission and vision statement provides direction.

Cooperation in any relationship is the key to survival. In the business world, these cooperative forms or collaborations are exhibited in various areas of manufacturing. Anyone involved in libraries is well aware of the role of collaborations or partnerships. Examples of the collaborations you participate in on a daily basis include: construction agreements, collection and technology partnerships, donor and political arrangements.

Partnerships or collaborations develop because:

- No library can develop all of the necessary technologies and solutions by itself.

- The costs of developing new programs are rising.

- Strategic relationships can bring credibility to the association.

- Small libraries can gain management expertise, distribution muscle and credibility.

- A large library acts as a credible reference that tells the market that the small library is a winner and that all libraries are connected.

Communication is the key to building relationships. When you are communicating with your customers, politicians, or donors, it involves as much listening as it does talking. You build relationships through this kind of dialogue. This communication strategy takes time, sometimes years, to build trust, consistency, familiarity, and confidence. It is difficult to build this communication strategy. It may start with a more formal communication and evolve into a personal friendship.

Customers set up expectations based on previous experiences with the library. They have a hierarchy of values, wants, and needs, based on data and their opinions. Libraries need to build a strong foundation by building strong relationships with their customers. Buying a one dollar tube of toothpaste does not involve much risk. However, nobody donates $1,000,000 to a library unless they have confidence, trust, knowledge, and a relationship. In order to raise that kind of money you have to offer something of substance, not just an image. Good relationships with customers are required to win a bond election, to build strong customer service, to secure funding both from private and public sources.

There are many relationships that a library will want to build. In the next sections, the following relationships will be discussed:

- Customer service;

- Leadership;

- Partnerships and leveraging;

- Voter marketing;

- Donor relationships;

- Cause-related marketing.

Customer Service

Customer service is quickly becoming the make or break factor for all companies. It is the source of "competitive advantage." Institutions that have good customer service dominate their industries. As you can see by the first efforts in the marketing planning process, a great deal of time is spent on understanding the potential customer. You understand what benefits they need, and what attributes are necessary for your programs to succeed. These efforts, however, were a one-time snapshot. Our customers keep changing. They age, grow more sophisticated, and their needs change. Therefore, you must constantly be aware of our customers changing needs and how to serve them in the best way possible.

Superior service is as important for libraries as it is for IBM, McDonalds, and Wal-Mart. Good customer service creates satisfied customers, who come back again and again. For libraries, good service will also result in customers voting for bond elections, contributing private dollars, and volunteering to support libraries. Poor customer service will result in lost elections and lost funding. It is as simple as that. Good customer service pays.

The library customer is more sophisticated, demanding, and educated than ever before. This customer has alternatives. If libraries are to survive and thrive, they must realize that they are there to meet the needs of their customers and communities. Libraries must reach out and meet specific customer information needs. Librarians need to serve customers even more personally.

The majority of unhappy customers never complain. In fact, almost all unhappy customers never complain about rude or discourteous treatment, most who are dissatisfied with the service they receive will not come back. Each of the unhappy customers will tell his or her story to a few other people. A smaller number of those unhappy people will tell his or her story to many.

There are some other rules including the 80/20 rule. 20 percent of your customers account for 80 percent of you business. It costs six times as much to get a new customer as it does to retain an old one. Those costs include advertising, special programs and library card signup programs.

There are barriers to good customer service and it is important to be aware of them.

- **The differences in people**. Most people are not sensitized to customers. It takes training and support to make the cultural change and create sensitivity to customers. Customers have more money, more choices, are better educated and more demanding than ever before.

- **Believing that customers are expendable.** Some customers are difficult, but they are not expendable. After all, people need libraries to help them get the information they need. Remember that every employee affects the actual experience of each customer. Customers generalize from one experience to the entire library.

154

- **Unwillingness to pay the price**. What is the price? The price is training and retraining. It is new reward and recognition programs. It is the ongoing commitment to quality. Budgetary problems are real, of course. Often librarians say that they cannot provide good service, because they cannot afford to hire the staff or buy the materials. The budget must be examined in view of customer service and priorities need to be changed. It is important to do some things really well, rather than provide more programs and services poorly.

- **Superficial commitments**. It takes organization-wide commitment to customer service to make it work. Each function of the library must be committed to customer service or the entire process can break down. Our customer relations are only as strong as the weakest employee within the library. Everyone in the library must take the responsibility to help the customer. Therefore, there can be no superficial commitments. It must be accepted throughout the organization.

- **Listening but not hearing, looking but not seeing**. You do not really take the time to listen to and watch customers. Yet, each customer's perspective is new and unique. If you will listen, your customers will ask the questions that you need to hear. All of the service superstars have managers who "walk about" and mingle with the customers. You must create wide ownership of the success of the library's customer service program.

Good customer service demands constant vigilance, training, and commitment. The demands include the following:

- **Changing the culture**. You need to examine all of your traditional ways of dealing with the customers. Policies and procedures have been in place for a long time and it is difficult to create an awareness that you need to change. You must get everyone involved so that everyone has a vested interest in achieving your customer service goals. You cannot continue to do things because you have always done them that way.

- **Creating a risk-taking environment**. Libraries have been bureaucratic in design. They have not encouraged risk taking. Customer service requires more authority by front-line staff. They must be trained to provide the customer with good service. Taking risks is the only way library employees can provide effective and efficient customer service. Getting people to take risks is a powerful way to improve efficiency and service.

- **Developing informed judgment**. Rules, policies, and accepted proce- dures, are often convenient to hide behind. In a customer-oriented environment, you expect front-line staff to make decisions and to use their judgment. They require training and support to do this. They also need access to good information in order to feel informed.

- **Delegating**. Trusting employees to make the right decisions and allow them to try, this delegation of responsibility is required in a customer orientation.

- **Providing autonomy and trust**. Creating an environment in which an individual employee can make a mistake is important. Creating an atmosphere of trust and autonomy enables employees to feel important and respected. These employees will provide the best service to customers.

- **Developing a reward system with incentives**. If you are going to change the culture, you must reward that positive (changed) behavior. The rewards stimulate all employees to seek positive reinforcement in this manner.

- **Creating systems of accountability**. Job descriptions, and forms that evaluate levels of customer service provide a basis of measuring performance. Accountability is the method by which the organi- zation puts the "teeth" in its customer service program.

- **The impact of leadership**. The library director sets the example for customer service for every staff member. Employees are all cus- tomers of the library director. Employees will treat customers the way they are treated by the library director.

Steps to Customer Service

A. Determine your potential markets

    1. Determine the segments of the market to be served. Understand their needs for services and products. Understand the barriers to service.

    2. Develop products and services for a targeted market.

    3. Develop marketing strategies for each targeted market including distribution channels, advertising, promotional channels.

4. Monitor the expectations with the understanding that customer loyalty has to be earned over and over again.

B. Establish an environment of customer service

1. Evaluate the present level of service quality

2. Clarify the service strategy

3. Educated the organization (preaching and teaching the gospel of service)

4. Implement new tactics at the front line and release the creativity of front line employees.

5. Reinforce the new orientation. Remember, the executive director sets the example

Customer service is a marketing strategy that leads to success. It is not a one-time event or training, but a program that infiltrates every system in the library. Customer service is involved in every customer interaction. It comes into play as customers obtain library cards, in delivery systems used by the library, in public access catalogues, telephone service and equipment, telephone inquires, library programs, products, and services. It affects the hiring of a customer service workforce. It is carried through employee orientation, programs to make employees aware of service, job descriptions, performance standards, as well as rewarding and motivating employees for good customer service. A library that provides good customer service is a fun place to work. The morale and enthusiasm of employees is high, and employees pass this enthusiasm on to customers.

Success Story 6.1
Developing Customer Service Strategies

Queens Borough Public Library,   **Jamaica, New York**

At the Queens Borough Public Library, one of three public library systems serving New York City, it is frequently said that customer service is one of the most important factors in running a successful library. Adhering to this idea, they have adopted a strategic planning process that is used extensively in library planning and operations. Staff members from every level of the library are recruited to serve on strategic planning work teams. They are also required to make suggestions, reengineer work processes, and align all work activities with at least one of the strategic directions.

The annual report is broken down into the four strategic directions listed below:

- state-of-the-art community libraries;

- books and reading;

- customer service;

- children and teens.

When a budget is requested for new initiatives, part of the justification is that the proposed initiative will further one of these strategic directions. Management reaffirms their commitment to the strategic directions and refers to them frequently. In short, the directions are pervasive throughout Queens Library's internal communications and culture. Any staff member asked why he/she performs any task—from sweeping to purchasing to book preparation—will relate his/her job to one of the strategic directions.

Customer service is the most important of the four strategic directions. The library's mission is for the people in Queens consistently to receive quality library service provided by dedicated, knowledgeable, experienced and diverse customer oriented staff. Their four components of customer service include the following:

1. Queens Library customers meet and interact with courteous and professional staff who provide collections, programs and services reflecting the diversity and unique character of each neighborhood.

2. Queens Library actively recruits qualified staff and provides compensation and benefits that are commensurate with the individual's qualifications and experience.

3. Queens Library provides a work environment where all levels of staff are able to advance their careers, receive continuing development and training, and are recognized and rewarded for giving excellent service to the organization.

4. Queens Library fosters intergenerational communication and cooperation.

The staff is encouraged to be innovative while improving customer service. Contributors are rewarded with positive recognition through the Employee Recognition programs and through a pay-for-performance incentive program. A dedicated strategic management analyst oversees the strategic planning process, under the supervision of the deputy director of customer services and the library director.

The Queens Borough Public Library administration has recognized that the employees are also customers and the employees have responded with creativity and enthusiasm. Together, they have built programs that are unique, imaginative and just what customers want. The library has consistently had a higher circulation than any other public library system in the country, according to the American Library Association. Apparently, customer service pays.

Thomas E. Alford, deputy director of customer service at the Queens Borough Public Library agrees that the measures his library has taken have been worthwhile. "At Queens Library, customer service is our top priority, and an integral part of the corporate culture. We challenge staff to proactively look for new opportunities to serve. It might involve outreach, it might be an improvement in the way we merchandize materials, it might be enhanced service to a particular demographic group or a brightening up of the physical space. We see the positive results in sheer numbers of people who use our facilities every year."

Success Story 6.2
Winning through Customer Service

Ruby M. Sisson Memorial Library,   **Pagosa Springs, Colorado**

Tucked away in the southwestern corner of Colorado, Pagosa Springs is a beautiful community. There are scenic railroads, hot mineral springs and Rocky Mountain wildlife. It is the gateway to the desert southwest. It is not a land of people or of libraries. In fact, the Ruby M. Sisson Memorial Library is the first library in the San Juan Library District and the only public library in Archuleta County. Lenore Bright, a library lover, arrived in the small community from the town of Greeley, Colorado on the eastern slope of the mountains. At that time, the only library facility in Pagosa Springs was one small room in the town hall. The librarian had left and Bright volunteered to pick up the pieces. It was not long before she became the library director, heading up an effort to build a bigger library. There were no professionals or grant writers to begin this daunting process. Bright met with her board and staff volunteers to write grants and organize events like auctions and bicycle races. They had land donated to them and raised $750,000 to build a new library.

The library was built in 1987 and in the beginning it had a staff of only three. Since then, the number of people working at the Pagosa Springs Library has grown to eight. These workers are very important to Bright and to the library. Working with the staff to provide an enjoyable and positive working environment, Bright has maintained flexible schedules for her employees and has created a training program so they may deliver the best in customer service. Learning from her examples, the staff delivers the same kind of service they receive.

Increasing literacy rates was identified as a challenge for Pagosa Springs as the library became committed to meeting the information needs of the community. The first need was for an adult literacy program using computers and training. They developed the first literacy program in a library in Colorado. The literacy program grew so much that it had to move to a separate facility. It has become so large that it now has a life of its own and is also offered at the Pueblo Community College program.

Lenore Bright does many things to keep close relationships with her customers. She invites them to join her for lunch and breakfast so they can tell her what they would like to see in library programs. She is an active and visible member in the community, attending the Chamber of Commerce meetings and other organizations. A friendly and approachable woman, she always listens to customers when they tell her what they need and want from the library.

The library is very customer service oriented as exemplified by the fact that the staff treats every one as a guest. They create hours that are convenient for their customers. The staff checks out materials to everyone who wants them, even to tourists and campers who are in the area for only a short time. Rarely is there a problem with lending materials to the temporary guests.

There is a growing Hispanic population in Pagosa Springs. To meet their needs, the library obtained a Spanish-language computer from the Bill and Melinda Gates Foundation. Although there is a Hispanic community, most of them speak English, as well, so the demand for Spanish-language materials is less.

It only took 14 years for this community of 11,000 to outgrow the library. Now there is an ever-increasing demand from Lenore Bright and her small but mighty library. She and her library staff have set out to raise another $590,000 in private gifts and grants. They need more computers for public access and they need to enlarge the children's section. Lenore Bright has raised $515,000 with no professional staff in order to make improvements on her library. She has done this by consistently providing good customer service to her donors from 14 years ago, when the library was just starting out, and has maintained almost all of her private supporters. Foundations on a state and national level have also contributed. The Bill and Melinda Gates Foundation have provided endless computer support. As Lenore Bright has seen, customer service pays off in staff loyalty and commitment, customer satisfaction and donations.

Understanding the "Law of Leadership"

Being the forerunner of a particular field is often more important than being a master of that field. Leadership can be achieved by being "the first" to accomplish something. For example, the name of the first place winner of a marathon is usually broadcast all over the news. Perhaps the runner-up is truly the better athlete, but the public will only hear about the person who "came in first."

Everyone wants to identify with a leader, a "winner." This is touted as the "ultimate competitive strategy." Libraries must recognize their leadership roles and toot their own horns. They must publicize, promote, and attract customers with their leadership strategies. Remember, people, politicians, donors, stakeholders, and customers want to be a part of a winning team.

Everyone realizes that the leading brand in any category is usually the brand that is in the prospective customer's mind. Consider the rental car business. Think how Hertz and Avis have both maximized their position in the market by saying, "We are Number One," or "We are not Number One, so we try harder." Often a first brand maintains its leadership, because its name becomes generic. Xerox became the name for copiers. Other famous names you will recognize include Kodak, Kleenex, Jeep, Scotch Tape, Jell-O, Band-Aid, and Saran Wrap. They are only a few of "firsts" that have become generic. Many firms have capitalized on this positioning, and so can you.

Libraries compete for many awards, which they can utilize to bring recognition and leadership to the institution. The Library of the Year, John Cotton Dana Awards, the World Book Awards, the Coretta Scott King Book Awards, LAMA Awards, Leadership awards, the Library of the Future Awards, Public Relations awards are among the hundreds of awards given to libraries. Take advantage of the awards to promote your library's leadership.

Success Story 6.3
Demonstrating Leadership

Denver Public Library,   **Denver, Colorado**

In 1999, Thomas Hennen, Jr., the administrator for the Waukesha County Federated Library System, published the first edition of *Hennen's American Public Library Rating Index* in the *American Libraries* magazine. This library rating index is the first and only ranking system for 9,000 of the nation's libraries. The Denver Public Library, for the third consecutive year, has been named the number one public library in the nation for library systems serving a population greater than 900,000. The factors tabulated for Hennen's American Public Library Rating Index include cost per circulation, visits per capita, and expenditures per capita. The index can be accessed online at www.haplr-index.com. The 2002 Hennen American Public Library Rating Index is based on information collected by each state in 2000 and submitted to the Federal State Cooperative Service (FSCS) in 2001.

The Denver Public Library was compared to 76 library systems nationwide on 15 major points focusing on circulation, staffing, materials, reference service and funding levels. The index scores, similar to a standardized test, were calculated from 1 to 1,000 with the Denver Public Library receiving a rating of 890. The total scores of all the libraries in Colorado gave the state a ranking of sixth best in the nation.

The Library immediately capitalized on the opportunity provided by the award. They conducted an advertising campaign using a variety of media. They produced banners reading "We're Number One!" Brochures and buttons were available for proud customers to wear. The motto "We're Number One!" became visible in every branch of the library and throughout the city, infusing a campaign that reinforced the enthusiastic support from community members. The community and stakeholders became aware of the library's leadership role in the library world. In addition to the signs, brochures and advertisements stating that the Denver Public Library was "number one," newspaper articles, radio, and television broadcast stations also featured the winning news. They organized a Customer Appreciation Day. The former mayor of Denver, Wellington Webb, presented the library with an award for fine service. "The Denver Public Library is delighted to be named the number one library in the nation," said Library Commission President Wesley Brown, "we are pleased the award recognizes our being good stewards of our funding and resources. In this uncertain budgetary climate, we are challenged in our work to provide top-notch service and build a collection that serves our customers well: the support of the citizens of Denver remains critical to our continued success."

City Librarian Rick Ashton also remarked, "Receiving the number one rating for the third consecutive year is an honor, not only for the library, but for the City and our taxpayers who contribute their excellent support. We are dedicated to serving the community and look to the citizens of Denver to champion our efforts."

This number one ranking shows the library staff, donors, customers, and the politicians and citizens of Denver that others recognize the wonderful job the Denver Public Library was doing meeting the needs of the community. The library sets a fine example of excellence, not only for other libraries nationwide, but for people and communities nationwide.

BRAINSTORMING 6.1 HOW CAN YOUR LIBRARY BE NUMBER ONE IN YOUR COMMUNITY?

These questions are designed to get you thinking about what makes your library stand out, and what words or key characteristics can help define your library as a leader in the community.

- What makes your children's program (or any other program) number one in your community? How is it unique? How does it stand out from all other children's activities?

- How is your library number one as the place for information?

- How else is your library unique within the community?

- What awards and distinctions has your library won? Why did you win those distinctions?

Partnerships and Leveraging

A library's credibility in a market depends on the relationships it forms. You can develop many types of relationships, including joint development of project, as well as distribution relationships. The creation of significant relationships in the marketplace can change credibility. For example, Microsoft's credibility in the software industry increased significantly when IBM decided to use the operating system for its personal computer.

Change is inevitable. Success breeds success. In the nonprofit world, "challenge grants" are an important way to raise funds (just listen to National Public Radio's fund-raisers). A group of members join together to leverage their money in the form of a grant that will stimulate new members to join. The station wins in two ways. It increases the support of old members and stimulates new members to join. They have leveraged past members to gain support of new members. This program strengthens the commitment of older members and offers them an opportunity to help. Everyone wins.

Throughout the nonprofit world, you leverage one donor against another, and one grant against another.

Success Story 6.4
Using Strategic Partnerships to Create Results

West Virginia Library Commission,   **Charleston, West Virginia**

West Virginia is a beautiful state, but also one of the most economically challenged in America. With a population of 1.8 million residents, it contains many small libraries that struggle to stay financially solvent and up-to-date technologically. Enhancing and building a connection among the state's public libraries was a challenge that was overcome through strategic partnerships and funding. The U.S. Department of Education provided $2.5 million and the Bill and Melinda Gates Foundation provided a grant to the West Virginia State Library Commission and to its individual libraries. The purpose of the funding was to help maintain a partnership between the libraries and all their catalogues, providing access to the Internet and full text databases.

After the money was supplied, one component remained for the commission to secure in this strategic partnership: the support of the state legislature. Unfortunately, West Virginia was experiencing a deficit in revenue from chemical, steel and coal companies. However, the state had just initiated a lottery system, which everyone hoped would bring the state out of its slump. The lottery funds were intended for education, tourism, and support for senior citizens. First, the West Virginia State Library Commission had to identify libraries as institutions of education. Secondly, they had to convince the state legislature to allot $1 million of lottery funds for libraries on an annual basis. Through a number of meetings and a great deal of communication, the state legislature realized that funding for libraries and technology was an important matter. Libraries benefit all members of the community as they are sources of education and culture. They agreed to provide annual funding. The legislature is currently happy with this partnership and is planning the next step in the relationship; they would like to establish a digital library that would provide remote access throughout the state. According to James Wagoner, "We are still doing everything we have always done. All we have done is expand and expand and expand."

It takes planning, funding and enthusiasm to repair a damaged library system. The success story of the West Virginia Public Library System is a wonderful rags-to-riches tale, and revives faith in the partnering of libraries with their respective local and state governments. It seems West Virginia could be on its way to having an extensive and strong network of libraries. They certainly have the spirit and determination to create one.

Success Story 6.5
Creating Partnerships and Strategic Alliances

Mississippi Library Commission,   **Jackson, Mississippi**

There are 47 library systems in the state of Mississippi, with each system serving one to five counties. How does a State Library Commission provide the incentive, creativity, and the strategic relationship to help smaller libraries become major players in the technological age? Small libraries need equipment, training, communication, and, of course, money. How can the State Library Commission enhance the image, connection, professional leadership, and power of all of its libraries, especially its smaller ones? Through funding at private, state, and federal levels, the Library Commission of Mississippi was able to buy new equipment for their smaller libraries and conduct intensive training sessions in public relations, subsequently weaving their libraries into a tightly knit, high-tech system.

The Mississippi Library Commission sought to strengthen the role of marketing and public relations through partnerships among its libraries. There were three sources of money in the state library system including: (1) money and equipment from the Bill and Melinda Gates Foundation for computers and software, (2) federal funds from the Library Services and Technology Act (LSTA), and (3) state money. The commission realized that if each of the smaller libraries was given $5,000, they would be able to buy an up-to-date computer, graphic software, a digital camera, or a scanner. They contracted with the company Solinet, based in Atlanta, to develop a class to teach Microsoft Publisher and scanning techniques.

Two days of marketing and resource training were provided for directors and employees of smaller libraries. Each library was to spend their $5,000 as needed. Some purchased computers while others purchased digital cameras or other equipment that would allow them to develop brochures, bookmarks, signage, and newsletters. One library bought a color copier with their funds and established a mini print shop. They took digital photographs and sent them to their local newspapers to show the public the ways in which they were enhancing their resources. This program allowed the libraries to maximize their effectiveness, show their professionalism, and enhance their images throughout the state of Mississippi.

The partnership has benefited the forty-seven public library systems and raised the level of library service in Mississippi. The Library Commission continues to expand the capability of the small library through the LSTA program. The LSTA is currently sponsoring regional marketing and public relations workshops using marketing professionals. They have invited various media representatives into these workshops to teach librarians how to maximize their marketing and public relations skills, with special focus on customer service. Sharman Smith, Executive Director of the Mississippi Library Commission says, "Most of us did not grow up with public relations tools in mind. This is a changing mindset for librarians. We need to develop the partnerships in order to enhance the quality of library service in this rural state." The Mississippi State Library Commission shows that it knows how to adapt by improving their library system with the changing times.

Success Story 6.6
Leveraging Makes All the Difference

Shelby County Public Libraries,   **Columbiana, Alabama**

In the mid-1980s, the Shelby County Public Libraries realized that they needed to make some changes. They had to enter the world of automation, but they were a small system of libraries with little money, still operating with card catalogues. Shelby County, Alabama (population: 143,000) boasted a total of 11 libraries, each branch operating independently with its own library board, city council, and director.

In the beginning, the library system could only take small steps. Each library got one fax machine to provide interlibrary loan. Eventually they established a dial-up automation system but soon realized they needed more access points than a dial-up system offered. Thanks to the leadership, direction, vision, political intuition and commitment of their leader, Barbara Roberts, the Shelby Information Network (SIN) was created.

At the same time, the library began the long process of looking for money and writing grant applications. They asked every funder that turned them down for a reason, learning from their mistakes, until finally, the Bill and Melinda Gates Foundation offered the Shelby County Library System a grant to provide computers and other much-needed equipment.

The leaders knew the Gates Foundation could provide a greater opportunity if they used the grant the right way. As Mary Hedrick of the Shelby County Public Libraries says, "We realize in this age of technology, the changes we make today are seeds for the change we will make tomorrow.... Change begets change.... We were able to leverage one grant to ask for another." The library went on to ask the county for funds to match a Library Services and Technology Act grant for more computers and improved telecommunications capability. In addition, they wanted to connect to the county's fiber optic cable to have the ability to provide the county departments with Internet access. Mary Hedrick offered this explanation. "It wasn't a library thing alone. This project could benefit them, too. The Gates Foundation grant allowed us the opportunity to leverage what we where doing for the libraries in order to get additional county funds to expand and enhance services not only to our libraries and library users but to county employees also." By combining the libraries' need for improved telecommunications with the county's need for Internet access, the library was able to get more bang for the county's buck.

The project changed the way county officials looked at the library: this small library system had suddenly become a technology center. As the Library sought the funding and the access, they continued to consider the benefit to the county commission. In addition to the Internet access, the county's department heads would get direct access to the library's databases on CDs and allow them to search for articles to help them in their work. Now there are signs in the computer centers thanking the Bill and Melinda Gates Foundation and the Shelby County Commission for providing public access computer services. "We were good stewards of their money. We were serving everyone in the county. We were successful."

Shelby County Public Libraries are now entering a new automation project to move to a third generation Web-based county-wide automation system. "Only because of the Bill and Melinda Gates Foundation grant and commission support can we move ahead with this project. We are ahead of our long range plan by approximately five years." Mary Hedrick said. The new automation system is being funded by a $150,000 grant that was matched with $37,500 by the county commission. Again, the library was able to leverage services and opportunity to gain financing that will put technology in place to serve the entire county. "We bring something to the table. We try to give something back, to find ways that the funding sources, themselves, can benefit."

Recently, the library system found yet another way of saying "thank you." Shelby County opened its first juvenile detention center recently, and the library wrote a grant to provide books and computer access for the center. The county had the telecommunications system of the library placed within this new facility. "We are good partners and we look for ways to give back."

Asked for the secret of their success, leaders offered these key recommendations:

1. Take baby steps;

2. Stick your neck out, take risks;

3. Consider yourself a success if one grant out of 20 gets funded;

4. Give back, be a good partner;

5. Leverage one grant on another;

6. Say thank you;

7. Never stop planning for the next change, it is just around the corner.

Success Story 6.7
Taking Risks and Leveraging a Donation Leads to Success

Denver Public Library,   **Denver, Colorado**

The development office at the Denver Public Library received an unrestricted donation from an individual for $5,000. The library took a risk with the money. They hired a grant writer for three months. Then they applied for a grant from a local foundation to support a program in grantsmanship. A positive response came from the foundation in the form of $50,000 for a new program in grantsmanship. The administration, staff and grants employee then collaborated to apply for a National Endowment for the Humanities Challenge grant for $1.5 million dollars. This NEH grant would match every two dollars given by a donor with an additional dollar. The fact that the National Endowment for the Humanities recognized the library brought recognition and respect by local corporations and individuals. The original donor was very pleased by the return on her original investment of $5,000. The library staff took her to lunch frequently, recognized her and honored her formally. She said, "You know, I give $5,000 a year to several institutions. You are the only one that really said 'thank you'." Denver Public Library completed the challenge opportunity and successfully raised the $1.5 million. The donor was so impressed with the library that she left a very substantial estate to the library at her death.

Voter Marketing

As everyone knows, libraries live in the hip pocket of politicians. Elections are a way of life. Libraries have bond elections, as well as elections to increase the mill levy in library districts. Marketing principles assure successful outcomes in these elections.

Vision

Developing a vision as you are looking at election campaigns is the same process that you used at the initial stages of this manual. However, you are now developing a vision for a new building or a successful campaign to provide funding. Often a consultant can provide the link between your vision and reality.

Environmental Analysis

At this point you need to conduct an analysis of community needs and the community's ability to pay to meet those needs. You also need to analyze the appropriate timing for elections, identify specific segments of the population that will support the program, identify the organizational structure necessary to support the election process, and to identify funding sources.

The strategies and tactics within the promotion area are the key to success.

Tactic #1:

The first step is to work with the chairperson and the outside election committee to develop a fund-raising program to support the costs of an election. Those costs include promotional programs and polling and market research programs, as well as an outside advertising and public relations firm to provide professional assistance. Supporters can include the Friends of the library, the foundation, as well as individuals and corporations within the community.

Tactic #2:

Develop a vision statement. "A Great City Deserves A Great Library," and "A Library isn't a Library Until You Fill It," are both examples of vision statements from major, urban libraries.

Tactic #3:

Work with a professional advertising or public relations firm to develop a logo and complete graphic package. Develop a complete promotional plan. That plan will include strategies for press, radio, television, billboards, yard signs, brochures, and banners for each library. Develop time lines, action steps, and delegate authority.

Tactic #4:

Develop training programs for staff throughout the system. Staff become your best "sales" group. Although they cannot campaign on work time, they can answer questions for customers and provide information.

Tactic #5:

Develop a core of volunteers. These volunteers can be staff members, community volunteers, Friends and supporters of the library. Volunteers give speeches to community organizations and groups, distribute yard signs and brochures, hang banners, and carry signs at street corners and bring voters who need a ride to the polls.

Tactic #6:

The election committee develops letters of endorsements from community celebrities, institutions, press and media, corporations and individuals.

The success of an election requires positive relationships with politicians, communities, volunteers, corporations and institutions, staff, Friends and foundations. The process is supported by sophisticated market research at every step, along with targeting audiences and implementing a successful promotional program.

Success Story 6.8
Demonstrating Successful Voter Marketing

Broward County Library,   **Fort Lauderdale, Florida**

Broward County sits on the East Coast of South Florida between Miami and Palm Beach. The Broward County Library was a strong system and well regarded in the community. The 35-library system struggled to meet the needs of an exploding population growth in the area. The system needed new libraries and it needed existing ones renovated, retooled, and expanded with new materials and new technology. County funding however was limited to the construction of one new library per year. While the county commission recognized a need for expansion, they were reluctant to put a new bond indebtedness to a vote of the public. To achieve their funding goals, the Broward County Library would have to maximize voter marketing, using professional consultants, identifying their plan and target audiences, and listening to the community. Ultimately, the library prevailed. In a stunning three-to-one victory, voters passed a $139.2 million bond measure to bring improved library service to every community in Broward County, Florida. How did they succeed?

First, the library used professional market research assistance and paid careful attention to the results. After a library consultant helped the Broward County Commision formulate a clear facilities plan, the Foundation hired a market research specialist/election consultant to test their funding goals with potential voters. Focus groups were an important part of this research, allowing the library to identify the specific amount of money that voters would approve. The initial price of the expansion came to $262 million, but after holding focus groups, the library cut their proposed budget by about $122 million.

The election consultant also advised the library to move the budget vote from the November ballot, which normally attracts the highest number of voters, to March, which attracts "Super Voters," those who vote consistently in all elections. Though postponing the initiative would create an ever widening delay of needed services, the library once again heeded the results of market research.

By the time the county commission decided to place the issue on the March ballot, however, the library had only seven weeks to develop the program, produce the materials, and educate the voters. With less than two months before the election, rather than waste resources on people unlikely to vote or support the library, the library focused its efforts on its target audience. Library users and Super Voters, particularly Democrats, who had responded positively in surveys. The election consultant analyzed previous elections, overlaid election results onto zip codes and identified profiles of those most likely to vote in both November and March elections and the areas in which these people lived. The library identified three central goals for the campaign: develop a campaign committee, raise necessary funds to support the campaign, and win the election. To achieve these goals, the library set the following objectives:

1. Create recognition, awareness and support among "Super Voters" that would move them to vote "yes."

2. Generate citizen support in areas where new libraries would be built.

3. Target the library cardholders, as well as Friends of the Library.

4. Create a speaker's bureau and present 210 speeches to community groups.

5. Develop promotional campaign with strategies and action steps

6. Get endorsements from city officials, politicians, local celebrities, civic groups, educational institutions and newspaper editors.

7. Create partnerships with organizations to reach greater audiences.

8. Enlist three celebrities to endorse the campaign: Chris Evert, Dave Thomas, and Dan Marino.

9. Continue to use polling and market research to identify appropriate action steps that would lead to success.

The campaign committee was formed under the leadership of a dynamic community volunteer, Norman Tripp, an attorney and a recognized community activist. The committee, including Friends of the Library and the Library Foundation, as well as high-profile community leaders and activists from the financial and marketing area soon hired Pierson Grant, a professional public relations firm, to advise them on advertising, promotional and public relations strategies.

Developing strong partnerships was central to the library's public relations strategy. The League of Cities, Nova Southeastern University, Florida Atlantic University, Arvida/JMB Partners, Broward Community College, the School Board of Broward County and its PTA, and the Southeast Library Information Network all became partners. They placed full-page ads in local newspapers and sendt notices to their faculty, students, and constituents. The League of Women Voters staffed tables at all 35 libraries to distribute promotional materials and provided endorsements in local publications and mailings to their constituents at their own expense. Other partners included individual municipalities, Chambers of Commerce, homeowners associations, and local newspapers who supported the effort through editorials and advertisements. The county commission also determined that the election was not a controversial issue as no one was opposed to it, allowing library employees to lobby for the vote within the libraries.

Pierson Grant further helped the committee by orchestrating some of the promotion. They wrote and sent press releases to all of the print and broadcast media, with a substantial effort directed at the local papers and community news sections. They developed the positioning statement, "Better Libraries for the Better Broward. Vote Yes for Libraries, March 9th," as well as a logo for use on letterhead, fliers, bookmarks and other print pieces. A "Vote Yes" image was used on buttons, bus signs, street banners, palm cards and lawn signs.

In the end, the campaign committee raised $150,000 in cash and in-kind support from individuals, the Library Foundation and corporations. While this represents substantial funds, it is a relatively small amount of money to conduct a big promotional campaign to raise $139.2 million. These funds were further augmented by the tremendous support of the library's partners, who provided mailings and promotions at their own expense. In March, the budget passed unanimously in every precinct in Broward County, and the final count revealed

72.45 percent voted in favor of the measure. The successful community and organizational partnerships, the speaker's bureau, the celebrity endorsements as well as the targeted promotional campaign all contributed to the success. By hiring professional people, heeding their advice, and paying attention to market research and polling statistics, the library maximized their financial and human resources, targeted their market, and won the John Cotton Dana Award at ALA for public relations programs.

Success Story 6.9
Winning the Referendum

Rampart Library District,   **Woodland Park and Florissant, Colorado**

Woodland Park, Colorado is known as the "City above the Clouds," a beautiful and small town nestled in the pine trees. Nearby are ancient cliff dwellings, as well as the remnants of the mining industry that once flourished here. The other small town in the area is Florissant, Colorado, population 2,700 and home to the famous Florissant Fossil Beds, with its huge petrified redwoods and ancient, fossilized insects and plants. Until recently, the libraries in both towns were very small, a 1,200 sq. ft. log cabin with 23,000 items in Woodland Park, and in Florissant, a 300 sq. ft. library with no restroom facility and only 3,000 items, many of those donated. The original Rampart Library District had been formed in 1986 with a mill levy of 1.3 mills. Although there had been no increase in that mill levy for over 15 years, the community had increased in population by 65 percent while circulation increased by 24 percent. In 1997, a community based survey indicated that the citizens of the area wanted expanded book collections, Internet access, and better research materials for support of school studies, private study and reading areas, some community space as well as video and CD Rom collections. When the librarian for the Rampart Library District retired after thirty years of service, the board realized that they needed a full time director to run a campaign to build two new libraries.

Sharon R. Quay wanted to come home to work and live in Colorado. Although she had an MLS degree, she had never worked professionally in a library setting. Nevertheless, she applied for a part time position in the Rampart Library District. She had worked as the human resource director for a large corporation involved in mergers and transitions, and the board quickly realized that her vast experience was invaluable. Quay advanced to become the new director.

In 2001, the Library District did a feasibility study, assisted by an outside consulting firm, to discover if they had the community support, recognition and the private financial support to raise money for new libraries. The board and the new library director hoped to build new libraries in

Woodland Park and Florissant with a future satellite in Divide. The Woodland Park Facility would contain 29,000 sq. ft. with approximately one third committed for community use. The Florissant facility would be 6,700 sq. ft. with 40 percent for community use, including 600 sq. ft. for the Teller Park and Recreation center. The feasibility report came back with negative answers. People interviewed said that the libraries smelled musty, that there were limited programs and a limited collection. The library was not "on the radar" of many people within the community, while a new hospital and new performing arts center were considered greater priorities for private funding. "We were advised that we would not be able to compete in the private funding sector," says Sharon Quay. The district began to realize they had a better chance requesting tax funding, so, "We decided to try for a bond issue."

The libraries still had a lot of work to do to improve their image before the bond issue would become public. In the summer and fall of 2001, the libraries went through a major face-lift. More space was made in the Woodland Park Library so that they could hold storytelling within the facility. They did a major housecleaning, even wiping the books clean on a regular basis. They put gravel in the formerly mud parking lot and repainted in fresh, lively colors. They formed a second circulation desk and trained all staff in customer service. Young Adults operated a book sale three times a week, with the profits to go to the young adult collection, while the Kiwanis club ran additional sales at the local farmer's market to raise even more money. The staff started a summer reading program designed for families and not just adults, offering prizes and certificates for all ages. They added picnic tables and summer events, inviting other nonprofits to do programs in the summer. A paleontologist from the Florissant National Monument offered special programs to attract families. To end the summer, the Rampart Range District held a festival with puppets, prizes, demonstrations, and cotton candy, attracting 200 people. The library also launched a video as another effort in marketing. It was a successful summer in which the library "repositioned" itself in the eyes of the community.

The library made further efforts to reach out to voters when the board of trustees, Volunteers, and staff held their first community meeting to introduce the campaign ahead. The meeting was made open to everyone that was interested, and community leaders and activists received special invitations. They discussed the potential campaign, the state of the present and proposed libraries. Their mission statement became, "Something for everyone," emphasizing their goal to respond to the dynamics of a rapidly changing community. The board and the staff had also interviewed and selected an investment-banking firm for the bond. A representative from this firm was also on-hand to present information on financing a bond referendum.

A five million dollar bond mill levy to build both libraries was officially launched. The campaign demonstrated that the increase represented a $6 a month increase for the average family. They emphasized that the bond would cover construction costs for the new facilities and the operational revenues would cover the day-to-day operation of the buildings, staff, salaries, and utilities. The new libraries would provide new community event rooms, Internet access, study areas/reading areas, children's area, room for a special Colorado collection.

Soon, a speaker's bureau was formed and training programs were developed for a multitude of volunteers. In all over 60 presentations were made, to churches, civic and community organizations, the Senior Citizens Center, county committees, and many other private groups. The library also provided a handout that contained the most frequently asked questions about election issues, as a handout on donations to the library, whether major or small, and commemorative gifts.

The board interviewed for legal counsel on the bond issue searching for a firm that would help them understand the library issues. A separate election committee was formed and raised money exclusively for the election campaign. The Citizens for New Libraries raised $5,000 to pay for the election, mass mailing, yard signs as well as large signs on the highway.

In November, 2001 the voters were asked to approve the referendum to support a five million dollar bond mill levy to build both libraries and to provide operational revenues to cover the day-to-day operation of the buildings, staff, salaries and utilities. The election squeaked by, but the library still won and the construction process began.

Building on the momentum of the election, the library soon launched a fund raising campaign, seeking out grants, major gifts, and community participation. The staff raised $4,000, and developed an "Adopt a Book Campaign" that allowed individuals to come to the library and select the book that they would like to adopt. The El Pomar Foundation, which had turned them down a few years earlier came through with a grant for $25,000. The Gates Family Foundation in Denver provided support as well as the Boettcher foundation, the Adolf Coors Family Foundation. Other grants have been forth coming and those include the Bill and Melinda Gates Foundation, the Pikes Peak community Fund as well as the Women's Foundation of Colorado. Grand opening ceremonies are planned for November, 2003 for the new libraries in Woodland Park, CO, and April of 2004 for Florissant, CO.

Donor Marketing

Professional fund-raising programs employ all aspects of marketing. It is a field unto itself. The creation of a consistent fund-raising program is crucial to the growth, survival, and development of libraries.

To be most effective, fund-raising programs require the same steps: identification of a mission and core values of the institution, as well as an environmental analysis. You often develop a "Case for Support" that identifies the specific purposes for philanthropic funds. The relationships you build with donors including individuals, corporations, and foundations, are developed and strengthened over the years.

In fundraising programs, the visible areas of the campaign include membership drives, special events, corporate solicitations and other programs. These programs are supported through public relations, and donor recognition events. The evaluation step provides insight for the next year's efforts.

It is not the purpose of this book to go into details of raising money. There are enough books written about that already. However, there are various campaigns, including the annual campaign, the capital campaign, and the endowment campaign, that are crucial to the ongoing financial health of the library, and the purpose of this section is to help you understand these campaigns.

Success Story 6.10
Raising Money with "The Little Library that Could"

Angel Fire Library,   **Angel Fire, New Mexico**

Stephanie Rawlins Gerding, the continuing education director at New Mexico State Library, coordinates a statewide training program and internal staff training. She was excited to share the story of Angel Fire, New Mexico with me. (A version of her article has also been printed in the magazine *Computers in Libraries*, Volume 23, Number 2 in February, 2003.)

Angel Fire is a small resort community of just over 1,000 residents, located three hours north of Albuquerque in New Mexico. This village is popular in the summer for outdoor activities, but Angel Fire really comes alive in the winter for ski season. With a large resort and many cabins, visitors to this village are often repeat customers. However, the true strength of the community comes from the year round homeowners.

As longtime board member Martha Lassetter tells it, the library was begun in June, 1978 by a group of friends at the Angel Fire Resort Country Club, waiting for the State Library Bookmobile to arrive. After a few cocktails and still no Bookmobile (it was destined never to arrive due to a flat tire), the friends decided that the village was long overdue for a permanent library;

175

they started it then and there with a $300 donation and a love of reading. Since its inception, the Shuter Library has been directed and staffed entirely by volunteers. The library board members took turns being director, each with one day a week to run the library. The library had approximately 42 volunteers, including a husband and wife team who took one day together.

Ask library board director Debby Clanton, and she'll tell you that the impetus for this small library to make major plans for a new building, computers, an automation system and to seek grant funding and other methods of fund-raising all were greatly facilitated from its first computer, from the Gates Foundation in 1999. According to Debby, customers first started seeing the library as an actual benefit and significant value when that resource was added. Residents started coming into the library to e-mail friends and relatives. Patrons appreciated that they could use the computer to check stock quotes and search the Internet. Seeing a large foundation make an investment in their library caused community members to increase their support, both financially and through volunteer work. Soon the library staff was planning for more computers and getting fund-raising underway.

In 1999, Shuter Library's volunteers established a fund-raising campaign. They called the campaign the *Love Your Library Fund* and set a goal to raise $200,000 to build a new library extension. They held fashion shows, golf tournaments, raffles, benefit dinners, luncheons, and flea markets. They sold helicopter ride drawings, baked goods, books, and golf shirts. They established a memory wall in their library with plaques for sale for $100 to commemorate loved ones.

The first $40,000 came from a private donor with stipulations that the funds be matched, the donor have the privilege of naming the library, and use of a specific building contractor who would build at no charge as part of a donation. The Shuter Library Board composed and mailed a letter to every property owner in the valley soliciting donations at various levels in return for a wall plaque. The Shuter Library also submitted successful grant applications and raised funds for matching grants. They received grants from the Taos Community Foundation, the M.A. Healy Family Foundation, the William and Flora Hewlett Foundation, the McCune Charitable Foundation, the U.S.D.A. Rural Development Initiative, the East Texas Charity Foundation and the Nobel Foundation. A volunteer who had no grant writing experience took on the responsibility of writing grants. Joan Salas says that once you compile the data for the first grant, the rest are easy, as many require the same information. She has completed around 10 grants and seven were awarded to the library.

The success of the Shuter Library is a direct result of the hard work of its volunteers with their immense energy, excitement, and true will to succeed. They visualized their success. When the volunteers began their fund-raising, they hoped to raise enough to build a new library extension. In 2000, they abandoned those plans when they realized they could set even higher goals, including constructing a brand new building. Goals are very important in fund-raising and should represent achievements that you are reaching for, not just a checklist of outcomes you will have no difficulty accomplishing.

The Angel Fire community is very small. Their initiative, enthusiasm and dedication took them on a path that few undertake. This is an example of a library whose needs reflect their individual community. What works for the large urban library in Seattle would not work for them. They planned and coordinated the fund-raising effort that their community needed.

Developing a fund-raising plan, setting time-based goals, having deadlines and due dates helped the Shuter Library stay on course. They did not lose their vision when they ran into a few hurdles. Stephanie Rawlins Gerding reminds us that foundations and corporations prefer to contribute to local enterprises, and they usually see libraries as a worthy cause.

In June of 2001 the Shuter Library of Angel Fire opened the doors to its new building. Early 2001, the library staff realized that they had received more grant funds than expected. They decided to do something to standardize their circulation process. Though they faced many obstacles, they proved that no goal is too lofty for an enthusiastic, can do attitude. Shuter's staff contacted the State Library to ask for assistance on selecting automation systems. Overwhelmed at first by the large task in front of them, they proceeded to make headway in contacting automation vendors. Within two months, they had selected a vendor, learned to use the software to create their MARC catalog records and had purchased two staff computers. Remember that these were all volunteers without professional library experience.

The Shuter Library knew that having public access computers was extremely important to the Angel Fire community, so that became an early goal for fund-raising. In addition to the residents using the computers for e-mail, other customers were using the computers for different purposes. They were used by parents who were home schooling their children, residents working on resumes and contractors e-mailing bids.

Winter of 2002 produced groups of international students who were employed at the ski resort and who were eager to communicate with friends and family through e-mail, again validating the idea that public access computers would play a large role in the new library. At that time, the library had purchased two additional public access computers to supplement the Gates Computer. Since then, the Shuter Library has added a fourth computer, which has helped with the summer visitor traffic and will help ease the wait for returning international students in the winter.

Debby Clanton said, "What I'm really proud of is that the community could pull together and do something like this. It's all community; we had all the support we needed. "The library was always careful to keep residents informed of what its goals were and how progress was coming.

Through articles in the local newspaper, the Shuter Library volunteers kept residents excited about the new building. They advertised the steps they had determined were needed to raise money, and each step included a new fund-raising event. They were also inventive in how they solicited and accepted help. The library made major progress when the Angel Fire Resort donated land for the new building.

Libraries are fortunate because they immediately bring credibility to fund-raising requests just by their reputation and the services they provide. A great deal of the Shuter Library's success comes from the infectious enthusiasm and joy of its volunteers. The fund-raising is not going to stop any time soon, however, because in April of 2003 the library achieved yet another goal. Due to the success of the Shuter Library the decision was made to hire a full-time library director, liberating the "daily directors" to return to board member status. The new director, Rebecca Marshall, states, "I was amazed at the spirit of cooperation and teamwork displayed by these hardworking volunteers....They are like a large extended family, all with a different talent to offer." The group is comprised of a variety of age groups, from seniors, to middle age, to high school age volunteers who manage to laugh and tease each other through any difficulty.

Stephanie Rawlins Gerding comments, "If you are looking at ways you can implement fund-raising in your community, you should start by examining your community needs. Then you will be ready to identify goals that you want to work toward. Fund-raising goals should convey a vision or a sense of how the library could be in an ideal future; they should convincingly generate excitement about the future. The goals should not be unrealistic or beyond the library's grasp, but they should not be a piece of cake either. Then you are ready to start researching grants and brainstorming on fund-raising appropriate for your community." Take a lesson from the pros at Angel Fire's Shuter Library; stay committed, excited, and confident that you can do it.

Understanding the Annual Program

The money libraries require to assist their operational needs every year is called annual funds. The fund-raising campaign designed to meet annual needs is called the annual campaign. This type of campaign includes membership programs, special events, and corporate and foundation support.

The vast majority of time is spent on the annual campaign. Libraries use several strategies, including the familiar book sales, as well as direct mail, special events, telethons, and personal visits. The purpose of the annual campaign is to get donors to give repeatedly; you want to build a base of donors who give money every year. It is essential to analyze how a person becomes a donor to a library and how, ideally, that person increases their support of and loyalty to the library.

People go through three phases in relationship to the library. The first phase starts when an individual hears or reads about a group they believe in and decides to make a donation. That donation is called an "impulse" gift. Even if it is large, it will not reflect what a donor could really afford and it generally reflects a shallow commitment to the organization. The relationship the donor establishes with the library is crucial for the future. That donor is thanked for his first gift and given other opportunities to become invested in the organization. If a donor has given for two or more years, you call them a "habitual" donor. These people see themselves as part of the organization, although not a big part. Once a donor gives a larger gift to our organization than he/she does to other ones, the donor becomes a "thoughtful" donor. (Kline, 2001: 19–22)

A library or other organization can expect to retain about two-thirds of their individual donors every year. The loss of donors can be attributed to various reasons. In planning fund-raising strategies, you need to develop programs that will entice new donors to join the family. Organizations need to cultivate their "habitual" donors to become thoughtful and convert their "impulse" donors to become habitual ones. There is a considerable effort given to upgrading strategies. These efforts are all built upon relationships.

Both special events and membership programs serve to build relationships. They create communication, visibility, awareness and invite participation. See their benefits as demonstrated within Figure 6-1.

FIGURE 6-1 Special Events	
Special Events	
Type	**Benefit**

• Book Sales
• Sporting Events
• Theatre
• Auctions
• Author Dinners
• Recognition Events
   - Benefits & Balls
   - Recycling junk cars
	• Create participation
	• Bring media attention
	• Create visibility
	• Generate excitement
	• Bring new donors into donor pool functions

Individual Giving	
Type	**Benefit**
• Membership • Major gifts	• Greater opportunities for participation and communication • Greater "involvement" • Provides unique opportunity for recognition
Corporate Philanthropy	
Type	**Benefit**
• Matching funds • Volunteer support • Sponsor events • In-kind support	• Stimulates employee involvement • Participation in community • Provide high quality, unique advertising • Maximizes participation while not utilizing cash

Each of the different annual fund programs—membership drives, book sales, special events, corporate philanthropy, individual gifts, as well as foundation grants—requires "prospect research," identifies donor segments, develops a "product" or a "unique selling position," and provides prospective donors opportunities to give. Incentives are used, and they can be as minor as the address return labels you receive in direct mail solicitation or as sophisticated as naming a new children's center of the library after the donor. Strategies are identified; promotion plays a big role, as each gift requires specific recognition and appreciation. Pricing strategies involve the pricing of donations, as well as the costs associated with the acquisition of gifts. A campaign tends to position an institution with individuals, corporations and foundations.

Creating a Capital Campaign

Libraries and other institutions have campaigns to raise funds to purchase or improve their building, collections, equipment, and technology.

These campaigns are known as capital campaigns. Capital needs can range from new computers, to the cost of building or refurbishing an entire building. Donors who give to the capital campaign usually have given to the annual fund. Through this fund, they have come to believe in the cause and they have the resources to help with a special gift. These gifts are given only a few times in a donor's lifetime and are usually requested in person. A great deal of research goes into the development of a capital gift. There is a careful match between the donor, solicitor, and the institution. In fact, the relationship between the institution, the donor, and the solicitor is the very key.

A capital campaign is built upon the framework provided by the annual campaign and occurs at special times. The first step is to make a case for the institution. A case statement is used to educate donors about the opportunities to give, provides them the opportunity to be a part of the development of the program, provides communication and entices donors to become larger donors. The case statement provides the tool with which to do feasibility testing (market research) to determine if the goal of the campaign is feasible. After the feasibility test, the institution must identify donor segments, research prospects, design strategies, and recruit leadership and volunteers. The selling in this case requires individual consideration. Major gifts become a specialized area. The efforts in this area can lead to substantial, once-in-a-lifetime gifts to the library.

FIGURE 6-2 Nine Surefire Ways to Get the Big Gift

Nine Surefire Ways to Get the Big Gift

1. Involve their family
2. Honor their life's work
3. Respect their values
4. Answer their questions
5. Ennoble their lives
6. Honor their family name
7. Showcase their talents
8. Give them financial security
9. Make sure that the right person asks

Using an Endowment

Libraries and other institutions often need to develop a long-term permanent income stream to ensure financial stability. This income comes from the interest generated through endowed funds, or funds that come from gifts of stocks and bonds, wills and bequests, and trusts. The organization invests the money and uses the interest from that investment to augment its annual budget. The principal is not spent. A campaign aimed at developing those gifts is called an "endowment" campaign. The endowment acts like a savings account.

Endowment funds can be raised in many ways, but most often they are raised through planned gifts, such as bequests. Donors usually have a personal relationship with the library.

To make a substantial planned gift to the library, a prospective donor needs to have a strong relationship with the institution. Planned gifts come out of assets and can include gifts of stocks and bonds, life insurance, or bequests. The relationship to the library is the key for success. Endowment campaigns require all of the marketing steps of prospect identification, cultivation, prospect research, strategy development, sales, and promotion. They depend on a consistent, close, personal, and strong relationship for success.

Understanding the Importance of Board Development

Development of a foundation board is a crucial step. The people on the board *authenticate* the library to other individuals and enable the library to extend those personal relationships. This group of people is responsible to the library and to the government for the actions of the organization. They are chosen because of their long-term vision and their commitment to the organization. Board members contribute their skills in various areas including legal, financial, and advertising. In addition, they bring their lists of prospective donors and contacts. Their power, influence, community connections, wealth help to "position" the institution as one worthy of support. Developing a strong board of influential people requires research, strategy, change as well as challenge for board members. Strong, influential people want their time used effectively. They want to make a difference. They want to know what is expected of them. The vision of the institution must be expansive enough to for them. Board members can be top corporate executives, trust officers, CPAs, CLUs, a professional in media or advertising, attorneys, financial planners. They can also include an ethnic cross section of the library, as well as representation from the geographical areas of the library.

There must be a strong link between the foundation board and the library. The library must provide the leadership, guidance, and assistance that are necessary to ensure that the foundation will proceed in a direction that is compatible to the library board and the administration. They must proceed in the same direction, be on the same team. Foundation board members often have different characteristics from those of the board of the library. They need "care and feeding." There are successful foundation traits and they include:

- Active participation by the director of the library;
- Clearly stated goals and objectives;

- Foundation board members feel ownership in the library;
- Strong staff support;
- Strategic and fund raising plan in place.

Inspiring Others to Give

The author acknowledges the input of Arthur C. Frantzreb of McClean, Virginia for the following:

"Creating the desire to give, then to give generously, then to give recurringly, then to give ultimately by bequest is the continuing challenge of staff personnel, officers, governing board members, and volunteers alike. Those who find the secret to the challenge succeed; those who do not move on."

The organization must have leadership (e.g., board, trustees) that positions itself in several dimensions to earn the confidence it seeks.

This positioning would include:

1. Building a governing board composed of powerful members of influence or affluence or both;
2. Setting a marketing strategy to promote its integrity, its values, its services, its potential;
3. Communicating its values and promoting its directors in every media form to the 10 percent of its constituents who hold in their hands and hearts the power to affect the destiny of the organization;
4. Studying its constituency resource principals to ascertain their interests, concerns, ideals, and personal nuances;
5. Ascertaining the personal needs to those few constituents, so as to set a strategy for an eventual investment solicitation;
6. Creating an asset-builder/building psychology among all other constituents.

This is quite an order. Nonetheless, this is what philanthropy is all about. All the rest is mere fund raising—a set of mechanics.

Success Story 6.11

Setting the Standard for Excellence in Private Philanthropy, and Donor Marketing

Seattle Public Library Foundation,   **Seattle, Washington**

The Foundation for the Seattle Public Library was formed in 1980 as a fund-raising group for the library system. An executive director, Terry Collings, hired in 1989, developed the board of directors for the

Foundation. This fund-raising board has a separate agenda from the library board and has been extremely successful in soliciting donors to improve the library.

The first task of the Foundation was to develop lasting, committed, dedicated relationships with new board members. Terry Collings recognized that the nominating committee of the Foundation board was the single most important committee, because it focused on developing the necessary relationships with prospective members and philanthropists of the library. One board member, who was well-connected in the city of Seattle, eventually became the Foundation president and head of the nominating committee. One of the ways in which he strengthened the Foundation was by searching his network of powerful people and adding some to the board. The Foundation built upon these relationships which helped form more important relationships.

The library developed a building plan and the Foundation put together a vision statement for improving the library's excellence. The goals the library then pursued, with the help of the Foundation, would improve the library tenfold. Nine years of persistence, relationship building, research and development strategies were needed in order to build a team that would create a successful Seattle Public Library.

In 1998, the library won a bond election for renovating and building new facilities. Immediately following the successful bond election, the mayor of Seattle asked the Bill and Melinda Gates Foundation to provide a "leadership gift" for their capital campaign. This gift was their key to success, not only because it was a generous one, but because it also served as a "lead" gift, stimulating more philanthropic contributions to the campaign. Board members themselves contributed over $4 million to start the campaign, which was to be used for construction, collections, and programming needs. The Foundation was ready to begin improving the Seattle Public Library.

The Seattle Public Library Foundation honors their current donors as a strategy for motivating prospective donors to make major gifts. This strategy does not entail "winning" a donor, as much as it means understanding the desires of the donor and making the right match. For example, an established Seattle philanthropist wished to memorialize her late father who loved history. After suggesting the library name the History and Biography Collection in the new Central Library after her father, she was delighted. She then donated generously. Similarly, a family foundation, that in the past had donated money to the library for literacy programs, wanted to distinguish the matriarch of the family, who was in poor health. In exchange for their generous donation, they honored their mother by naming the Literacy, ESL and Multilingual Center in the new library after her. Other spaces recognize the donors themselves, illustrating the different needs and motivations of the donors. Understanding these motivations is the key to successful donor solicitation.

Another important example of successful donor marketing strategy is shown by a relationship built and nurtured by a library staff person, which resulted in annual support from a small family foundation. The husband and wife team of Caleb Canby and Theresa Mannix head their own small family foundation, the Mannix-Canby foundation, making donations in the Seattle area. They enjoy supporting smaller community-based projects that benefit children. "Our foundation is about four years old and consists of just my husband and myself," said Mannix. "We want to fund programs for at-risk youth and programs that address the basic academic needs of those children." They funded the Global Reading Challenge, a program in which teams of fourth and fifth graders from public schools read ten books each and compete with the other teams in a quiz bowl. Readers of different skill levels are represented on each team. This was a program that matched well with their personal values. Mannix agrees with the Seattle Public Library Foundation about the importance of building partnerships. "We like to meet the people who are running the program. We want to get a sense of their enthusiasm. We want to see evidence that the programs we fund are successful." The librarian who organizes and manages the Challenge keeps in touch with the donors, invites them to attend the competitions, and provides them with success reports at the end of each cycle. The relationship formed and strengthened between the donors and the library has secured the Mannix-Canby Foundation as supporter of the program for four consecutive years. They are even committed to funding the next two years. It is *everyone's* job, not just the job of the Foundation, to build relationships that keep our libraries vibrant and vital.

Success engenders more success. The success of the library's bond election, the generous gifts, support and endorsement of Board members and political officials has improved the Seattle Public Library. Terry Collings acknowledges the offering of choices within the campaign as a key element of its success. Providing personalized collections and programs, capital expansion, and technology for their donors ensures there is something for everyone. The Seattle Public Library raised $77.5 million through their own efforts. Even with a depressed economy, their community campaign has been a bright spot, receiving 1,000+ donations every month through direct mail and telemarketing. At this time, the library is moving forward with vigor toward an Endowment campaign, allowed by the previous success of their donor solicitation.

The Seattle Public Library has had the vision, built the necessary relationships, positioned the library, supported and encouraged the board, and done the necessary strategic planning and research in order to make it the best it can be. They have developed strategies, tactics, promotions, communications, and programs which have systematically moved them toward excellence. They set the example for libraries throughout the world.

Cause-Related Marketing

The last area of relationship marketing is *cause-related marketing*. Nonprofit organizations often develop campaigns to raise money through cause-related marketing alliances with corporations. These partnerships are usually executed at the store level; for instance, "Buy my product and we'll donate X cents to the cause for each purchase you make." Cause-related marketing takes place in many libraries as they work with for-profit organizations to support summer reading programs. On a grand scale, you see cause-related marketing in action at the Olympic Games and other large events.

These types of relationships are a win-win arrangement for both parties. The consumer buys a product that is already on her shopping list and suddenly she or he is elevated from the status of a mere shopper to that of a social benefactor. What is in it for the corporation or "brand?" Of course, they get to be a good corporate citizen and to generate funds for a needy organization, "positioning" themselves as a good guy. However, they also do it because it stimulates sales and increases profits. The value of the donation to the nonprofit is usually minor compared to the brand's profit in extra sales. Sponsors also benefit from a halo effect by associating with a cause. Charities also love these promotions, because they do provide money and free publicity for the cause.

Some brands, including Ben & Jerry's Ice Cream and Newman's Own products, have actually institutionalized cause-related marketing as a part of their positioning. Their commitment to charity conveys to the public that their company is dedicated to earning money for a good cause.

For libraries seeking to do cause-related marketing, the image of the library is the important item. Companies are looking for exposure and promotions. Programs, the Summer reading program, and kids activities and events, are all candidates for cause-related marketing programs.

Sponsorships are closely related to cause-related marketing. Often a corporation wants to tie itself to the image of a library or other nonprofit institution. Sponsorship of a major event identifies that corporation with the customer who attends that event. In arranging such a sponsorship, it is important that you know who will attend the event, numbers of individuals in your target market who will see the promotion of the event and reach of the event. Television coverage adds to the effectiveness of the sponsorship. The critical words within the definition are commercial, partnership, and mutual benefit. The same objectives are driving both the fundraising and the marketing strategies, image enhancement, awareness, relationship building, and loyalty.

The development of a cause-related marketing programentails several steps.

1. Develop the project and budget. Identify targeted markets.

2. Identify benefits to both parties.

3. Develop a timeline.

4. Bring the proposed partner in on the planning. Identify partner's goals and objectives.

5. Remember that the partner wants quality, timeliness, and seeks to reach a targeted market.

6. Create visibility for the partner.

7. Deliver a quality program.

8. Evaluate the program.

Example: VISA (credit card) and RIF (Reading Is Fundamental):

Visa decided to link with a cause. They conducted a study identifying 70 percent of cardholders felt reading was important. Visa hoped supporting reading would create a large increase to their card usage. Visa developed a strategy after realizing they could best promote reading by contributing to a reading organization.

Parenting Magazine and *The Chronicle for Higher Education* recommended RIF. Visa and RIF developed a campaign together. Every time a cardholder used a Visa card, the company donateda percentage to RIF.

References

Kline, Kim. 2001. *Fundraising for Social Change.* San Francisco: Jossey-Bass.

Ries, Al, and Jack Trout. 1994. *The 22 Immutable Laws of Marketing, Violate Them at Your Own Risk.* New York: HarperCollins Publishers.

CHAPTER 7
Marketing with Technology

In the past 30 years, technology has reshaped the library environment, affecting market research, customer expectations, as well as customer interactions. To succeed in the digital age, libraries need to reposition themselves as organizations, where services continually changing and improving. They must use the power of information technology to provide public services. Many times, people view their local library as a recreational resource or a support to education. They have to make the change and be given the opportunity to recognize the library as the center of information technology and information in a variety of formats. The emphasis is shifting to visual information in a variety of formats and away from book-oriented activity. The technology allows users instant feedback and communication with customers. It is changing the very definition of the word, "circulation." Now there is access to information resources and providers anywhere in the world, through a variety of means.

The Internet offers people the ability to communicate via computers and make available vast quantities of information. Digital libraries are rapidly developing, with libraries scurrying for funds. Material is published on electronic journals, electronic publishing, telecommunications, networks, geographic information systems, online catalogs and bibliographic systems, optical information systems, software programs, library consortia, and vendor relations. States are developing their virtual reference service and virtual library to provide personalized service, answering questions direct from the user 24-hours a day. All of this responds to customer needs almost before they are aware that the need exists.

This chapter discusses the impact of technology on libraries, from a marketing perspective. Database marketing and Web sites both offer libraries the opportunity to reposition themselves by taking advantage of new programs, relationships, and partnerships. The possibilities are end-less, the opportunities are great, and the rate of change is accelerating.

What is Database Marketing?

Marketers have used database marketing—marketing through the use of database information—for 20 years, but new technology continues to energize it. More and more applications are being developed that allow businesses to tap into their customers. In the commercial world, companies are using database technology to pinpoint customers on a global scale. Businesses use database marketing to track their customers, and to target their advertising, to understand their customers, to track their inventory, and to reach their customers individually. Every time you use a grocery card, charge something on a credit card, use a gasoline card, or subscribe to a magazine, you contribute information to a database. Amazon.com, for example, tracks customers' purchases and matches those purchases with demographic information to identify additional needs.

Libraries are all too familiar with databases, but they are just now entering the arena of database marketing. Currently they offer access to hundreds of information databases. They develop collaborative rela-tionships to provide collection databases. They maintain a database of their cardholders. They are beginning to develop databases regarding donors, members and friends. University libraries are compiling stu-dent, faculty and campus information and integrating those databases with information.

Databases offer libraries the opportunity to learn more about their customers. They have unique marketing ability to capture information about our customers and create life-long relationships with our customers. They provide resources for a new generation of professionalism in mar-keting. New skills are required in database marketing. Those skills include technology skills, marketing skills and database management skills. This area has become a field in itself.

Strategically, the role of database marketing is to help identify target audiences and to facilitate an ongoing relationship between the library and the customer. The database can become the heart of a market research intelligence system. You can analyze your database to determine customer penetration (where your customers live), frequency of use, formats of material used, and circulation of materials. You can work with census reports and user databases to help you focus your efforts in customer development, and to stimulate support in the election process. You can make futuristic forecasts as well as evaluate circulation statistics immedi-ately and instantly.

Three Types of Databases

1. The Historical Database

The first type is a passive, or historical, database. The data is limited to name, address, and telephone.

2. The Marketing Intelligent Database

A marketing intelligent database is specifically designed to allow professionals to analyze data for marketing information. A marketing intelligent system gathers information on the customer to enhance the institution's ability to understand its customers. This type of database tabulates fields of information concerning a customer. It allows you to cross-tabulate fields and compare information in unexpected ways. The goal is to learn from the current and past customers to predict the propensity of the future use.

In this area, libraries are beginning to use their customer databases to study segmentation, to examine "market penetration," to overlay their customer database on the census database for success in elections. Some libraries are using their database information to communicate with customers via e-mail. They are sending overdue notices electronically.

Mark Ellis, Manager of Reference and Information Services at the Richmond Public Library, shares a famous example in the use of database marketing. It is called the story of beer and diapers. It seems that through the "mining" of database literature, professionals determined that people were buying beer and diapers at the same time. The marketer studied the situation through the database and came up with this analysis: mama is at home with the infant. She calls her husband and asks him to pick up some diapers on the way home. While he was making the stop for diapers, he picked up some beer for himself. The discovery of this relationship was made through the cross tabulations within the database. It is called database "mining" and leads to some unexpected discoveries. Data mining allows us to discover nonintuitive relationships. It allows a supermarket to discover the opportunities for them when they put the baby diapers next to the beer. It probably would have never occurred to them before database marketing came into existence. The library landscape is full of database marketing possibilities. "Likewise in libraries, you miss opportunities to better serve our customers by not making full use of the data we've collected," says Mark Ellis.

3. The Integrated Business Resource Database

The most sophisticated database is an integrated business resource database. It captures the entire information resources of an organization. It integrates customer service, finance, distribution, as well as inventory, research, and marketing. The catalogue company L. L. Bean is a good example of an integrated business resource. Their kind of database allows them to track their customer relationships to products and services, balance inventory, keep track of financial accounts, and identify customer preferences.

Library Uses of the Database

Database management and marketing can be effective tools for understanding the use of collections, for weeding purposes, for purchasing new products. You can identify the profile of a "good" customer and then find new customers that look like current customers. You can design specialized communications programs to reach new, infrequent, or moderate users, while heavy users can receive communication that promote loyalty.

Databases allow us to study segmentation of different branches and identify needs for collections in specific areas. You can conduct market research on small groups of people, offer test marketing for new products and services. You can personalize your services to individuals. You can say, "thank you" and ask customers if their experience was a good one. You can create a system that recognizes complaints and gives customers feedback. You can communicate individually with your customers. You can send e-mails for late notices. You can use direct mail applications.

Constructing a Database

The database is only as powerful as the data it contains. The data you gather is crucial in database marketing. If you do not collect the correct data, or do not keep the data updated, the database will never be used to its full potential. While libraries have been dealing with collection databases, as well as research, periodical, and information databases from the beginning, they are just beginning to deal with customer databases.

First, you have to have basic, credible information on your customers. If you are aware of the benefits that come from a data-driven marketing program, you formulate a data-development strategy. You then begin to collect more information on your customers. You can use that information to develop better programs to support both the library and the customer. The database becomes your information and intelligence resource.

The data that you collect about your customers is limited by the willingness of the customer to give you information. There are three types of data that you can collect. The first is called *compiled data*. It represents demographic information. Libraries most frequently acquire this type of information. *Behavioral data* represents information collected about customer attitudes, purchases, and financial information. In the case of libraries, it would be materials checked out, fines, renewals, and program participation. The third level of data is called *modeled data*. In this form of data, commercial organizations collect individual and census-level data to develop models of consumer purchase behavior.

These databases are then laid over other databases. The concept implies that people who have similar cultural backgrounds, financial means, and perspectives gravitate toward one another. Because of this kind of database technique, several models have been developed to gather the households in those groups into marketing groups. You probably recognize some group titles. They include "Blue Blood Estates," "Shotguns and Pickups," and "Good Family Life." By overlapping a library database on a modeled database, a library can understand voter characteristics in elections or understand market penetration in various neighborhoods.

The library must transform or organize data into information to be useful and to support the decision-making processes. How do you build a more active database? Currently you have basic information on cardholders, including name, address, and telephone number. That data often elapses, because you do not check expired cards and addresses. Given the frequency with which data changes, you must create a card renewal program to maintain the database. You must develop a proactive maintenance program to use the cardholders' database effectively.

Mark Ellis, Manager of Reference and Information Services at the Richmond Public Library, in Richmond, British Columbia, comments that the Richmond Library began "warehousing" their circulation records in 2000 to improve their understanding of where their branch users were coming from. For example, they studied their Chinese collection. By "mining" the database, they were able to determine that many of their customers for the Chinese collection came from Vancouver. According to Ellis, the warehoused circulation data also "made it possible for us to employ implicit personalization on the new Web site. The home page now allows you to log in with your personal library card number and telephone number. When you log in, your circulation activity comes up on the computer. If the Web site identifies you as a teenager, the information for teens is instantly displayed. The same is true for other segments. The book covers that are displayed on the home page are drawn from the statistical category from which the customer most frequently borrows. Without the warehoused circulation data, this type of service would be impossible to offer."

The staff at the Richmond Public Library developed a list of the things that they wanted to know about their customers. That list was more inclusive than information usually obtained for a library card.

- Name

- Address

- Telephone

- Age

- Sex

- Patron category (adult, junior, home services, etc)

- Statistical category (the Richmond Public Library is geographic)

- Home branch/branch most used

- Language preference

- Borrowing history

- Program registration

- Family relationship (parent/child)

- Associations established through data mining

- Combination of the above

FIGURE 7-1   Statement of Patron Confidentiality

PATRON CONFIDENTIALITY – JAMIE LaRUE, DIRECTOR, THE DOUGLAS PUBLIC LIBRARY DISTRICT

"Sometimes I joke about it. Now that King Soopers and Safeway have foisted their credit cards on me (in exchange for some terrific discounts), I know that they can also track my purchasing habits.

Not that my habits are all that weird. I buy tortillas and beans. I buy pre-grated cheese. I buy pre-chopped salad. I buy lots of fruit and have a fondness for squash, and more rarely, cauliflower.

I like wild rice. I buy more chicken than beef. I have a weakness for sausage (both chorizo and Italian). I LOVE organic apple juice.

And now you know everything they know.

But occasionally, just to throw them off, I buy something I don't want, don't need, won't use. Try to profile ME, will they. Hah!

Childish? You bet. But I'm aware that with the advent of computers, it's getting far too easy to collect such data, both on the individual level, and the aggregate.

On the one hand, I understand that such data gathering is good business.

First, you have a really good handle on who buys what. That means you can identify both your customer base, and their preferences. Together, that translates to good inventory control. You stock what your customers want.

Second, you can target your advertising very precisely. You can generate coupons at the register for just those items people buy. That brings them back for other purchases. You can generate mailings (or sell lists for other people's mailings) for products most likely to appeal to them.

Together, these strategies mean more sales. They also mean, for many customers, that they only get the advertising that interests them.

FIGURE 7-1 (cont.)

So why not do the same thing in the library world? To check out a book or unlock a database, you already need (and probably already have) a library card. It would be simplicity itself to build patron profiles.

Many of our patrons have checked out literally thousands of books, videos, and tapes. Just by cross-tabbing our data files, we could easily determine that Ms. B- chechs out mostly children's books, the odd mystery, and Vogue magazine.

It wouldn't be hard to take that one step further. What are her FAVORITE children's and mystery writers? When we get a new book, why not send her an e-mail to say we got it? Better yet, why not put it on hold for her automatically?

This would be good for her (less work to get more books). It would be good for us (less work for more use). So why don't we? Why not adopt cutting edge technologies to push our inventory?

Well, librarians have a bias. We think that your transactions with us are nobody's business but yours. Every time we buy an automated system, we demand that it deliberately throw historical data away.

That's worth highlighting. At this writing, there is NO public library computer system that gathers and stores the pattern of your library use.
How come? Because we hesitate to create a record that somebody else (NOT you) could ask for.

Maybe you're reading a book about mental illness. Maybe it's about divorce. Maybe it's about sexual dysfunction, or substance abuse, or bankruptcy.

If we don't preserve such information, then nobody can get it from us.

The recent decision of the Colorado Supreme Court (Tattered Cover versus the City of Thornton) says that "The First Amendment...protects more than simply the right to speak freely... it safeguards a wide spectrum of activities, including.... The right to receive information and ideas."

To librarians, the ideas you receive from the public library- the most comprehensive collection of intellectual artifacts imaginable, whose value is far beyond what even the wealthiest of our citizens can afford- are PRIVATE.

That means that the books, magazines, and web pages you read are nobody's business but yours, for whatever reasons you may have.

That means that the videos and DVD's and music you borrow from us, not to mention the questions you ask of us are, utterly confidential.

Frankly, sometimes this troubles me. We could offer you way better service. We could make your interactions with the library far more efficient. Librarians are really, really smart about just what technology can do.

But we've held ourselves back. Why? Because when it comes right down to it, we think that what YOU think about shouldn't be part of a governmental file.

What do you think about that? You can reach me at (720) 733-8624 or at jlarue@jlarue.com.

☼ BRAINSTORMING 7.1 WHERE ARE YOU?

1. What is your current use of your customer database?

2. How do you maintain your customer database?

3. What information do you collect?

4. What are the restraints? What is your privacy policy?

Balancing Ethics and Database Technology

Customer privacy is a major issue among libraries. You will find significant disagreement among professionals in the library field regarding database marketing and privacy.

It is important that libraries maintain honesty with their customers. Database marketing allows us to develop a dialog with our customers. How can you use the data to provide the services your customers tell you they want? You must listen to the customer, create advisory boards to advise you on privacy issues, and turn privacy issues from a threat into an opportunity. The technology of the future will force you to be creative with database marketing, while respecting the need to maintain the privacy of your customers.

The Richmond Public Library, in British Columbia, has researched provincial and federal legislation, as well as the American Library Association and the Canadian Library Association to help them develop a privacy policy. In this particular case, the staff at the library does not see what is being produced by the interactive software and database. It is simply information that is between the customer, the software, and the database.

Developing Web Sites

The Internet was originally designed for research and scholarly communication. As it grew, new applications appeared and multiplied. By 1990, business services began to connect to the Internet, along with entertainment and informal communication. Now, more than 58 million people worldwide are connected to the Internet.

The Internet brings with it some exciting uses of the Web site of your library. You can reach nontraditional groups of customers; you can collaborate with other organizations including city and county governments, schools, arts organizations, community organizations and newspapers. The Internet site of your library can be a source of information for library users. The Internet site of your library establishes a presence in homes, schools, workplaces, and community centers. Anywhere there are computers, you can take advantage of the library's resources.

A collection of links to online resources is necessary as you build your Web site. How do you build an online collection? It takes time. The online collection grows and changes. You have to employ a systematic approach to including and deciding which sites offer the information that is most suited to your collection. Several directories on the Web can be useful as you examine which sites to include.

The design of your Web site has a direct impact on your customer's impression of your library. You want to create a very favorable impact. In fact, you must make a good first impression. Your "book" on your library will be judged by its cover. This Web site serves as a platform for your mission, your services, programs and catalogues, as well as linkages and communication about library programs. It can serve to demonstrate the involvement of the library with the community. You can use the Web to publish traditional promotional style material. However, the Web offers opportunities to do much more. It allows you to reach the customer in ways that you have never reached them before as well as to offer specific services to that customer. The Internet can open new roles, as well as serve to "reposition" the library.

Think Before You Design

The purpose of your site should guide the design of the site. Be clear on these four steps before you attempt to design a Web site.

- **What is the goal of the site?** What do customers hope to gain by using the site? What is its purpose? Do you want to communicate library programs? How will the site reflect the mission of the library?

- **What is the design message?** Keep it simple. Keep it consistent. Make it lots of fun. Present the electronic resources available in your library to the public. For some users, the Web site is their introduction to the Internet and what it has to offer. What image do you want to convey to your audience? Remember that this design message comes across by the look you create. Be progressive, sophisticated, intellectually stimulating, as well as entertaining and fun in your message. The message sets you apart from other organizations.

- **Who is the intended audience?** As in every marketing program, segmentation is the key to success. Target your Web site to specific segments of your audience. Make it easy for specific segments to get to the connections that are appropriate.

- **What is the content of this site?** Customize the template to include the information most relevant to the users of your library. Create a Web site that is easy to navigate. Provide a link on each page back to the home page. Think outside the box of the catalogue of the library alone. Provide access to information of all types.

Your new Web site also provides opportunities for partnerships. In fact, technology mandates that you develop partnerships to handle the rapidly expanding information services. Libraries have an opportunity to play a leadership role in developing their own local community networks and partnerships. They can draw on their experience and proficiency to organize community information on networks. They can help people select information resources, design the user interfaces, and promote the community along with individual participants on networks.

To do this, libraries must create effective communication channels—they must develop infrastructures of suppliers, vendors, partners, and users. The relationships with all of these people will sustain the library, maintain their position in the community, and kept the library on the technology edge. Libraries must do all of this with gusto, enthusiasm, leadership, and commitment, to retain the position in the information industry.

Some things to keep in mind while developing your Web site:

- **Get the help you need.** Professional consultants are available to assist you in every stage of Web site design. Many libraries have established Web site departments within the library staff. Professionals are essential, since you want your library Web site to be well designed, functional, and interesting. Professionals will save you time, energy, and mistakes.

- **Build your Web team.** Is your Web site to serve a marketing function? Can your Web team report to a technical area within your library? You will need employees to manage the groups and lead this project. Make sure that individuals from all areas of the library have input into the design of the Web site.

- **Publicize your Web site.** People will not use the Web site of your library if they do not know that it exists. In order to maximize the impact of your Web site and provide effective technology services to the community, you must actively work to publicize your site. Use the library's current outreach efforts to include information about your Web site. Include the address on newsletters, stationary, overdue notices, and yellow page listings. Think about signage within the library, as well as promotional pieces, such as bookmarks that describe the Web site.

- **Maintain and Update your Web site.** Once you build a Web site, the tendency is to relax and say that the work is done. However, it is then time to start thinking about maintaining, updating and testing the Web site. Establish a maintenance schedule. Visitors that see outdated material on your Web site probably will not return. Test your Web site to make sure that links are working. Provide a way for all of your users to give feedback and point out broken links.

Personalization

As with all things, the Web site is evolving. In the early stages, Web sites were content-based sites. Customer-focused sites now offer individual customers the opportunity to personalize the sites. Personalization is a relatively new and challenging area of Web content delivery. Libraries have been reluctant to take up personalization as an innovation, primarily because of privacy issues, although they have been aggressive in adopting automation technology. There are two types of personalization. They include *explicit personalization* in which users pick functionality and lay it out on a personal home page. The user can have personalized pages called My Views, which present the information and services chosen by the user. They can change the look and feel of their user interface by selecting from different color schemes. In *implicit personalization* software behind the site infers user interests from their behavior on site—past or present, and then customizes the content presented accordingly. The user does not have to invest any effort in setting up a profile, but then they cannot explicitly control what happens on the site either. This type of personalization gives you the power to create implicitly personalized content on the Web site. Special postings or notifications can be sent to the user, as well as automatic e-mail- notifications.

Personalization helps recreate the human element that understands the customer and offers the personalized touch. It is an ever-growing feature of online services. Will personalized service become part of the customer's definition of good service? Are customers expecting personalization? Personalization allows the library to anticipate the customer needs, and make the interaction efficient for both parties. It builds a relationship that encourages the customer to return for subsequent encounters. It has been described as being about building customer loyalty by building a meaningful one-to-one relationship.

Examples of personalization in the nonlibrary world include those typified by MyYahoo, which allows you to personalize your Web site and Amazon.com, which uses its personalization as a marketing tool. GMBuyPower allows you to select the make, body style, color (both interior and exterior), and price, and locate the nearest dealer for your car. Wells Fargo Banks offers full service banking activities via your personalized Web site. Financial institutions and retail institutions offer full personalization. The entertainment industry (including television listings) are beginning to provide personalized guides where one can pick viewing times, genre, and channels.

User satisfaction is the ultimate aim of personalization. It puts the user at the center of the interaction and tailors the interaction to meet his specific needs. If the needs of the user are successfully met, it is likely to lead to a satisfying relationship and the reuse of the services offered. There is often a distinction between customization and personalization. Customization or explicit personalization occurs when the user can configure an interface and create a profile manually. The look or the content is explicit and is user-driven. In implicit personalization, the user is in less control. The content that is offered is based on tracking previous decisions.

The Success Stories in the chapter examine four great sites that illustrate various types of Web site design. Each of the libraries has used elements of either implicit or explicit personalization in the design of their Web site. Brarydog at the Public Library of Charlotte and Mecklenburg County is an animated creature complete with a rap that appeals to young adults. The site allows for explicit personalization. It serves as the center of their program. However, the Web site is used for a total program involving teachers, schools, librarians, and other educators.

The Seattle Public Library Foundation uses their Web site to build a personal relationship with their donors. Their Web site provides a presence, which gives donors the information they need, provides donor recognition, as well as education and makes donors feel appreciated for their support. It provides awareness and offers opportunities to participate online. It is an important part of their community campaign.

North Carolina State University has employed many innovative Web site techniques that allow students and faculty to develop a personal interactive relationship with the library. Users can find sophisticated information resources, have research abstracts and documents sent to them by e-mail, and can be alerted to new information. North Carolina State University is one of the pioneers in the field.

The Richmond Public Library, in British Columbia, Canada has used their Web site to galvanize the community. They focus on the customer and the community, providing links to the Newspaper, community services and centers, musical and theatrical programs, citizenship tests, drivers license information as well as library resources. They offer online services that allow you to check and pay library fines, pay for programs as well as sign up for a library card. Their goal is to make their Web site a valuable source of community information. They are providing individual personalization on their Web site. This personalization acts much as Amazon.com does, alerting customers to new additions to the collection that will appeal to them individually.

Benefits and Rewards of Richmond Public Library's Approach to Internet Services

When people learn about the Richmond Public Library's Internet projects, they become amazed that the library is using this technology to enhance its services. Aside from enjoying recognition from the library community, the library's payoff comes from being the treasure of Richmond. The mayor frequently praises the library publicly for their technological achievements. A neighborhood group campaigned to open a much-needed new library branch in their area. After much advocacy and fund-raising, the neighborhood group was successful in their campaign and the city agreed to build a new neighborhood branch with money from the city budget, community groups, and sponsorship from local businesses. The community made it happen, because they wanted to help make their library system thrive.

The Richmond Public Library has won many prestigious awards for excellent service and innovation. In 2003, the library was awarded the Gale Group Award for Excellence in Reference and Adult Library Services. The library was also awarded the CLA/Information Today Award for Innovative Technology. These national awards both recognized the library's outstanding collection of online interactive resources. In 2002, the ABC Canada Literacy Foundation Grant was awarded to them for their "Share the Stories" book collection. The funding went toward purchasing board books with thick, durable pages made especially for babies and toddlers for their beginning stages of literacy. The Richmond Public Library also won the 2002 Canada Post Literacy Award for Community Leadership in recognition of the nearly 1,900 programs sponsored by the library that serve the diverse needs of the Richmond community. Over 55,000 people were educated through programs such as ESL conversation circles, after-school tutoring for children, a reading buddies program, programs in computer literacy, a writing contest for young adults, and an immigrant orientation program. The Canada Post Literacy Award acknowledged Richmond Public Library for contributing to literacy in the community. In 2002, the library also received the ExplorASIAN Canadian Heritage Award for Community Building Through Arts and Culture. This award acknowledged the library's significant contribution to strengthening the community infrastructure so that culture and arts may flourish there. The *Library Journal*'s "Movers and Shakers" identifies the leaders and innovators of the library world. Cate McNeely, Richmond's Deputy Chief Librarian, was recognized in the category of "Visionaries" as a mover and shaker for her leadership in the library field. This nomination recognizes "those individuals who are enhancing the way we provide service, who are making us think about what we do and how we do it, who are creating new models for others to use."

Whether it be improving their successful Web site, getting the community involved, or winning myriad awards, the Richmond Public Library is paving the way for all Canadian libraries to apply new and innovative methods to their own systems. Perhaps in the future, with the presence and growth of new technology, libraries will be the center of society. The example set by the Richmond Public Library and its local residents shows us the benefits an excellent library can bring to an active community.

Success Story 7.1
Creating an Innovative Web Site Design

Richmond Public Library,   **Richmond, British Columbia, Canada**

In the Richmond Public Library, reference statistics were declining for several years as customers found it was easier to get information on the Internet than through the library. Mark Ellis, manager of the reference department, began getting his staff more involved in Web development. He said, "rather than trying to reinsert librarians into reference transactions, we need to facilitate the use of the Internet in the Richmond Public Library. By doing this, our productivity will increase and the staff will be free to do more Web development and instruction." Therefore, librarians in the reference department became involved in Web development in addition to their other duties. Shirley Lew, one new, full-time librarian has become the Web-coordinator. She monitors, maintains and develops new Web services and has taken the Web site to new levels.

While the library's Web site has always been on the forefront of innovation, it is now exceptional. You can view it at www.yourlibrary.ca. The Richmond Public Library has used their Web site to focus on the customer and the community. They have developed seven sections in the design of their Web site:

1. My Library Account

This area's one-step processing provides the ultimate in customer service. Here customers can accomplish things like applying for a library card, checking due dates and/or fines for overdue materials, changing addresses, renewing material, and checking material on hold.

An area called "My Picks" allows the customer to register for special service and offers a personalized Web page. Customers can be automatically informed via e-mail when their new favorite titles in books, videos and DVDs arrive in the library. It allows customers of the library to place holds on material and browse the collections online.

This system allows for customer interaction and has had an impact on all areas of the library, especially circulation, collections and acquisitions. The customers' increased demand has forced the library to review their circulation and development processes so they may decrease the time required to get materials to the customer. Customers usually want new books and new materials right away. The library has recognized that it needs to make the delivery process more efficient.

2. Find Books

This is the second section of the Web site. The Richmond Public Library has made it easier for the customer and produced a one-stop section, which focuses on the reading, listening, and video needs of the customer. Links to sites that offer reading suggestions are provided.

The most popular services in this section are the new acquisitions lists, which show the library's new fiction and nonfiction books, children's books, DVDs and videos, and music CDs. The lists feature cover art and each title has a link, which takes customers directly into the library catalog for holdings information. From this catalog, customers can also place holds on materials.

The *Find Books* section is changing the way people use the library and is creating an explosive demand for materials. Customers enjoy the convenience of browsing the collection from home through the Web site. The library realizes that people want to read, but need suggestions on what to read. "Public Libraries have always been in the business of helping people with reading suggestions, but that role has been overshadowed by the onslaught of the Internet and the Information Age. With our new Web site, we've utilized technology to merge the reading world with the Web to great success," said Shirley Lew. "The tremendous response has caught us off guard. The sudden demand has caused us to reorganize how we do things." If a customer finds that Richmond Public Library does not own something they desire for the collection, they can fill out an online Purchase Suggestion Form. "We have found that the community wants to be involved in collection development," says Lew. "The community is taking ownership in a way they have never done before."

3. Online Resources

This area of the Richmond Public Library Web site provides links to core reference resources on the Web. The purpose of this section is to help customers find answers to their questions from the convenience of home or work at any time of the day. "We'd like our librarians to do more Web development and to think of the Web as a way to deliver reference service," says Shirley Lew. "That is how people want information." If there is a high demand at the reference desk for certain types of questions, the library tries to develop a Web solution. Through *Online Resources*, a customer can search through subscription databases, do a job search, and work with health or business indexes. They can also get telephone directory information.

Richmond Public Library provides an interactive Web-based citizenship test. This test allows Richmond's large immigrant population to practice the Canadian Citizenship exam online and have it graded instantly. "While the creation of this test was motivated by service to our own customers, it has found a national audience evidenced by the e-mails we receive from elsewhere in Canada," according to Lew. The citizenship exam is a good example of the technology the library is using to provide service and community-based information.

For those who can't find answers to their questions through the Web site, there is an e-mail reference service called Ask Us. Questions are answered within 24 hours.

4. Computers at Richmond Public Library

This area of the Web site is user-friendly and designed to encourage customers to use library computers. Here, a customer can prebook a library computer online. There is also an Online Learning Centre where customers can learn computer and software skills through the Web, a service provided in partnership with a private company. Providing this service is Serebra Corporation, a company that develops online learning modules on computer topics such as XML programming and MS Word, as well as on professional development topics such as project management and customer service. There is a fee for the online courses and a percentage of sales go to both the service provider and the library.

A section where customers can register their laptops is available. Customers can bring their own laptop to the library and receive Internet access at no charge. This section also showcases the many computer-tutorial programs at the library. There are workshops just for seniors that teach e-mail, Internet, and Microsoft Word usage, as well as basic introductory courses for the computer novice.

5. What's On

The fifth area of the Web site, *What's On*, provides detailed information and online registration for programs in the library, which are organized by community groups. The library features quality programming for all ages and interests. Promotion on the Web site has really helped certain programs, such as Story Times, Teen Times, and Chinese Culture Programs, become popular. The energy of the librarians has been refreshed by the enthusiastic response to library programs. Let's look at the Teen Programs, for example. A council of teens plays an active role in library programs and community events. Teens can choose to be a "Reading Buddy," "Teen Tutor," or "Cyberteen." As a Reading Buddy, teens work with children in the community to develop their reading skills. Teen Tutors help kids with their homework. Cyberteens are paired up with Cyberseniors, helping senior citizens use computers and surf the net. The Richmond Public Library Web site supports these programs with online applications and information.

6. Community

This section features a one-stop location for all community information. Community organizations like Volunteer Richmond, community centers, political parties, local music and theatre, and local businesses are linked to the library's Web site. There is also a link to the online edition of the local newspaper, The Richmond Review, to which library staff contributes weekly book reviews and articles on computers and technology. This section of the Web site provides one-stop shopping for your cultural appetite.

7.   About Us

This section contains the mission statement, strategic report, the library's goals and vision, information about Ironwood, the "Library of the Future," and more. Since this section contains so much information, it generates heavy traffic from other libraries, who wish to learn more about the Richmond Public Library. Browsers of the site's "About Us" section frequently link to the information about the progress of Ironwood, Richmond's high-tech library branch that boasts multiple high-speed Internet ports, a large music collection, a beautiful children's area, digital reference centers, and teaching resources to aid the community in preparing to use progressive technology.

Success Story 7.2
Introducing the Brarydog Web Site

Public Library of Charlotte and Mecklenburg County,   Charlotte, North Carolina

Brarydog.net was created by the Public Library of Charlotte and Mecklenburg County to serve as a personal reference tool for both local library cardholders and Internet users throughout the nation. Its primary users are young adults. With Brarydog.net, students can bring their favorite online resources and Internet sites together to create a personal online library. It is designed to provide Internet users with easy access to information, and is personalized to meet each user's research needs.

The library has developed several Web sites, each offering a different service to their users, including reader's advisory for children and adults (www.readersclub.org, www.bookhive.org), access to select health and business resources (www.healthlinkplus.org, www.bizlink.org), and bilingual children's storytelling (www.storyplace.org). In addition to organizing and presenting information in a user-friendly manner, the library decided to develop a site for students to simplify their access to online resources. The "My Library" personalization concept evolved into "brarydog.net," offering students a customized one-stop center for homework help. The animated character Brarydog adds a special dimension of fun for teens.

How it works

To access Brarydog resources, the user creates a login with a user name and password. Then he or she can select which resources to display. Library cardholders have access to "premium resources," including subscription data bases, Web resources, and photo archives which can be opened by using a library card number. The user can also choose a search tool, background, and text colors. Once the page is created, the user is greeted by Brarydog when they log in, and their personalized page is displayed. Users can then use any resources to which they have access without requiring further authorization.

Brarydog.net is updated through feedback from users, gathered from workshop sessions and comments sent in through the site. Web site usage statistics are utilized and evaluated for market research purposes. Updates are created in response to all the feedback and include changes to the instructions for creating pages, the expansion of the research help area, and a "study break" area. These additions assist in broadening the scope of the site and increasing its usage. Remote usage of the Public Library of Charlotte and Mecklenberg County Web sites is among the highest in the country, with nearly 450,000 external visitors a month.

The Brarydog.net Web site is the nucleus of a cooperative effort that has developed between the library and the community. As the site was being developed, the library recognized the importance of working with the school system and community. In order to maintain this collaboration, the library hired a Brarydog coordinator. The Brarydog coordinator acts as a liaison between the libraries and the schools, as a trainer for students, teachers and parents, and as a PR representative for the Web site's presence and services. Brarydog is also the library's mascot, making appearances at many community events. The presence of Brarydog as a homework assistant and ambassador for the library creates a brand that has been very well received in the community. Response from parents, teachers and students has been very positive: "I can't imagine life without Brarydog!" one satisfied user insists.

Brarydog.net exemplifies the approach of the Public Library of Charlotte and Mecklenburg County to fulfilling their mission of "meeting the public's information needs," while embracing and incorporating technology. Offering both an information gateway and a strong link to the community, Brarydog.net is an inventive method in delivering traditional library services.

The Public Library of Charlotte and Mecklenburg County has also been a pioneer among libraries in developing "service sites," providing remote services to a specific user population rather than just providing information about the services and collections of the library. PLCMC began this development back in 1998 with the creation of BizLink (www.bizlink.org). Designed to provide business users with easy access to the best in library and Internet resources, the site maintains its own separate identity and URL. "We wanted patrons to identify with the business service first," explains Library Director Bob Cannon, "and then discover that it was developed and created by a public library." The model was successful in satisfying the business community's needs. Today, the PLCMC family of Web sites consists of ten unique service sites:

- **BizLink** (www.bizlink.org)—Recommended Internet and print resources for the business patron, with emphasis on the local community.

- **BookHive** (www.bookhive.org)—A children's book review site, with mascot Zinger the Bee, designed to help kids locate books to read and allow them to share comments on their favorites.

- **Brarydog** (www.braydog.net)—A customizable research companion developed to assist middle and high school students with homework assignments.

- **Hands on Crafts** (www.handsoncrafts.org)—An online interactive studio on North Carolina's rich craft heritage; designed for kids.

- **Health Link** (www.healthlinkplus.org)—Recommended Internet and print resources for consumer health and medical information.

- **Reader's Club** (www.readersclub.org)—A reader's advisory site for adults and teens offering more than 1,000 staff reviews and recommendations for both fiction and nonfiction.

- **StoryPlace** (www.storyplace.org)—Interactive stories and activities for children in English and Spanish.

- **The Charlotte-Mecklenburg Story** (www.cmstory.org)—A rich local history archive with numerous online exhibits and thousands of images covering the region's past.

- **Novello Festival** (www.novellofestival.net-information)—A Web site about the library's nationally acclaimed Novello Festival of reading and book publishing.

- **PLCMCC** (www.plcmc.org)—The library's main site providing information about events, program services, including all nine of its additional service Web sites.

Success Story 7.3
Revising a Web Site to Meet Customer Needs

Seattle Public Library,   **Seattle, Washington**

In 2001, the Seattle Public Library Foundation (foundation.spl.org) had a rather small static Web page. It provided information about the foundation mission, leadership gifts, and the board of directors, but the Foundation knew their Web site needed more. It needed to reflect the right image to the customer, to represent the library's progressive environment. The Seattle Public Library Foundation recognized that their Web site needed to reflect the excellence of their campaign. The Web site also offered them the opportunity to acknowledge gifts, recognize board members and encourage new donors to give to the library. Their unique Web site was developed with help from the Foundation staff. Now, the Seattle Public Library Foundation stands at the very heart of information technology, making a big difference to the library environment in the city.

The Web site project began when a special team was formed to find the right design and development firm to identify and meet the needs of the library's customers. "We needed to step up our presence," said Jonna Ward, who administers the community campaign for the Foundation, "but at the same time, we realized that Web sites can be very costly and very time consuming." The search team, including members of the Foundation and library staff, quickly determined their own needs: they wanted a design firm that loved the library, one that would be motivated by the project's visibility, willing to work for a highly discounted rate. They identified and contacted a handful of firms, all of which responded with written proposals. After telephone interviews, three finalists were selected for site visits, before a final choice was made.

The total revision process took about six months from the release of the RFP to the launch of the new Web site. Jonna Ward, who led the team, described three central aspects to making the design a success: 1) Working with a dedicated and committed team; 2) Identifying and understanding your key audiences and what's important to them; and 3) Having a strategic vision and roadmap that frames your decisions on content, functionality, and design. Since launch, easy-to-use management tools have also allowed the Foundation to update the site on a monthly basis, transforming it into a dynamic brochure. Even someone who is comfortable with a software product like Microsoft Word could update the site. With new content about initiatives and events, success stories, leadership gifts, and underwriting opportunities, the foundation presents itself as a winning organization raising money for an important civil institution. It takes the opportunity to communicate about what has been accomplished and what remains to be done while demonstrating good stewardship of donors' gifts.

The new Web site guides an individual through five main areas. In the first area, *Your help matters*, detailed explanations of various funds are complemented by a series of success stories revealing the importance of private gifts. The second area, *Who We Are* identifies the role of the Foundation with the library and provides background information on the board of directors, staff members, and supporters as well as financial management. In the third and fourth sections, *Ways to Give* identifies how a donor can contribute to the foundation—whether through the site, phone, fax or mail—while *Planned Giving* explains wills and bequests, stocks and bonds, and trusts. Finally, *Corporations and Foundations* offers companies and organizations information on potential partnerships with the library.

Success Story 7.4
Leading the Way into the Future with Web Site Design and Services

North Carolina State University Libraries,   **Raleigh, North Carolina**

The North Carolina State University Libraries (www.lib.ncsu.edu) provides a rich and diverse range of electronic resources and services to support the teaching and research missions of North Carolina State University (NC State). Through its innovative programs, the libraries have given NC State a competitive advantage and has won national and international recognition and awards, including the Association of College and Research Libraries' "Excellence in Academic Libraries Award" in 2000. The central D. H. Hill Library plus four branch libraries offer many elements of a digital library, including content-rich access through its Web site, access to online and offline electronic resources, online reference, and circulation, borrowing record and renewal services. Network connections are available for use throughout the main and branch libraries, and Web access is available via clusters of public terminals, computing facilities, and laptop computers loaned for in-building use. The libraries continue to encourage creative and innovative involvement in developing the potential of the Web, led by the Web Strategy Team, Web Development Librarian, and the libraries' Web publishers, who are responsible for the content, currency, and accuracy of the Web pages.

The libraries' homepage is the gateway to a diverse range of Web content and services structured to guide users and make information easily and quickly accessible. This is a fine balancing act as the libraries serve a diverse community with different levels of expertise and needs. Central to providing such services and resources is strong Web site architecture and design, integrating eXtensible Markup Language (XML) technologies and content management. With the establishment of the libraries' Learning and Research Center for the Digital Age (LRCDA), it is anticipated that there will be greater awareness of Web-related issues as well as further investment in Web-based activities and development.

The libraries also leverage Web technologies to develop and provide innovative services and resources, create a rich learning environment, as well as market, promote, and publicize those services and resources. While many users will continue to seek direct assistance in person or via telephone, the Libraries must constantly look for ways to develop its Web site and virtual environment. As Carolyn Argentati, Deputy Director of Libraries, observes, "It is impossible to overestimate the power of the Web in reaching out to our users with an ever-evolving mix of content and services that supports research, instruction, and public service. The phenomenal increases in Web access statistics that we have seen in recent years may only be the beginning."

The following is a brief list of some of the key resources provided on the Web site:

- **NC LIVE:** A digital resource initiative encompassing all community colleges, public libraries, private academic institutions, and public academic institutions in the state of North Carolina. It offers all state residents Web-based access to a wide range of online information resources. The Libraries hosts the NC Live help desk librarians and serves as a primary server site. NC LIVE staff recently developed a single search interface for easier access to multiple electronic resources.

- **Electronic Reference and Research Resources:** Users have access to the libraries' online catalog, a Database Finder, an E-journal Finder, and research guides by subject. Also available is an innovative tool that searches across core and related Z39.50 databases for the subject selected by the user and presents the resulting hits. Assistance and training in the use of a variety of databases for both instructional and research needs are also provided on the Web site. These include instructional and "how-to" pages, as well as subject guides. "SearchAssist" is an innovative Web-based search and retrieval service. LOBO2, the libraries' online basic orientation Web tutorial, facilitates an understanding of the research process and resources available. This tutorial won the 2003 ALA/*Information Today*, Inc., Library of the Future Award and is a measure of some of the innovations and collaborations necessary in developing Web services.

- **Virtual Reference Service:** The Libraries launched a Web-based online "chat" virtual reference service in January 2000, allowing the reference enquiry process to take place in real time. This is especially valuable for users who are unable to come to the physical library. Through the Web, the user has a direct communication link to a reference librarian, and the shared Web browser enables the librarian to demonstrate immediately to the user the process of searching for information through the libraries' Web site, online catalog, databases, and electronic journals. While there will always be a need for face-to-face reference service, innovative technology is used to supplement and enhance the Libraries' reference service.

- **MyLibrary@NCState:** This user-driven, customizable Web interface allows users to create a subject-oriented Web page that lists information resources available from the libraries, including full-text and bibliographic databases as well as direct access to librarians. Several prepared layouts are available, and users can also set up their own. It is platform independent and accessible from any computer with an NC State username and password. This feature is part of the personalization services available from the libraries and enables a more focused Web interaction for the user. A number of libraries in the United States and international are currently using or adapting the script originally developed at the libraries, including Auburn University, in Alabama, George Mason University, in Virginia, Lund University, in Sweden, and the Norwegian University of Science and Technology, in Norway.

- **Geographic Information Systems (GIS):** Computer-based systems that facilitate the input, storage, manipulation, and output of geo-referenced data. Interactive Web-based mapping applications make data resources easily accessible for novice users. The successful implementation of GIS services at the libraries earned the Environmental Systems Research Institute (ESRI) 2001 Special Achievement Award in GIS. The libraries were chosen from more than 60,000 organizations worldwide as the winner of this award.

- **Design Library Image Collection:** A Web-accessible collection of over 50,000 digitized images of slides in the areas of architecture, interior design, graphic design, and product design. There are thumbnail and full-size images, and the accompanying records include cataloging and indexing information. Users are able to search the collection, and faculty members have access to the "Portfolio Builder" to select images for presentation and class use. A module for student presentations is under development. An attractive Web interface and layout was designed to give this product its distinctive look and feel.

- **Transactional Services:** Users can check their borrowing record to see items on loan and can renew items online. Web-based forms are available to request interlibrary loans, items not on the shelf, photocopied materials, and electronic reserves. The libraries' electronic reserve system was among the first to couple the existing integrated library system's reserve module capabilities with digital materials. Web-based forms are also used to request specific documents, campus delivery of library materials, and assignment of Faculty Research Studies.

Other Web-based efforts at outreach and promotion include Friends of the Library (FOL) and name branding. The Friends of the Library program, together with the Development Office, coordinate and manage donor gifts and corporate partnerships. The Friends Web site reflects its mission and provides information as well as online membership registration. The latter is a Web-based form located on the Libraries' secure server to ensure privacy and security.

Some vendors like LexisNexis now allow institutional branding of the services to which they subscribe. The libraries have taken advantage of this by designing an appropriate logo to promote and highlight to the NC State community the role the libraries play in bringing those services to them.

For an increasing number of users, the Web site is the library at least some of the time. Providing rich Web content and easy access to information is, therefore, central to the mission of the NC State Libraries. Technology is transforming the world of education and information, and, with the foundation of resources already established, the libraries will continue to leverage the Web and Web technologies to enrich its presence and better serve the information needs of the NC State community.

Anticipating the Future

The information economy and the digital revolution will continue to change the library of tomorrow. Libraries will fundamentally need to rethink the processes by which they deliver customer value. They will have to change from being archival, historical, and reference institutions, to ones that play an active role with their customers. They will need to involve their customers in the act of codesigning their desired products. They will need to be creative in programs, products and funding arenas. They will need to explore strategic partnerships, networks, collaboration, fee-based services, philanthropy, and coordination, as well as merchandizing and alternative funding scenarios. They need to be the very center and strength of the community as they provide free access to information. They need to embrace technology, as that technology will continue to provide new opportunities for delivery of service. The day of the *Virtual Library* is already here.

Libraries are changing their delivery of service every day. Drive-up windows, automated check out, and online services are proliferating.

Libraries are creating an atmosphere pleasing to customers, providing outreach services, engaging in partnerships and creating advisory groups of customers. They are seeking to develop the hours of service that meet customer needs. They are also discovering their own strengths as they enter collaborative relationships with other corporations and entities. They are developing alliances and cooperative relationships with other libraries. They will continue to maximize their coordination within communities, counties, states, and within the Northern Hemisphere, as well as the world.

There are three ways to ensure success in the new Electronic Age. They include the following:

1. Put the customer first.

Develop hours of service, programs and collections to meet the customers' needs. Find a way to extend those hours. Hire friendly staff that walk around the library interacting with customers. Listen, listen, and listen some more. Personalize the service through the Web site. Develop a merchandising approach to the collection.

2. Build and actively manage a database.

In the case of libraries, they have already built one of the best databases for the community. They need to maintain that database by correcting information on a regular basis. They need to build a proactive database instead of a passive one.

Database marketing will be so significant in the future that it should not be ignored. Libraries have the opportunity to build additional databases that will allow them to personalize services in the future. An e-mail database will allow direct communication to customers. A kid's database formed through participation in events and programs will allow the library to communicate with individual children with a newsletter or e-mail about activities for kids, favorite authors or special programs.

Allow customers the choice of whether or not they want to be alerted to new items in the collections of which they have an interest. Perhaps they would be delighted to know that a new book on childcare has arrived or that their favorite author has just released a new book. Give them the choice and let them decide.

Donor databases are essential to the philanthropy process. These databases allow you to reach donors and potential donors in a personalized manner while not violating the privacy issues of the cardholder database.

3. Develop a clear concept of how the library will take advantage of the Internet.

The library already uses the Internet to provide research, access to information in their collection, as well as access to informational databases, journals and research collections. The computer promotes collaboration between libraries and library systems and provides up to date technical services. Through the Web, the library can also provide information about other community services and programs. The library can run forums, book reviews and discussions.

Pay attention to your Web site. Update it, update it and update it again. Make it interactive. Provide the access that the customer needs 24-hours a day.

Success Story 7.5
Creating the Library of the Future

Richmond Public Library,   **Richmond, British Columbia, Canada**

The experimental Ironwood Branch of the Richmond Public Library in British Columbia opened its doors five years ago. Ever since that time, librarians from across North America and as far away as Europe and Australia have made pilgrimages there. This branch serves as a prototype of the library of the future.

The first thing that visitors see at this Ironwood Branch is a quote from Groucho Marx "Outside of a dog, a book is man's best friend. Inside of a dog, it is too dark to read." Obviously, this library is different. "With the quote we are saying to our visitors 'come on in and enjoy yourself,'" says Cate McNeely, deputy chief librarian of the Richmond Public Library. There are attractive wooden display carts of CD's with listening stations, and books are displayed everywhere. There is a "living room" with a corner reading area, river-rock fireplace and comfortable chairs. Food and drink can be enjoyed in this comfortable library setting. In addition, staff "walk the floor" to assist customers, rather than wait to be approached at the desk. Collections are merchandized in a large array of appealing and ever changing displays.

The Ironwood branch is highly automated. There is a lively Web site (www.yourlibrary.ca) that offers quick access to newspapers, community activities and research.

- Customers use three automated "express" checkouts that resemble bank ATM machines. Over 95 percent of borrowers use the automated check out. This frees up staff to provide more value-added services such as extensive programming and long operating hours (74 per week).

- There is an 18-seat computer learning and training center, five digital kid's stations, six digital reference stations and 13 additional Internet stations. Software ranges from the Encyclopedia Britannica to Microsoft Office. The high-tech resources include:

- 18 Compaq computers running "Windows NT" in the Ironwood computing centre. They have Microsoft Office, unrestricted Internet access, and a variety of children's games.

- Six Digital Information stations for teens and adults. These have CD reference titles and links to reference related Internet Web sites and these stations are filtered.

- 13 Compaq computers with full Internet access.

- The children's area has five computers with games and educational programs. The children's Internet stations are filtered.

- Library Online to pay late charges, register for programs, and library cards, and book computers.

Cate McNeely says, "Libraries face urgent, expensive and competitive demands. First, they must provide computer access so that no one is left behind. Secondly, they must make the library an exciting and appealing destination for all ages with easy to browse collections, extensive programs and long open hours." "People have always expected to find bestsellers at the library," adds McNeely. The challenge "is to make sure we have more copies, and that they are better displayed, especially for all of those people who prefer to browse rather than use the catalogue or search the stacks."

While the library is high tech, it is also very high touch. The interior design is more like a contemporary bookstore. The "living room" has comfortable chairs with coffee vending machines and a magazine and newspaper collection. The children's area has a red wooden barn that hosts storytimes. "Add comfortable chairs and a homey atmosphere in the "living room," and you can see that we've taken a chapter out of the retail experience," McNeely says. "Our strong marketing makes it easier for a person to come into the library and find what they want."

"The library is becoming a destination. People of all ages, types and interests can come here and enjoy themselves," according to McNeely. "Public libraries will survive and thrive in the next millennium, but only if they are willing to change to better meet our customer's needs. Libraries are dynamic organizations responsible to their communities and affected by the same societal and economic changes as other organizations. As such they must continually change in order to remain viable," says McNeely.

Recent awards include the 2003 Gale Group Award for Excellence in Reference and Adult Library Services; the 2003 CLA/Information Today Award for Innovative Technology; the 2002 Canada Post Literacy Award for Community Leadership; the 2000 Canadian Library Association/Information Today Award for Library Online, the 1999 BC Library Association Merit Award for the Ironwood Branch, and the 1999 Canadian Library Association/FAXON award for PR and marketing. The Richmond Public Library is setting the pace, "thinking outside the box" and leading the way to the library of the future.

215

Cate McNeely says, "There are plenty of libraries offering coffee services and merchandizing their collections. The library of the future needs to discover what the customer really wants and deliver exactly what the customer wants. Customers want more convenient and longer hours. They want service on the weekends and in the evening. They want more programs. They want friendly, knowledgeable staff walking around and providing assistance. They want the collections to be merchandized. They want personalized service via e-mail. Listen to the customer and give them what they want. That is the library of the future."

BRAINSTORMING 7.2 IDENTIFY YOUR LIBRARY'S USE FOR THE INTERNET NOW AND ITS POTENTIAL USE IN THE FUTURE.

- List the various ways to use the Internet.

- Note the ways your library currently uses the Internet, including notes on how your library could improve those uses.

- Use the chart on the next page to explore ways in which you would like your library to use the Internet in 3–5 years.

Ways to Use the Internet	Our Library Now	Desirable in 3–5 Years
Provide access to information 　Library catalogue 　Information databases 　Journal articles 　Books and Bytes 　Magazine Articles		
Customer Opportunities 　Kid's Club 　Young Adults 　Fiction 　Poetry 　History 　Genealogy 　Business		
Information Services 　Library Cards 　Renewal 　Fine Payment 　Reserve list		
Community Services 　City Services 　Drug, Alcohol, Handicapped		
Information 　Mass Transit		
Information 　Social Services 　Arts, Theatre, Music		
Web Site 　State of the Art Graphics,Sound and Video		
Weekly News Features Donor Information Customer Interaction E-Mail Option		

Appendixes:
Marketing Tools
You Can Use

APPENDIX A

Step-by-Step Marketing Plans

The two sample marketing plans are intended to give you an idea of how marketing plans come together, what steps must be taken, and what order the plans should take. You have been given a lot of information, and these two plans are a small way to synthesize everything.

The sample plans differ in significant ways. The first sample, "Developing a Spanish-Language Program for Preschoolers," is a very specific plan with a specific audience. The second sample, "Developing a Shakespeare Festival at Your Library," is a more general plan aimed at a potentially wide audience. You can also see that one plan is essential to library service while the other is less so. The strategies for developing the plans, however, remain the same. There will always be a specific process to your marketing plans that will help you execute them successfully.

1. Developing a Spanish-Language Program for Preschoolers

The staff of the Inland Public Library recognized in their strategic plan a need to serve new members of their community. After examining the population and assessing the strengths and weaknesses of their service to the population, they recognized a need to serve Spanish-speaking families. While there are many segments within this population—preschoolers, young adults, adults, professionals, and seniors—the library has decided to develop individual programs to meet the needs of each specific group. Combined, each of these necessary marketing plans will fulfill the library's greater obligation to serve this community. This sample marketing plan will target the preschool audience.

Environmental Analysis

As you will recall, this analysis includes segmentation, demand, customer decision-making process and competition. For this particular marketing plan, you have a defined audience, Hispanic preschoolers, but even this limited audience requires in depth study in order to develop the service and the appropriate strategies and tactics to make the program a success.

221

Segmentation

This audience can be divided into several groups if you examine them closely enough. Segments are marked by language, schooling, location, economic factors, and family size. A list of potential segments includes:

- bilingual Hispanic preschoolers;
- monolingual Spanish-speaking Hispanic preschoolers;
- monolingual English-speaking Hispanic preschoolers;
- preschoolers with bilingual parents;
- preschoolers with monolingual Spanish-speaking parents;
- preschoolers with monolingual English-speaking parents;
- preschoolers enrolled in preschool;
- preschoolers who are cared for at home;
- preschoolers enrolled in part-time or full-time day care;
- preschoolers from single-parent homes;
- preschoolers from working parent homes.

Demand

Each segment will have unique demands of the program and the library should be prepared to meet those demands for the different users. The following table provides selected segments and their respective demands.

Segment	Factors influencing demand
Preschoolers with monolingual Spanish-speaking parents	• content • language • educational value
Preschoolers enrolled in preschool	• time • price • educational value • location
Preschoolers from single-parent homes	• time • price • location • concurrent activities for older children
Preschoolers with monolingual English-speaking parents	• content • language • educational values

Even with so small an audience, there are many demands within each segment. Though many segments share similar demands, many other segments differ on what will make worthwhile programs.

Customer Decision-Making Process

Anytime a program is directed at children, the decision-making process is complicated. Children's programs must be convincing to both the parents and the child.

The decision-making process of children is influenced by how fun, active, engaging, and enjoyable the program is. Putting on a bilingual story time would be appealing to children, but it may be something they already get at preschool. Fun activities combined with bilingual story time might make the activity more appealing and influence the child to remain interested.

The decision-making process for parents might involve some similar criteria, but will also include concerns about the schedule of the program (the time or day of the week), the educational bonus the program adds to the child's life, the cost of the program, and the safety of the facility.

Competition

The local theater could be running a similar program on Saturdays, which would influence when you schedule your program. Because the local YMCA might fund trips to the zoo on weekends, that could reduce the number of children in your program. The community's largest preschool might schedule field trips every Thursday or library trips every Tuesday, which might tire the children and make them less receptive to your program.

Market Research

This is a program that the library deems necessary. It should be able to back that up by research. Because this program is important to the community, and because it is directly related to the function of the library, it is important to invest serious research time into the design and assessment of the program. This is the type of program that the community expects and for which the library will be held accountable.

Secondary information

Census information as well as demographic information is available at the Chamber of Commerce, or even in the library. Perhaps, that information tells you that the Spanish-speaking population has increased by 30 percent in the last ten years. Interviews with the ELS program in town reveals a significant increase in people of Spanish-speaking origin, who are learning English.

Primary Information

You gather information through conducting interviews with members of the Hispanic community. You speak with individuals in the Latino

Chamber of Commerce, religious leaders, people active in literacy programs and ELS programs.

Perhaps you develop a focus group similar to the one previously mentioned in this book. All of this would tell you if the need truly exists, the barriers to and the need for service. It would help you determine the collection needs, facility needs, staff needs, catalogue needs, and program needs. It would also help you identify communication and promotion tactics that would be effective.

You develop information regarding your target audience. You use market research to understand the demand, the customer decision-making process, and the competition of your conceived program for Spanish-speaking children and their parents. Now with a solid understanding of your audience you are ready to establish marketing goals and objectives for this audience.

Writing the Plan

Goal

The library will develop services and bilingual story hours to meet the needs of Spanish-speaking preschool children and their parents.

Objectives

1. To hold two bilingual story hours each month;

2. To attract twenty Spanish-speaking children and their parents twice monthly;

3. To develop a diversified collection of children's material in the Spanish language to support this audience;

4. To generate $20,000 in grant funds to support this program.

P Strategies

At this point, you move on to sizing up the details of potential marketing strategies: product (service), place, promotion, and price. The additional strategies include positioning and politics.

Product (Service) Development

The service requires at least one animated staff member, fluent both in Spanish and in English, as well as children's literature. It requires the commitment of the library staff to become versed in at least basic Spanish to help the influx of Spanish-speaking patrons. The program will require you to post bilingual signs throughout the library. Without a corresponding commitment to develop collections in Spanish and to increase materials in Spanish, this program is doomed to fail. The product should carry some appeal to both parents and children, both of whom will be involved.

Take a look at the other Ps to develop additional strategies for this program.

Place Strategies

- The large children's reading room;
- Launch the program with festive decorations and food;
- Scatter the growing collection of Spanish children's books throughout the reading room for parents and children to view and check out.

Pricing Strategies

- Approximate amount the library budget can afford to spend on the program;
- Apply for grant from the city;
- Appeal to booksellers or Hispanic organizations to supply books and materials.

Promotion Strategies

- Posters, brochures and bookmarks distributed in the library, through the preschools and day cares, through Hispanic organization mailings and in advertisements in Hispanic newspapers;
- Scheduled interviews with local press and media;
- PSAs to local media outlets.

Positioning Strategies

- Recruit mayor or city official to become involved with the first program;
- Recruit Hispanic leaders to participate and bring their children;
- Recruit local sport figures or celebrities to participate;
- Recruit a prominent English and Spanish Speaker to present a bilingual program;
- Encourage an all-preschool day where all preschoolers and their parents are encouraged to participate in a special bilingual program;
- Encourage after-program discussions with the parents.

Politics Strategies

- Opening day speech by mayor;

- Encourage Hispanic political organizations to participate and cosponsor a program.

The Last Important Things

Staying on Schedule

This program may be part of a large-scale campaign to attract Spanish-speakers to your library or it may be the first test your library conducts to see if it can launch a larger campaign. Either way, this process will require scheduling.

Identify librarians to talk to the media, the preschools, and the parents. Identify librarians or volunteers to write the grant. Set collection goals—100 books by December, 150 by January. Make sure to allow enough time so that word can get out and your program will be attended. Special days, like the mayor's visit will require a strict schedule of contacting the mayor and scheduling a day, touching base to make sure that date still works, forwarding the program to the mayor's office so she has time to rehearse and coordinating with media outlets for ample coverage.

Staying on Budget

Even though there is no cost to parents and children for this program, there is a cost to the library. The cost comes in the form of brochures and promotional material, materials and collection, staff time to coordinate as well as to offer the program. All of those costs need to be identified, along with the source of funds.

Collection and facilities:	
Preschool Spanish Collection	$5,000
Technical Service	$500
Personnel	
Outreach Coordinator (1/2 time) to conduct story hours and offer library services	$10,000
Technology	
Web site conversion package	$2,000
Promotion	
Brochures and flyers	$500
Total	$18,000
Revenue Sources	
Library operating budget	$9,000
Special Grant from the City	$9,000

As mentioned earlier, there may be other financial supporters and the library may be so bold as to develop additional marketing plans to appeal to the Hispanic community organization, the local bookstore or copy center.

Designing the Marketing Tactics

This is the area of your marketing plan that becomes visible. You develop public relations strategies, tactics, and action steps. You also develop promotion tactics and action steps. You actually identify who will be responsible, the date that a brochure will be complete and the actual cost of each step. Look back at Chapter 5 to review how to create an action plan in more depth.

This marketing plan was a very simple one. It is time to try a more complex example with more than one target audience. You will see how different tactics and action steps are coordinated to come together at the same time to provide success.

2. Developing a Shakespeare Festival for Your Library

The staff of the Seaside Public Library recognized in their strategic plan a need to strengthen their position within the community. For the Seaside Public Library, unlike the Inland Mesa Public Library, this was a project that they wanted to accomplish, not that they had to accomplish. After looking at their strengths—enthusiastic staff, strong Friends group, small community, and nearby amphitheater—they decided to establish an annual program that will position the library as a cultural leader in the community, and a headliner for the arts. They want to use a marketing planning process to design and implement a Shakespeare Festival in the community.

Environmental Analysis

The environmental analysis includes segmentation, demand, customer decision-making process, and competition. In the previous sample marketing plan, for Spanish-speaking preschoolers, your audience was limited. This is a broader program, with a wider audience and multiple segments, demands, customer decision-making processes, and competition. This marketing plan will attempt to address the whole of the audience and will demonstrate a more extensive marketing plan.

Segmentation

Many segments of individuals would like the opportunity to see a Shakespeare play in an outside environment. Shakespeare enthusiasts can be segmented by age, location of residence, education, and economic factors. Therefore, a Shakespeare lover's audience probably consists of several segments:

- Families looking for activities of quality that are free and educational;
- English teachers, at both the high school level and the college level;
- Students in high school and college;
- Senior citizens;
- Friends of the library;
- Potential individual sponsors;
- Potential corporate sponsors;
- Book club members;
- Adult fans of Shakespeare.

Demand

First, you have to evaluate the potential demand from each of these segments. When you develop a marketing plan, various factors will affect the demand for the product or service. In the case of this proposed Shakespeare Festival, for each segment, those factors might include content, price, time, educational value, quality, or attendance.

Segment	Factors influencing demand
Families	• content • price • time
Teachers	• content • educational value • time • price • quality
Students	• content • educational value • time • price • location
Seniors	• price • time • location • access (wheelchair access; proximity to stage; audio aid) • safety
Sponsors	• prominence • benefit • attendance • promotion • quality
Shakespeare fans	• quality

As you can see there are many demands within each segment, and many segments share similar demands. Some demands can be easily met, while others might require work or extra effort on the part of the library staff or organizing committee.

As you begin to estimate the potential demand for the service, you must identify how many individuals there are in each segment. When you begin to assess the actual numbers of individuals in each segment, who might want to attend a Shakespeare Festival, you can decide which segments of the market will become your niche markets for this particular service.

Customer Decision-Making Process

In this case, the factors affecting demand provide a guide to the decision-making process of the customer. This process, of course, varies with the segment of the customer base under consideration.

The decision-making process of customers who would enjoy a Shakespeare Festival depends on such variables as: the actors, the facility, the availability of parking, the convenience of time, and the promotion and pricing strategies.

For teachers the decision-making process might also involve the appropriateness of the performance for classroom application, as well as the pricing and transportation package.

There will be strong student attendance if the festival is required, or if teachers offer extra credit incentives. Price and transportation will also play an important role. For senior citizens, the customer decision process will be based on price, transportation and safety.

Many of the sponsors will make their decisions based on the benefits offered when they become a sponsor. Increased benefits will encourage them to sponsor at a higher level.

Competition

Although it is unlike that any other Shakespeare Festival will occure at the same time, competition for all of the segments identified will come from other school and social activities, television programs, and other cultural events. Careful selection of day of week, time, and location will serve to minimize competition. Cost will certainly be a factor.

Market Research

No project can afford to have mistakes, so market research is always suggested. Understanding customers is the key. Simple methods like interviews, research, and informal discussions will provide the necessary information to plan a program or project.

Research can be conducted to gauge the attraction of certain plays (comedies or dramas, *Hamlet* or *Much Ado About Nothing*). You can conduct research to find out where students might be commuting from to help your library offer some sort of transportation. Research could also help you find out what organizations traditionally sponsor arts programming, which individuals are champions of the performing arts, and which businesses might offer in-kind contributions. Conducting solid research will save the company time and effort when it comes to putting the program together.

Writing the Plan

Goal

The staff of the Seaside Public Library will initiate, develop and produce an annual Shakespeare Festival in the town of Seaside. The goal is to position the library as a leader in cultural outreach in the town.

Objectives

1. To have an average audience size of 300 people per night;

2. To generate press and media coverage to excite the community through the newspaper, TV, and radio;

3. To secure $5,000 worth of in-kind donations from an advertising agency, to design a graphic package that will include a logo look, graphics, and media plan;

4. To receive a grant from the local arts council in the amount of $2,500;

5. To obtain $10,000 in corporate sponsorship and individual sponsorships;

6. To develop a VIP night gala event with the cast and sponsors. This black-tie event will provide special benefits to this group.

P Strategies

Marketing strategies are the next major issue to address: product (service), place, promotion and price. Additional strategies include positioning and politics.

Product (Production) Development

Consider now the actual product of the Shakespeare play itself. You realize that you need professional assistance to develop a quality theatrical production. Therefore, you determine that by hiring a professional director and two professional actors, you will be able to develop a quality production.

Selecting one of Shakespeare's comedies will increase the participation of families, which will increase community demand for the product. You also know that a quality product will increase the demand. Therefore, the more professional you can make the production, the more response you will have. Customer decision-making process is influenced by professionalism of presentation, as well as other factors previously discussed.

Place Strategies

- Location: the outside, open theater beside the library;

- Advantages: provides ambiance, convenience, and is free.

Pricing Strategies

- Apply for grant from the local arts council to support the program;

- Seek sponsorships for advertising and media coverage;

- Seek local company support for professional fees of director and actors.

Promotion Strategies

- Posters, brochures, bookmarks distributed to bookstores, coffee houses, and through the library itself;

- Personalized letter or e-mail campaign to English teachers at private and public high schools, as well as faculty at nearby colleges;

- Scheduled interviews with local press and other media;

- Public Service Announcements to all local media; listing in all local events calendars;

- Development of volunteer committee to encourage ticket sales locally;

- Personalized invitation to Friends of the library;

- Displays and special discussions within the library.

Positioning Strategies

- Production will feature professional director and actors;

- Special after-performance discussion for educators and students;

- Community involvement in cast and crew make this an opportunity for the community to come together in support of the arts.

Politics Strategies

- Opening night speech by mayor;
- Donation basket for local arts organization.

The Last Important Things

Staying on Schedule

In a planning process, it s often best to develop a notebook for the marketing plan. Included within the planning document would be a section for strategies and strategy work sheets. There would be another section with actual marketing tactics. Included within that section would be action work sheets. These working documents allow you to identify exactly how long each step requires and the coordination of all of the planning events. It also allows you to realize the impact of a deadline that is missed.

The most common error in the marketing plan is developing an unrealistic schedule. Specific steps that have been identified to create a successful program often are ignored altogether or compressed until they lose their effectiveness. Usually these efforts occur in the promotion strategy area. Therefore, the attendance at the specific program is lower than desired. The result may be demoralizing to both staff and volunteers.

A scheduling strategy is developed for the general production, fundraising, publicity and advertising, outreach, and for each of the segments. For example, two librarians are identified for school outreach, tackling the student and educator segments of the audience. They will be responsible for contacting educators in the semester prior to the scheduled performances. Scheduling class visits one month prior to the performance to advertise directly to classes and students, and contacting the school office one week prior to the performance to make sure the festival is advertised in the school's daily announcements or weekly newspaper.

Staying on Budget

Now that you know the parameters of your program, costs come into clear view. You have decided that this is to be a free event to the families, community, Shakespeare lovers, students, senior citizens, and teachers within your area. It is to be a gathering and celebration, but it is not without cost. Even though you do not charge admission, you must have a source of revenue to pay expenses. Therefore, your first job is to delineate just exactly what your expenses will be. Then you need to create a marketing plan, to decide who will help you with the expenses and what they need to do so.

A simple description of the budget would look like this:

Program		BUDGET	
Cost		**Total**	**Expenses:**
Professional Staff			
• Coordinator		$2,000	
• Two professional actors		$2,000	
• Director		$1,500	$5,500
Facility			
• Lighting and sound		$5,000	
• Props, sets, technical equipment		$2,000	$7,000
Promotion			
• VIP affair		$1,000	
• Graphics design, logo book, applications		$1,000	
• Posters, banners, brochures		$1,500	
• Invitation		$1,000	
• Play bills		$250	
• Mailings		$250	
• In-kind media support		$500	
		$3,000	$8,500
Total			**$21,000**

Because you are looking to drum up outside funding, you should also create a table for that.

Program			
Amount		**Total**	**Revenues**
• Grant from local arts council		$2,000	
• In-kind media sponsorship		$3,000	
• Corporate sponsorship		$10,000	
• Individual sponsorships		$3,000	
• Friends		$1,000	
• Library		$2,000	$21,000
Total			**$21,000**

In the budget, you have said that you want to get a grant from the local arts council, develop corporate sponsorships, identify a media sponsor, as well as identify individual sponsors and ask the Friends of the library for $1,000. Each of these segments requires a mini marketing plan integrated within this overall plan. Each segment will have individual characteristics and must be treated uniquely.

Looking Closer, Planning Wiser

This project offers the opportunity to develop several mini-marketing plans for raising funds. The following are individual plans for each of the sponsors.

Corporate Sponsor Plan

Goal: To raise $10,000 from corporate sponsors.

What kind of corporate sponsors are you looking for? (**segmentation**) You are looking for sponsors who will benefit from associating with a community project of quality who want to present an image of integrity and support of the community. Candidates for corporate sponsorships might include a local bank, an investment service company, real estate companies, and legal firms. What is the **demand?** Firms are asked for support on a continual basis, so the quality and the uniqueness of this offering will affect their willingness to support it. **Competition**—who else will be asking for their support and sponsorship? **Customer decision making process** will depend on several things. One of the most important items is who does the asking. A second determinate is how much publicity and recognition will they receive. A third criteria will be, who else is sponsoring this event.

You actually identify potential corporate sponsors, create **strategies** including pricing (how much are you asking for), promotion (the kind of promotion they cannot buy), in a place that is unavailable to them otherwise. You identify who should do the asking, what benefits you can offer them. You begin with the corporate sponsor that you have identified to be the primary sponsor. If you are raising $10,000 you might look for one sponsor at $1,500, two sponsors at $750, four sponsors at $500 and so on. You will also try to identify specific items for them to sponsor. For example: a corporation could be your sponsor for the professional actors. They can also be the general sponsor or sponsor the VIP event.

The effort to acquire corporate sponsors will require staff coordination and a volunteer team effort. This also requires individual action steps with follow up and expressions of appreciation.

Individual Sponsors

Goal: To generate $3,000 in sponsorship from individual philanthropists and leaders. Obviously you need to identify specific individuals (segmentation) who will be enthralled enough to provide extra funds for the effort. What do you have to offer that would entice such individuals? Obviously, the benefits that you provide for Individual sponsors are different than those provided for corporate sponsors. Generally, individuals do not need the kind of public recognition. However, they do need special acknowledgment and special treatment. You need to invest some extra effort to identify potential candidates, identify who should ask and for how much. Again you will develop specific strategies, tactics, and action steps to acquire individual sponsors.

Arts Council Sponsorship

Goal: To obtain a $2,000 grant from the local arts council.

You identify the application process, deadline dates and requirements of the council and submit your grant proposal. Through this process, you have once again identified the arts council as a segment, identified the demand, the competition, and the customer decision-making process used by the council in order to maximize your opportunity. As far as strategies, you have developed a proposal (product) to be delivered at the appropriate place and time (place) for the appropriate price. You have also identified the recognition (promotion) that they require. You have created an action step process to make sure that this application is timely and that it meets all requirements.

Friends of Library Sponsorship

Goal: To obtain $1,000 from the Friends Group

They need to be treated as an additional segment. What is the demand for their funds? What will encourage them to support this program? Customer decision-making process. What kind of competition is there for their funds? Again, what are the specific strategies to ask the Friends. Product (preparation of proposal request), Place (timing), Price (amount to be asked), and Promotion—What do the Friends need in recognition?

You need to recognize all of these segments that are providing funding for this special event. This VIP event will provide a benefit for corporate and individual sponsors, as well as for volunteers, library staff, Friends, and other people who have worked to support the Shakespeare Festival. This event also requires a mini-marketing plan integrated within the total event. The segments that this will serve have been identified. The demand meets the need of people, sponsors, and volunteers to be an integral and intimate part of a winning team. The customer decision-making process will be influenced by a personal invitation.

Audience Development

Now that you have created your various marketing plans in areas of funding the program and the actual product, you need to develop plans to cultivate specific audiences. You have indicated in your original planning that this event would attract 50 families, book clubs, Shakespeare fans, teachers and students, Friends, as well as a general adult audience. You need to develop a specific marketing plan for each segment, along with strategies, tactics and action steps to maximize the attendance.

Target Audience #1—Family Audience

Segment: family units, the average of which comprises four individuals. You would like to have 50 families in attendance at the festival for each of the three evenings.

Demand: there are 30,000 cardholders within the library. You estimate that this represents 10,000 families.

Competition: other events in the community, television, or other entertainment.

Customer Decision Process: the parents will probably make the decision when it comes to family participation. The success of the event will depend upon promotion and enthusiasm of parents.

You need to develop special offerings that make the product attractive to families. The price is right to encourage family participation. Special promotion will make a difference, as well the promotion of "every one is going."

The marketing tactics and action steps will identify the specifics of each step, as well as the responsibility and time required.

Target Audience #2: English Teachers and Their Students

Segment: English teachers and their students.

Demand: depends on school curriculum and programs.

Customer Decision Process: students will attend if they are given extra credit, while English teachers will relish the event, especially if they are given special time to plan their teaching around the event. Special promotional tactics need to be developed for this group to maximize their attendance and involvement.

Competition: depends on timing and other factors.

Target Audience #3: Friends of the Library

Segment: Friends of the Library.

Customer Decision Process: they will support the attendance of this event if they are involved and invited. Their involvement as a sponsor serves to encourage their participation. Their role as volunteers also enhances their role.

Target Audience #4: Book Clubs and Organizations within the Community

A personal letter or contact to each organization will maximize their attendance and participation

Target Audience #5: General Adult Shakespeare Fans

Segment: general adults.

Demand: hard to estimate the demand. However, the town has a population of 30,000 people. Demographic and census information indicates a higher than normal level of educated people.

Customer Decision Process: The customers will base their decision on the festival based on the proposed quality of the production and the time.

Competition: other activities and events.

Marketing strategies of product, place, promotion and price will also be considered in this group. The promotion strategies and tactics will be very important so that there is a general knowledge of the occasion to encourage attendance.

One-Day Marketing Workshop

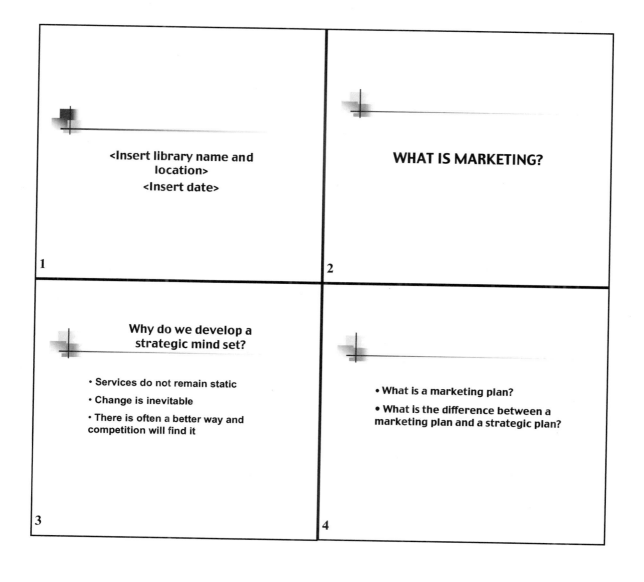

The Strategic Plan

- Participatory process that identifies the library's place in the environment of the future.
- Comes first
- Gets everyone in the institution on the "same page", going the same direction.
- Identifies goals, objectives, and priorities of the institution

5

Marketing Plan

- Focuses on problems, weaknesses, strengths and opportunities
- Builds on strengths
- Capitalizes on opportunities
- Strengthens weaknesses

6

The first step....

ENVIRONMENTAL ANALYSIS

or

SITUATIONAL ANALYSIS

7

ENVIRONMENTAL ANALYSIS

- Who?
- How many?
- Who/ what is my competition?
- What will make them want to use my services?

8

SEGMENTATION

- Who?
- Differentiate by demographic, psychographic, lifestyle, economic differences

9

DEMAND

- Potential numbers of people in each segment
- Concentrate on areas of greatest demand

10

Customer Decision Making Process

- What affects your decision to use a service?
- What affects your customer's choice?
- Decision making process depends on:
  1. availability
  2. convenience
  3. displays/merchandizing
  4. sales
  5. promotion

11

COMPETITION

- Time
- Weather
- Other organizations
- Activities
- Materials

12

Market Research – Getting the Facts

- Secondary Information
  1. Standard and Poors
  2. Census Data
  3. Voting records
  4. Other sources

13

Market Research – Getting the Facts

- Primary Information
  1. Qualitative Information
     - Focus groups
     - Interviews
  2. Quantitative Information
     - Surveys
     - Telephone Interviews
     - Polling

14

Market Planning Process

The Process

Program Objective

Environmental Analysis

Demand

Segmentation Competition

Decision Making

Research

Opportunities/Problems

Tactics

Strategy

15

Getting the Information You Need

- Pay for it
- Build partnerships with colleges, universities
- What is the cost of a mistake?

16

GOALS & OBJECTIVES

- Goals are broad
- Objectives are quantifiable

17

MARKETING STRATEGIES

- Product
- Place
- Price
- Promotion

18

Market Strategies

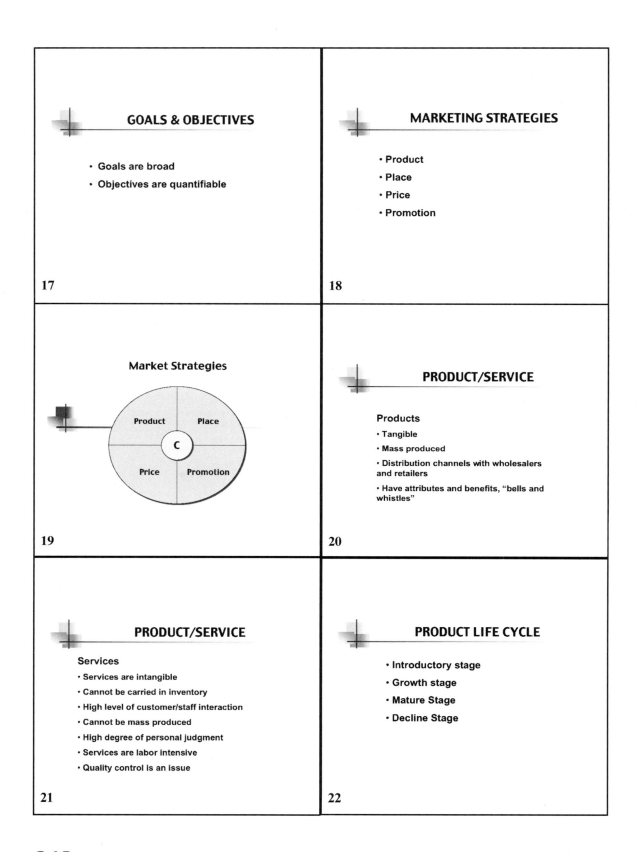

Product | Place
C
Price | Promotion

19

PRODUCT/SERVICE

Products

- Tangible
- Mass produced
- Distribution channels with wholesalers and retailers
- Have attributes and benefits, "bells and whistles"

20

PRODUCT/SERVICE

Services
- Services are intangible
- Cannot be carried in inventory
- High level of customer/staff interaction
- Cannot be mass produced
- High degree of personal judgment
- Services are labor intensive
- Quality control is an issue

21

PRODUCT LIFE CYCLE

- Introductory stage
- Growth stage
- Mature Stage
- Decline Stage

22

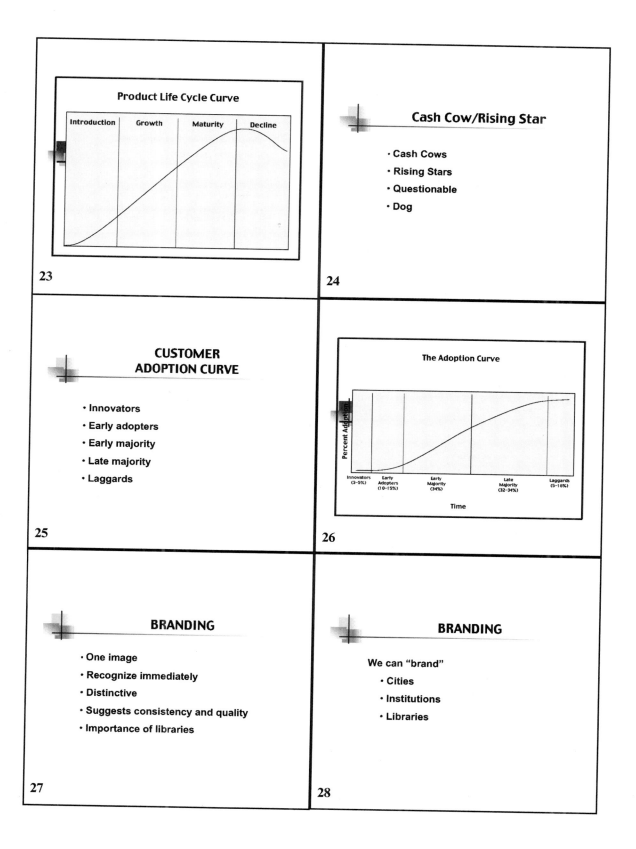

Product Life Cycle Curve

| Introduction | Growth | Maturity | Decline |

23

Cash Cow/Rising Star

- Cash Cows
- Rising Stars
- Questionable
- Dog

24

CUSTOMER ADOPTION CURVE

- Innovators
- Early adopters
- Early majority
- Late majority
- Laggards

25

The Adoption Curve

Percent Adoption

| Innovators (3–5%) | Early Adopters (10–15%) | Early Majority (34%) | Late Majority (32–34%) | Laggards (5–16%) |

Time

26

BRANDING

- One image
- Recognize immediately
- Distinctive
- Suggests consistency and quality
- Importance of libraries

27

BRANDING

We can "brand"
- Cities
- Institutions
- Libraries

28

NICHE MARKETS

- What is a "Niche"
- Strength of finding a "niche"

29

PLACE

- The physical place, building, facility
- Distribution channels
- Access
- Networks, collaborations
- Partnerships
- Includes things as book mobiles, books by mail, web sites, digital information

30

PRICE

- All organizations deal with price
- Tuition
- Budgets
- Fares
- City, county budgets
- State budgets
- Federal Budgets
- Alternative funding

31

PROMOTION

- Sales, promotion and libraries
- Promotional campaign leads to marketing tactics

32

PROMOTION

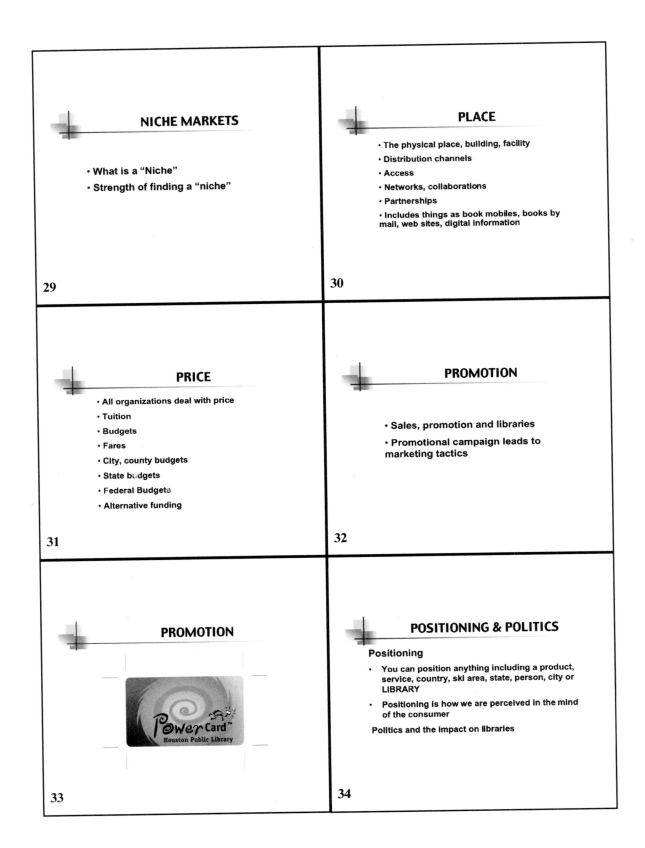

33

POSITIONING & POLITICS

Positioning

- You can position anything including a product, service, country, ski area, state, person, city or LIBRARY
- Positioning is how we are perceived in the mind of the consumer

Politics and the impact on libraries

34

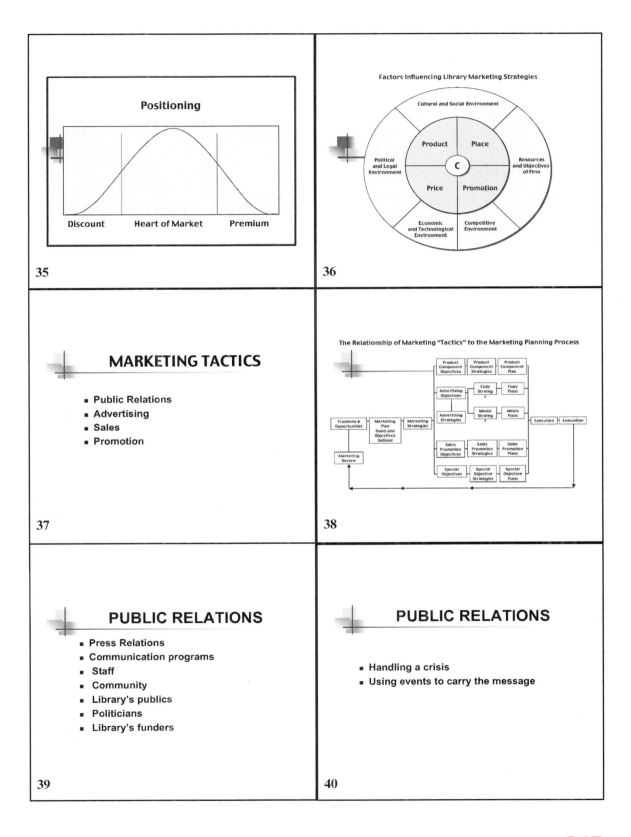

Positioning

Discount   Heart of Market   Premium

35

Factors Influencing Library Marketing Strategies

36

MARKETING TACTICS

- Public Relations
- Advertising
- Sales
- Promotion

37

The Relationship of Marketing "Tactics" to the Marketing Planning Process

38

PUBLIC RELATIONS

- Press Relations
- Communication programs
- Staff
- Community
- Library's publics
- Politicians
- Library's funders

39

PUBLIC RELATIONS

- Handling a crisis
- Using events to carry the message

40

PROMOTION & ADVERTISING

- Sales
- Promotion
- Advertising

41

DEVELOPING AN ACTION PLAN

42

THE EVALUATION PROCESS

- Review original Goals and objectives
- Review decisions regarding segmentation, demand, customer decision making process, competition
- Review each of the marketing strategies
- Was the product of service appropriate?
- Was the price or funding adequate?
- Was there an issue with the promotion?
- How about the distribution channels?

43

2. My Marketing Plan

The last step of a workshop about marketing planning is designed to be a participatory step. At this point, each participant or group of participants is to design their own marketing plan. I have found this to be a crucial step in a marketing workshop. I circle the room and work with each group to help them work on each step. It is in this phase that they must truly apply all of the information they have learned previously within the workshop. It is in this stage that they truly begin to understand the concept of marketing planning.

Concept of Project:

Author: (the individual or group working on the plan)

_____

Description of project:

_____

_____

Relationship to Strategic Plan of Library or Organization:

_____

_____

Environmental analysis:

_____

_____

Segmentation: Who are the customers that will be targeting in this project? (I find that librarians tend to make projects too general. I want a separate marketing plan for each individual segment.

_____

_____

Demand: How many potential customers are there?

_____

Competition: Who/what is the competition?

_____

_____

Customer Decision-Making process: What will make your customers that you have selected decide to use your product/service?

_____

_____

These steps tell you that you need more information. Therefore, you are going to look at acquiring more information about your "target market." You are going to do some hypothetical market research.

Market Research:

Secondary: (Participants usually try to remember just what is secondary and primary research? When I remind them that secondary research is information that is already available, they say "Oh, yes" and start to think about their local school, Chamber of Commerce, or what information might be available that would be helpful.)

_____

_____

Primary: (I remind participants that primary research is information that they must obtain themselves. Marketers talk about focus groups, interviews, and community forums. Those are qualitative forms of research. Quantitative information comes through surveys and polling.

_____

_____

Qualitative?

_____

_____

Quantitative?

_____

_____

Marketing Goal(s): In this category, I help participants design goals and objectives. Marketing goals are broad, while objectives are quantitative. Here again, it is easier if they think about one segment of the market. It is a lesson in how to focus more precisely. The goal is not to develop new services in an area. The goal is, rather, to develop service in a new area to one specific audience, such as senior citizens.

Objective:

_____

_____

Objective:

_____

_____

Objective:

_____

_____

Marketing Strategies: After they have developed their goals and objectives, I ask them to develop the marketing strategies for their marketing plan. The first strategy is concerned with the actual product or service that they are designing for the individual target market.

Describe your product or service:

_____

_____

Place is the next strategy. I ask them several questions regarding "place."

_____

_____

Where are you going to offer your product? Describe the access to the service or product. How are you going to distribute your product or service? What distribution channels will you use? What hours will your library be open to provide service? Are you going to use electronic services?

_____

_____

Price is the third strategy. Price does not simply mean how much you are going to charge the customer. It does mean how are you going to pay for your product/service and where those funds will come from.

_____

_____

The fourth P in the traditional four Ps of marketing refers to promotion. How are you going to promote the new product or service? Can you outline your promotional program?

_____

_____

The fifth P is called positioning. How are you going to position your new product or service? How does it add to the way your institution is perceived by the target audience? By the community as a whole?

_____

_____

Marketing Tactics: This area identifies the action plan for every promotional program used to encourage the target audience to participate in your new product or service. While you discuss advertising programs, you also discuss public relations and promotional programs. The key element here is to identify the step-by-step process required to coordinate these efforts. This is the visible part of marketing. You are able to design each step in an effective way, because you have identified the correct segment or target audience, you have analyzed the decision-making process, and you have identified the marketing strategies in the appropriate way. Now, timing is the absolute key. You may think that you can do more than you really can. Also, deadlines are optimistic. If deadlines to produce flyers or newspaper articles or advertisements are not met, the entire program suffers. In this area I ask participants to tell me the specifics of each program and then to draw up a timeline.

Identify public relations program:

_____

_____

Promotional action steps

_____

_____

Sales Program

_____

_____

Advertising Program

_____

_____

I work with groups or individuals as they develop a marketing plan for them to take home. At the end of the session, a spokesman for each group presents their project and marketing plan for the whole group. This exercise helps people apply the information that they have learned during the day-long seminar. The project is almost always a real project that pertains to their library, so it is very meaningful to participants.

Index

About the Author

Suzanne Walters served as the Director of Marketing and Development for the Denver Public Library through their successful bond election and capital campaign.

She has also served as the Director of Marketing for the Regional Transportation District of Denver, responsible for the implementation of the 16th Street Mall. In addition, she has served with Adolph Coors Golden Recycling Company to develop nationwide programs of aluminum recycling. She has been the Development Director for a small private college as well as the Statewide Volunteer Coordinator for KRMA TV (PBS).

Her MBA comes from the University of Denver, Daniels School of Business.

Suzanne currently is a consultant and president of her own consulting company called Walters & Associates located in Denver, Colorado.